Storytime Magic

400 Fingerplays, Flannelboards, and Other Activities

Kathy MacMillan and Christine Kirker

AMERICAN LIBRARY ASSOCIATION

Chicago   2009

Kathy MacMillan is a freelance writer, American Sign Language interpreter, librarian, and storyteller. She has contributed articles to *Public Libraries*, *American Libraries*, and many other professional journals and is the author of *Try Your Hand at This* (Scarecrow Press, 2006) and *A Box Full of Tales* (American Library Association, 2008). She was the library/media specialist at the Maryland School for the Deaf from 2001 to 2005 and prior to that was a children's librarian at Carroll County Public Library and Howard County Library. Kathy holds a Master of Library Science from the University of Maryland, College Park, and through Stories by Hand (www.storiesbyhand.com) presents storytelling programs that introduce sign language to thousands of children and families each year.

Christine Kirker has been a children's library associate with the Carroll County Public Library in Maryland since 2005. She has developed and presented many programs for children of all ages and offered many educational outreach programs. She also launched a monthly Art Explorers program at the library where children discuss the lives of featured artists and explore their techniques. In Christine's latest project, Uniquely Hand Made, young people design and decorate clay hands to represent their own unique spirit. After graduating from the University of Maryland, Baltimore County, Christine spent ten years as a research analyst for the university's Office of Institutional Research.

American Sign Language graphics are reproduced from *American Sign Language Clip and Create 4*, courtesy of the Institute for Disabilities Research and Training Inc.

Pattern illustrations are by Melanie Fitz.

The paper used in this publication meets the minimum requirements of American National Standard for Information Sciences—Permanence of Paper for Printed Library Materials, ANSI Z39.48-1992. ∞

Library of Congress Cataloging-in-Publication Data
MacMillan, Kathy, 1975–
    Storytime magic : 400 fingerplays, flannelboards, and other activities / Kathy MacMillan and Christine Kirker.
      p. cm.
    Includes bibliographical references and index.
    ISBN 978-0-8389-0977-5 (alk. paper)
    1. Children's libraries—Activity programs. I. Kirker, Christine. II. Title.
    Z718.3M253 2009
    027.62'5—dc22
                                                 2008030266

ISBN-13: 978-0-8389-0977-5

Printed in the United States of America
13 12 11 10 09   5 4 3 2 1

This book is dedicated to our children, Ashleigh and Sean Kirker
and J. X. MacMillan. They are the reason behind all we do.

Contents

Flannelboard and craft patterns can be found on the book's website, at www.ala.org/editions/extras/macmillan09775. Look for website material wherever you see this symbol: **WEB**

Acknowledgments

We would first like to thank Melanie Fitz for her beautiful illustrations, which went from "just a few" to "can you do two hundred by the end of the month?" Melanie, thank you for sharing your talent with us.

Special thanks also to Craig Patterson, Aimee Gladfelter, Amber Haslinger, and the other Carroll County Public Library staff members who contributed directly or indirectly to this project.

A big thank you to Laura Pelehach, who first saw the potential in this project and nurtured the seeds for it even as she transplanted herself to a new garden.

Thank you to Corinne Vinopol and the Institute for Disabilities Research and Training Inc. for their continued support and their dedication to sharing American Sign Language with the library community.

Thank you to the many librarians, past and present, who taught us everything we know and continue to open our eyes to all the things we don't.

Introduction

Welcome to *Storytime Magic,* your treasure trove of fingerplays, flannelboards, action rhymes, and more. Unlike many resource books for programming, which give you a preset menu for each theme, this book presents storytime à la carte. As any veteran of storytime planning knows, finding the books is the easy part—but what do you do in between? If you're tired of the old standbys, or if you're just looking for something new related to a specific theme, *Storytime Magic* is for you. We have compiled hundreds of fresh new ideas to add life to any storytime. Most of the ideas here are original, but we have also included some lesser-known traditional rhymes and songs. In this book, you'll find

fingerplays
action rhymes
songs, all set to familiar melodies
rhymes to sign, with accompanying illustrations of the American Sign Language (ASL)
    signs
flannelboards, with patterns
stick-puppet stories and rhymes, with patterns
crafts, with patterns
other games and fun activities

Entries are arranged in themed chapters, or you can use the index by title and first line at the back of the book. Each chapter also includes a theme-related list of recommended books for storytimes as well as Quick Tips boxes throughout to help you enhance the early literacy component of your programs. We hope you enjoy our *Storytime Magic.*

Flannelboard and craft patterns are shown in miniature in the book. The full-size patterns can be found on the book's website, at www.ala.org/editions/extras/macmillan09775.

The sign-language art images in *Storytime Magic* have been created using *American Sign Language Clip and Create 4,* a software product of the Institute for Disabilities Research and Training Inc. This CD-ROM contains more than five thousand sign-language art images that can be used to easily create any number of products (e.g., worksheets, cards, banners). It also contains six templates that automatically generate bingo cards, crossword puzzles, and finger-spelling scrambles using any of the five thousand sign-language images you select. Four games are included in the software. To purchase a copy or learn more about the institute's other ASL-accessible software, visit their website at www.idrt.com.

[WEB]

Chapter 1

Storytime Tips for Every Age Group

Every storytime programmer has a unique style and approach, but the tried-and-true techniques in this chapter will make your planning easier, help you identify the needs of your audience, and make your programs more fun.

GENERAL PROGRAMMING TIPS

Choosing a theme will generally make your storytime preparation easier. However, the younger the group, the less necessary a theme becomes. Theme should always be secondary to age appropriateness. All programs should use a variety of formats: books, flannelboards, storyboards, puppets, storytelling, or videos. This helps to engage the listeners. Plan on using a variety of materials: songs, fingerplays, bounces and tickles (for babies), riddles (for older children), and the like. Use your imagination. The possibilities are endless.

Playing music as the group enters is a wonderful way to set the mood. You may have a particular welcome song that you like, or you might play music appropriate to your topic. Remember to introduce yourself to the group at the beginning of the program. Set a warm and inviting tone by welcoming participants by name. Check out the "Hello and Good-bye" section in chapter 16 for songs and rhymes to open and close your programs. When planning the order of your program, try to start out strong. An activity song such as "If You're Happy and You Know It" is usually the best way to get the group together and focused. You want to let the group know right away that they are in for a special experience. Make storytime a *different* place from the rest of the library.

Strive to make your programs as participative as possible. This has different meanings for different age groups. See the individual age-group guidelines for examples. Try to pick songs with motions built in (for example, "Head, Shoulders, Knees, and Toes"). If you are planning to make up motions to go with the song, plan in advance what those motions will be.

Don't forget to practice! Know the songs and stories well enough that you don't have to keep your eyes glued to the page. Make eye contact with the participants. When presenting stories, be sure to move the book so that everyone can see the pictures. Tilt the top of the book down toward the listeners to minimize glare. You can even write words to songs and fingerplays on a display board. This will make it easier for you to see them and will allow parents to join in (if applicable).

To maximize library connections, set up a display of library materials that may be checked out by the participants. Keep the materials age appropriate and try to include a variety of formats (books, music, videos, etc.). Try to keep the materials theme related, but remember that an unrelated display is better than no display at all. Make sure to announce that the items in the display may be checked out. (You would think this would be obvious, but to most patrons it isn't.)

Do the hardest material at the beginning of the program. This usually means the longest story. Save the most active parts of the program for last because they will divert the group's attention. Occasionally you will have trouble if members of the group get antsy or cause disruptions. How you handle this will depend on the age of the group. The key is to remain calm and try to maintain the group's focus. See the sections below for ideas that work with specific age groups.

And most important of all, have fun! If you are not excited about the program, there is no way you can expect the kids to be!

ALL AGES/FAMILY STORYTIMES

When planning an all-ages storytime, choose a theme that will appeal to a wide age range. Generally, the more generic your theme, the easier your planning will be. For example, Silly Stories, Let's Have Fun, or any animal theme can be readily adapted to a diverse audience. You don't really require a theme, but it will help you to plan more easily. Remember, when all else fails, Librarian's Favorites is always a good theme!

Employ a variety of props and story styles: books, puppets, lap theater, storycards, flannelboards, magnetboards, storytelling . . . Make use of your prop collection! Plan to use several songs and fingerplays. If you can tie them in to your theme, great. If not, there are lots of wiggling-type songs and fingerplays that are very useful. (You can use "Shake Your Sillies Out" for just about anything!)

Pick materials aimed at different age levels. You may find some books, props, and so forth that would be suitable for any age. (Simple fairy tales generally fit this category.) Many materials, however, will be specifically aimed at one end of the spectrum. If you choose these materials, make sure you have alternatives that would appeal to other ages. When planning your program, think in or's. Always have options in case you have more of one age group. For example, if you are planning to read a Goldilocks story, have an older version (James Marshall's *Goldilocks and the Three Bears*) and a younger version (Byron Barton's *The Three Bears*) prepared. Be flexible. Give yourself enough materials so that you can change your program if necessary.

With a wide age range, it is especially important to start out strong. Usually an action song such as "If You're Happy and You Know It" is the best way to begin. Grab audience attention right from the beginning. Then do your longest story presentation while you really have their attention. Alternate stories, songs, and fingerplays. If you alternate movement activities with the sitting-down times, you will keep the children's attention. A sample program might be song, hardest story, fingerplay, song, story, fingerplay, activity, song, craft.

During a program for a wide variety of ages, there may be some distractions. If the children get antsy, try to do something (a song, a fingerplay, audience participation cued by a word or action in a story) that will grab listeners' attention. Don't expect to get through more than three stories (four if you're lucky). The key to working with children is interaction. Anytime you can incorporate an interactive element, you will keep the children's attention.

You will occasionally find that parents want to sit in the back and talk rather than be involved. If you announce at the beginning that grown-ups are expected to participate, you may dispel this problem. If you do get chatty grown-ups in the back, try to involve them in the story or song. For example, you might ask the children a question such as "Who knows some farm animals?" After the kids give their answers, say pleasantly, "Let's see if the grown-ups in the back know any." If they haven't been paying attention before, they will after that! This is an easy, playful way to get the grown-ups back in the game.

If you are offering a craft activity, pick one that can be modified for younger and older children. For example, in a monkey program, you might have the children make simple stick puppets; the younger children could make one while the older children might make a whole set and act out the Five Little Monkeys rhyme (126).

Remember that the most important thing is to have fun. If you aren't having fun, your audience can tell. Your energy level will usually determine that of the storytime group.

BABIES

The storytime portion of a baby program generally runs about fifteen to twenty minutes in length. Follow up with playtime. With this group, it is more important to have age-appropriate materials than it is to have a theme. If you do choose to use a theme, pick something centered on a young child's world, such as Bedtime, Playtime, or Animal Sounds.

Consistency is important in this age group. Try to use the same opening and closing routines from week to week (songs usually work best). Repetition is also key. Do not hesitate to repeat songs, fingerplays, or even stories throughout a series of programs because doing so reinforces concepts. Programming for this age group relies more on fingerplays and song activities than on books per se.

In choosing your stories, try to keep them interactive. This can include stories that invite participation (such as making animal sounds) but also stories that allow questioning (What animal do I see on this page?).

Use a variety of formats. Large board books can work, as can big books, flap books, or picture books with large, clear illustrations and minimal text. Flannelboards, magnetboards, storyboards, puppets, and lap theaters also add interest. Try to use props in conjunction with the stories (for example, a hen puppet with the book *Big Fat Hen* by Keith Baker). Or try concert reading: provide each parent with a board book of the title you are going to read and have everyone read together. This will provide an experience for the babies that is at once intimate and communal.

Fingerplay is a generic term that covers all sorts of activities that will work with babies: bouncing, tickling, clapping, rocking. The key is to use activities that are simple enough to be performed by the target age group.

Make it clear from the beginning that the babies are not expected to always sit still. Integrate movement into the program as much as possible. Let the parents know that it is OK to step out of the room for a few minutes if their babies get fussy. Also make it clear that the adults are as much a part of the program as the children. Enable participation whenever possible. Post the words to songs and fingerplays so that the grown-ups can participate.

Babies respond especially well to the sound of the human voice, especially singing. Using tapes or CDs is fine, but don't underestimate the power of simply singing a tune — nothing grabs a baby's attention quite like it. If you are uncomfortable singing without a tape, stick with familiar songs (such as "The Wheels on the Bus") that the parents will sing with you.

Try to use a variety of stimuli. Babies are fascinated by virtually everything, and the best ideas are generally the simplest (and cheapest): bubbles, crepe streamers, beanbags, brown paper bags, jingle bells, shaker eggs, or colorful scarves. Because this age group responds best to one-on-one interaction, try to use materials that will foster pairing. Tickles and bounces encourage the caregiver to interact with the child. You may want to use a song or rhyme that incorporates each child's name in turn, or have a stuffed animal or puppet that will greet each group member individually.

When planning your program, always keep the hardest material at the beginning. A sample plan might be opening song, fingerplay, hardest story, fingerplay, song, story, fingerplay, closing song, craft. Keep any activities that will redirect the attention of the group for last; don't expect to blow bubbles in the middle of the program and then get the group back together for a story. Whenever possible, point out ways that storytime materials can be used on a day-to-day basis. For example, you might introduce a fingerplay with "This is a good rhyme to say at bath time."

TODDLERS

During toddler storytimes, make it clear to caregivers that they are just as much a part of storytime as their children. Encourage them to participate whenever possible. Post fingerplays and songs so adults can sing along. Explain that children are not expected to sit still during the program. Build movement into the program. Let the adults know that it is OK to take children out of the room for a few minutes if they become disruptive.

Repetition and predictability are important with this age group. Try to keep the same opening and closing routines from week to week. Feel free to repeat songs and fingerplays throughout the session. When presenting a song or fingerplay, go through it at least twice. You can also reinforce comprehension by repeating stories in different formats. For example, after reading *The Three Bears*, retell the story with a flannelboard.

Toddlers' programs can rely on a theme, but the theme is less important than age appropriateness. Feel free to use activities that do not exactly go with the theme if they will enhance the program. Themes should be simple and related to the child's world. Stories for this age group should be simple and brief, and interactive when possible. Two- and three-year-olds respond especially well to participatory stories and are eager to share their newfound knowledge. Find ways to make your program as participative as possible. For example, have children help you count five little flowers as you put them on the flannelboard. Big books, flap books, flannelboards, storyboards, and puppets all offer appealing story presentations.

Remember that this age group is curious about *everything*. They will walk right up and point to the pictures in a book, or try to take flannelboard pieces from the board. If you are using an especially appealing item, such as a puppet, consider taking it around to greet each child in turn; that will satisfy the children's desire to touch it.

Music plays a big part in programming for this age group. Try to use songs with definite activities attached (such as "If You're Happy and You Know It"). Feel free to use props such as beanbags, hula hoops, or streamers during the songs. Playing CDs works well, but singing a cappella gives the presenter the flexibility to change the length of a song as needed. It also grabs the children's attention. Choose familiar songs that parents can sing with you or simple songs that they can learn quickly.

As always, plan to do your hardest material first and save big activities for last. A sample plan might be opening song, fingerplay, hardest story, fingerplay, song, story, fingerplay, fingerplay, song, craft. Programs for toddlers may include a simple craft. Two- and three-year-olds can usually manage crayons and even glue sticks with an adult's help, so they love any activity that enables them to scribble and glue or apply stickers. Have fun! This age group is just so thrilled to be in storytime that you can do no wrong in their eyes.

PRESCHOOLERS

Programs for preschoolers should always relate to their specific interests. Themes should be broad enough to encompass a variety of stories. Choose stories that have engaging texts, keeping in mind that the attention span and comprehension level of a three-year-old differ from those of a six-year-old. Try to include materials that will appeal to both. Choose stories that are fairly brief, with large and colorful pictures. Make sure that you like the stories you choose; if you are unenthusiastic, the kids will be able to tell.

Use a variety of formats: flannelboards, storyboards, puppets, and storytelling as well as books. Always plan an extra story and song to allow for last-minute changes if you have leftover time or the group gets restless. Plan to use a variety of music and fingerplay activities to allow variety. Repeat fingerplays at least twice. Use the fingerplays and songs between the stories as stretches.

At the beginning of each session, go over the rules with the children. Include such courtesies as keeping your hands to yourself, listening during the stories, and raising your hand if you have something to say. If children are beginning to get disruptive during a story, incorporate their names into the text. For example, say, "Daniel, do you know what that crocodile said? He said . . ." This may distract them from whatever mischief they are getting into. Remember that even though this age group can sit through longer stories, they still need breaks in between. Don't expect then to sit for too long without wiggling. Be ready to adjust your program, if necessary, in response to their needs. A sample program might be song, fingerplay, story, fingerplay, story, song, fingerplay, story, activity, song, craft.

Prepare a display of theme-related materials. Include a variety of formats. If possible, take a few moments to booktalk a few of the titles at the end of your program.

ELEMENTARY SCHOOLERS

Programs for elementary school children tend to be theme related. The most successful themes provide a hook, such as The *Titanic* and Other Disasters. Tying a topic to a popular person or character is another effective method—for example, a mystery program about Scooby-Doo. Themes should draw on the many interests of school-age kids, from foreign languages to animation to science. The specific age group can be chosen in relation to the theme.

School-age programs follow a lot of the same basic guidelines as preschool storytimes, but because the children have longer attention spans, there is an opportunity to use longer stories and a variety of activities and formats. Longer picture books work well with school-age children, as do storytelling, music, and video.

If appropriate to the topic, factual sections can be included. This could mean anything from sharing a variety of fun facts about the topic to creating a game or activity around those facts. Be creative. Try to use a variety of formats. For example, you might use a diagram or model to illustrate your points. Like all the other programs, this one will succeed best if it is interactive. Plan some activities that require participation.

Remember that even though these kids may seem blasé, they are probably not as sophisticated as you think they are (or as sophisticated as they want you to think they are). They still love to be read to (whether they admit it or not), and they really will get involved if you make the topic interesting.

The discipline guidelines for elementary school programs are essentially the same as for preschool programs: make sure the kids know the rules before you start the program. There are generally fewer discipline problems with this age group because they know how to raise their hands and take turns. However, if you find that individual members of the group are becoming distracting, try to engage the troublemakers. Have them help you tell a story or demonstrate a dance step.

These programs offer an opportunity to do more elaborate crafts because the kids are a bit older and there is more time. Prepare a display of items that can be checked out. These items should be related to the theme. Include a variety of materials: books (appropriate reading level, fiction and nonfiction, if applicable), videos, music. Take a few moments at some time in your program to booktalk a few of the titles and let the children know that they can check out material from the display.

A NOTE ABOUT USING SIGN LANGUAGE IN STORYTIME

This book contains many rhymes and songs to sign, each accompanied by illustrations of appropriate signs to use. American Sign Language can be incorporated into programming for any age group, and the benefits are many: it makes any program instantly interactive, it catches the attention of visual learners, it engages parents, and it adds a multicultural element to your programs as you introduce the children to another language. Plus, it's fun and kids love it. When introducing the signs, be sure to let the kids know that what you are doing is American Sign Language, a real language, not just made-up gestures. Demonstrate each sign slowly and repeat. Allow time for the children to do the sign and offer help as necessary. Kids of every age, from babies to teenagers, thrill to sign language used in programming. And don't worry if you don't know lots of signs—it's OK to just use a few signs for key words in a song, fingerplay, or story. For more information and creative ideas for using signs in programs, see *Try Your Hand at This: Easy Ways to Incorporate Sign Language into Your Programs,* by Kathy MacMillan (Scarecrow Press, 2006).

Chapter 2

All about Me

MY BODY

1   *In My Mirror*

In my mirror I can see
Two little eyes that look at me. *(point to eyes)*
Two little ears, one little nose, *(point to ears and nose)*
Ten little fingers, ten little toes. *(wiggle fingers, point to toes)*
One little mouth I open wide, *(open mouth wide)*
Two little rows of teeth hidden inside. *(point to teeth)*
A tongue that pops both in and out, *(move tongue in and out of mouth)*
Lots of joints that bend about. *(bend knees and elbows)*
When I look in the mirror, what do I see? *(mime looking in hand mirror)*
A beautiful person looking back at me!

2   *I Wiggle My Fingers*
(traditional)

I wiggle my fingers,
I wiggle my toes,
I wiggle my shoulders,
I wiggle my nose.

Now no more wiggles
Are left in me.
So I will sit still
As still as can be.

3   *Hair*
(to the tune of "Row, Row, Row Your Boat")

Brush, brush, brush your hair *(mime brushing hair)*
Each and every day.
Keep it shiny, keep it clean
And neat in every way.

4   *All about You*
(to the tune of "You Are My Sunshine")

You have two arms, they are for waving.
You have two feet to go stump, stump.
You have two eyes, they are for blinking,
And a bottom to sit with a bump.

5 *In My Mirror Craft*

MATERIALS: one copy of In My Mirror (1) for each child, one circle of aluminum foil for each child, glue, crayons, stickers, and other decorating materials

DIRECTIONS:
1. Glue the aluminum foil onto the paper with the poem to make a mirror.
2. Decorate as desired.

6 *Funny Face Picture Craft*

MATERIALS: one sheet of paper with an oval shape in the middle for each child, crayons, stickers, and other decorating materials

DIRECTIONS:
1. Use the oval to draw yourself with a funny face.
2. Decorate as desired.

See also Hello You! (364), My Fingers Can (372), Reach and Wiggle (373), and Wiggles (374).

MY TEETH

7 *I Went to the Dentist*

I went to my dentist and this is what
  she said:
"Brush your teeth with your hand on
  your head!"
Brush-a, brush-a, brush-a, brush-a,
  brush-a, brush-a, brush!

I went to my dentist and she said to
  me:
"Brush your teeth with your hand on
  your knee!"
Brush-a, brush-a, brush-a, brush-a,
  brush-a, brush-a, brush!

I went to my dentist and she said "Oh
  dear!
Brush your teeth with your hand on
  your ear!"
Brush-a, brush-a, brush-a, brush-a,
  brush-a, brush-a, brush!

I went to my dentist and she said
  something funny:
"Brush your teeth with your hand on
  your tummy!"
Brush-a, brush-a, brush-a, brush-a,
  brush-a, brush-a, brush!

I went to my dentist and what do you
  suppose?
She said, "Brush your teeth with your
  hand on your nose!"
Brush-a, brush-a, brush-a, brush-a,
  brush-a, brush-a, brush!

8 *Teeth*
(to the tune of "Shake Your Sillies Out")

You gotta brush, brush, brush your
  teeth each day.
Brush, brush, brush your teeth each
  day.
Brush, brush, brush your teeth each
  day,
To keep them healthy and clean.

You gotta floss, floss, floss your teeth
  each day . . .
You gotta visit, visit, visit the dentist . . .

9   Five Loose Teeth Flannelboard

See pattern 9. (Full-size patterns can be found at www.ala.org/editions/extras/macmillan09775.)

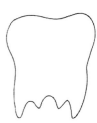

Five loose teeth and not one more
One fell out, and then there were four.
Four loose teeth as wobbly as can be
One fell out, and then there were three.
Three loose teeth, and I knew what to do
I wiggled one back and forth, and then
    there were two.
Two loose teeth, isn't this fun?

Wiggle, wobble, wiggle, and then
    there was one.
One loose tooth, wiggling just so.
I take a bite of an apple, and hey!
    Where'd it go?
No loose teeth are left in my gums.
I'll put them under my pillow and the
    tooth fairy will come!

10   Meet the Tooth Fairy

Invite a dental hygienist or dentist in your area to play the Tooth Fairy during a special storytime. Recycle an old prom dress or fairy costume and make a magic wand out of a dowel rod and silver glitter. The Tooth Fairy can make a grand entrance in your tooth-themed storytime, lead a tooth-brushing parade, share tooth-care facts, and hand out toothbrushes. This is a great way to involve your community.

> **Quick Tip:** Ask a dentist in your community to donate toothbrushes or dental floss to give out to storytime attendees.

11   Paper Plate Tooth Faces Craft

MATERIALS: paper plate for each child, yarn, puffed-rice cereal, glue, crayons

DIRECTIONS:
1. Draw a face on the paper plate.
2. Glue puffed-rice cereal onto the mouth to represent teeth.
3. Glue on yarn for hair and decorate as desired.

MY FIVE SENSES

12   My Eyes

My eyes can look left,
My eyes can look right,
My eyes can look ahead,
And see the sights.
I can close my eyes,
I can blink, blink, blink,
I can flutter my eyelids,
I can give you a wink.
But of all the things my eyes can do,
The best is when they see a friend like
    you!

13   What Sound Does It Make? Flannelboard

See pattern 13.

With my ears, I can hear
Things that are far and things that are
    near.
A fire truck just raced by,
Its siren let out a loud cry!
In my kitchen, pans and pots
Bang and clatter quite a lot.
When my doorbell starts to ring,
I hear it go ding-a-ling.

The helicopter flies without a stop,
And its blades go chop-chop-chop.
The birds in the trees sound so sweet
When they sing tweet-tweet-tweet.
When we pet the kitty's fur,
She curls up and lets out a purr.
When it's time to sit back down,
I take my seat without a sound.

14   How Does It Taste? Activity

Give each child a stick puppet with a happy face on one side and a sad face on the other. Show clip-art pictures of different kinds of food and have the children show whether they like the food or not by holding up the appropriate face. Some examples: french fries, cake, lemons, broccoli, peanuts, fish, chicken, spinach, apples, and cereal.

15   Touchy-Feely Bag Activity

Create a touchy-feely bag with an assortment of objects, some hard, some soft, some large, some small, and so forth. Have the children put their hands in the bag and describe what they are feeling and see if they can guess the object before they pull it out to look at it. Some items that could go in the bag are a small car, a block, a ball, a scarf, or a small stuffed animal.

Quick Tip: Because young children learn through their senses, activities like the My Texture Book Craft and Touchy-Feely Bag Activity lay the groundwork for later print awareness. Becoming aware of different textures and shapes will help children discern the differences between letters of the alphabet.

16   Hearing and Smelling Activity

Print clip-art pictures of things you hear (such as a phone, an alarm clock, birds, an airplane) and smell (a skunk, flowers, cookies, socks). Print enough noses and ears to give each child a set. Show the pictures and have the children hold up the nose if they smell the item or the ear if they hear it.

17　My Texture Book Craft

MATERIALS: booklet for each child (from pattern 17), feathers, fake fur, sandpaper, plastic wrap, aluminum foil, crayons

DIRECTIONS:
1.　Glue the items onto the appropriate pages to create a texture book.
2.　Decorate as desired.

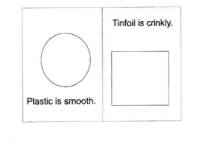

See also Shapes Touch Bag Activity (180).

MY CLOTHES

18　Fancy Me

When I get dressed up to go on the
　　town,
I always wear my prettiest crown.
With a big fancy dress the color of gold,
And my pinkest shoes, I'm beautiful,
　　I'm told.
My mom and dad pick me up at the
　　gate,
And we rush to the park for our
　　afternoon date.

19　Getting Dressed

Arms in sleeves, shirt over head
Pull it down just like I said.
Feet in socks, legs in pants
Pull them up and do a dance.
Feet in shoes, on goes the coat
Now we're dressed, and ready to go
　　out!

20　I've Lost My Sock Flannelboard

Use the sock from pattern 21 below. Make many pairs of socks from various colors of felt. (If you expect a large group in your program, make some socks striped, polka-dotted, etc., but do not make more than two socks of any one design.) Give each child one sock and keep the matching sock yourself. One by one, put the retained socks on the flannelboard, using the rhyme below to invite the children to come up and make a match.

I've lost my sock! I've lost my sock!
I don't know what to do!
Can you help me find my *(name of
　　color)* sock,
So that I will have two?

21   *Am I Ready to Go? Flannelboard*
See pattern 21.

I've got my pants on my arms and my
    socks on my head.
Am I ready to go? Yes or no?
I've got my hat on my knee and my
    shirt on my foot.
Am I ready to go? Yes or no?
I've got my sweater on my ear and my
    scarf on my ankle.
Am I ready to go? Yes or no?
I've got my shoe on my thumb and
    my belt on my leg.
Am I ready to go? Yes or no?

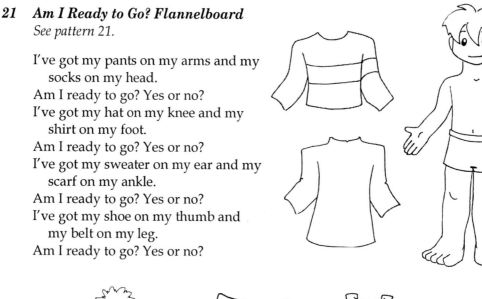

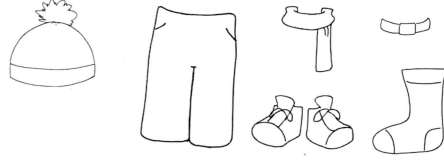

22   *Getting Dressed from Head to Toe Flannelboard*
See pattern 22.

On a cold winter's day, to avoid a sore
    throat
I remember to put on my warmest
    coat.
I add my socks and my boots too,
My mittens and hat,
And wooly scarf of blue.

23   When Do I Wear It? Flannelboard

See patterns 22 (above) and 23. Place a sun and a snowflake on opposite sides of the flannelboard. As you say the rhyme for each item of clothing, invite the children to guess in which season they would wear it.

I'm going to wear my *(item of clothing)*
    today, when I go outside to play.
It must be a *(winter/summer)* day!

See also Hat (90) *and* Design Your Own Pajamas Craft (130).

MY FEELINGS

24   Moody Days

On excited days I jump up and down,
I kick up my heels and make loud
    sounds.
On sad days I sit and moan,
I weep and wail and cry and groan.
On quiet days I think and rest,
I look around, and silence says it best.
On angry days I stamp my feet,
I shout and pout at those I meet.
On lazy days I sit and sit,
I do not want to work a bit.
On happy days, I smile big smiles,
I laugh and play all the while.

25   Some Days

Some days I'm happy,
Some days I'm sad,
Some days I'm very, very mad.
Some days I'm scared,
Some days I'm shy,
Some days I'm silly and pretend to fly.

See also The Mixed-Up Chameleon *Flannelboard (62).*

26   Best of All

I like my mom
And my dad too.
I like my brother
And the color blue.
I look in the mirror
And then I see
The best thing of all
Because I like me!

27   I'm Glad I'm Me
(traditional)

No one looks the way I do.
I have noticed that is true!
No one walks the way I walk.
No one talks the way I talk.
No one plays the way I play.
No one says the things I say.
I am special! I am me!
There's no one else I'd rather be!

ALL ABOUT ME: TEN GREAT BOOKS FOR STORYTIME

Horns to Toes and In Between by Sandra Boynton. New York: Little Simon, 1984. (for all ages)

From Head to Toe by Eric Carle. New York: HarperCollins, 1997. (for all ages)

The Mixed-Up Chameleon by Eric Carle. New York: HarperCollins, 1984. (for all ages)

Today I Feel Silly by Jamie Lee Curtis. New York: Joanna Cotler, 1998. (for preschoolers)

A Color of His Own by Leo Lionni. New York: Knopf, 2006. (for preschoolers)

We've All Got Bellybuttons by David Martin. Cambridge, MA: Candlewick, 2005. (for toddlers)

Taking a Bath with the Dog and Other Things That Make Me Happy by Scott Menchin. Cambridge, MA: Candlewick, 2007. (for all ages)

When You Are Happy by Eileen Spinelli. New York: Simon and Schuster, 2006. (for preschoolers)

Toby's Rainbow Clothes by Cyndy Szekeres. New York: Little Simon, 2000. (for toddlers)

Sometimes I'm Bombaloo by Rachel Vail. New York: Scholastic, 2002. (for preschoolers)

Chapter 3

Animals

BIRDS

28 Barn Owl

I met a barn owl. *(sign OWL)*
He turned his head, *(turn head while*
still making the sign for OWL)
He looked at me,
And this is what he said:
"I know I am a barn owl.
I flap my wings, that's what I do. *(flap*
arms)
But I have one question:
Whoooooo are you?"

owl

29 Five Little Geese Flannelboard

See pattern 29. (Full-size patterns can
be found at www.ala.org/editions/extras/
macmillan09775.)

WEB

One little goose heading south for the
winter, in a sky of blue,
Discovers another goose in flight, then
there are two.
Two little geese heading south for the
winter, flying high above the trees,
Discover another goose in flight, then
there are three.
Three little geese heading south for
the winter, in the sky soar,
Discover another goose in flight, then
there are four.
Four little geese heading south for the
winter, take a nap to revive,
Discover another goose sleeping, then
there are five.

CIRCUS ANIMALS

30 *The Animals in the Circus*
(to the tune of "The Wheels on the Bus")

The lion in the circus goes roar roar
    roar,
Roar roar roar, roar roar roar.
The lion in the circus goes roar roar
    roar
When the circus comes to town.

The monkey in the circus goes eee-
    eee-eee . . .
The elephant in the circus goes
    a-rooooo . . .
The poodles in the circus go jump
    jump jump . . .
The bears in the circus go growl growl
    growl . . .
The horses in the circus go gallop
    gallop gallop . . .

31 *Circus Animals*
(to the tune of "For He's a Jolly Good
Fellow")

Let's all go to the circus, let's all go to
    the circus,
Let's all go to the circus and have
    some fun today.
We'll see the elephant wave his trunk,
    we'll see the elephant wave his
    trunk,
We'll see the elephant wave his trunk,
    and then he'll say a-roo!
We'll see the monkeys jump up and
    down, we'll see the monkeys jump
    up and down,
We'll see the monkeys jump up and
    down, and then they'll say eee-eee.
We'll see the horses gallop and trot,
    we'll see the horses gallop and trot,
We'll see the horses gallop and trot,
    and then they'll say neigh.
We'll see the lion roar, we'll see the
    lion roar,
We'll see the lion roar, and then he'll
    say grrrrrr.

FARM ANIMALS

32 *Pony Ride*
(traditional)

Trot, trot, trot,
Go and go and never stop!
Trudge along, my little pony,
Where it's rough and where it's stony.
Go and go and never stop!
Trot, trot, trot, trot, trot!

> **Quick Tip:** Pony Ride can be used
> as a lap bounce with babies or as an
> action rhyme with older children.

33 *How Much Is That Piggy?*
(to the tune of "How Much Is That Doggy
in the Window?")

How much is that piggy in the pigsty?
    (Oink oink!)
The one with the curly tail. (Oink
    oink!)
How much is that piggy in the pigsty?
    (Oink oink!)
I do hope that piggy's for sale.

34   Rooster's Feathers Flannelboard

See pattern 34. Cut feathers out of different colors of felt. Place the rooster on the flannelboard. Hand out the feathers to children. Have the children decorate the rooster as you sing the following song to the tune of "Do You Know the Muffin Man?"

Do you have a red feather, a red
    feather, a red feather?
If you have a red feather, bring it up
    here now.
Repeat with other colors.

PETS

35   Call the Puppy
(traditional)

Call the puppy *(beckon with finger)*
And give him some milk. *(pour milk in
    bowl)*
Brush his coat *(pretend to brush)*
Till it shines like silk.
Call the puppy *(beckon with finger)*
And give him a bone. *(mime giving bone)*
Take him for a walk *(pretend to hold leash)*
And then bring him home. *(make shape
    of house with hands)*

36   I Went to the Pet Store
*Pause before the last word of each verse to
let the children guess the rhyme.*

I went to the pet store
And made a special wish.
The pet that I wanted
Was a very special *(fish)*!

I went to the pet store,
I went there at a jog,
To get a pet with a wagging tail,
It was a little *(dog)*!

I went to the pet store,
I went there just like that,
Because I heard a little purr,
It was a little *(cat)*!

I went to the pet store,
It had become a habit.
The pet I wanted now
Was a soft, white, fluffy *(rabbit)*!

I went to the pet store,
I'm sure this sounds absurd,
But the pet I wanted was
A colorful flying *(bird)*!

I went to the pet store,
It was no mistake.
What I really wanted now
Was a hissing green *(snake)*!

37   Little Poodle
(traditional)

I had a little poodle, *(hold up fist)*
His coat was silver gray.
One day I thought I'd bathe him,
To wash the dirt away,
I washed my little poodle, *(scrub fist
    with other hand)*
Then dried him with a towel. *(pat fist
    as if drying with a towel)*
My poodle seemed to like his bath,
He didn't even growl.

38   Puppy Dog, Puppy Dog

Puppy dog, puppy dog, wag your tail.
Puppy dog, puppy dog, let out a wail.
Puppy dog, puppy dog, jump for a bone.
Puppy dog, puppy dog, run on home.

39   *Puppy Time*

Puppy time, puppy time, we love
    puppy time!
One, two, three puppies barking at a tree,
Four, five, six puppies staring back at me.
Puppy time, puppy time, we love
    puppy time!

40   *Three Little Kittens*

Three little kittens going for a stroll,
    (walk in place)
The first one decided to take a muddy
    roll, *(roll arms)*
The second one ran through the
    garden chasing a mouse, *(run in place)*
The third one climbed to the roof of
    the house. *(pretend to climb)*
And when they all came home up the
    path, *(walk in place)*
Mama Cat said, "It's time for a bath!"
    (scrub)

41   *Three Little Puppies*
(traditional)

Three little puppies looking fresh and
    new,
One ran for dinner and then there
    were two.
Two little puppies napping in the sun,
One chased a little bird and then there
    was one.
One little puppy looking for some fun,
He headed off to catch his friends and
    then there were none.

42   *Two Little Cats*

Two little cats sitting on my windowsill,
One named Jack and one named Jill.
Run away, Jack! Run away, Jill!
Come back, Jack! Come back, Jill!

43   *Ten Dogs in the Window Flannelboard*
(traditional)

See pattern 43.

Ten dogs in the window for the whole
    wide world to see.
Look, someone is coming . . .
"You're the perfect dog for me!"
Repeat with numbers nine through two.

One dog in the window, she's as
    lonely as can be.
Look, someone is coming . . .
And here's a family.
One dog in the window, she's making
    such a fuss.
Look, they are all stopping . . .
"You're the perfect dog for us!"

44   *This Little Doggie Flannelboard*
(traditional)

See pattern 43 above.

This little doggie ran away to play.
This little doggie said, "I'll play all
    day."
This little doggie began to dig and dig.
This little doggie danced a funny jig.
This little doggie cried, "Woof, woof,
    woof! I wish I were big."

Quick Tip: When performing Two Little Cats (or its traditional counterpart, Two Little Blackbirds), use your right hand to represent one cat running away to your left and your left hand to represent the other cat running away to your right, and encourage the children to imitate you. This cross-lateral movement stimulates both sides of the brain and encourages the hemispheres to work together.

45　Dog's Colorful Day *Flannelboard*

See pattern 45. Based on the book by Emma Dodds (New York: Dutton, 2001). Dog gets messy as he gains spots of different colors throughout the day. This flannelboard story is a hit with all ages! Pass out mini scrubbers and ask the children to help you clean the dog when he takes his bath at the end of the story.

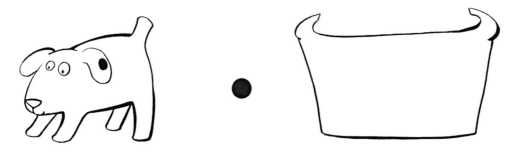

See also Someone Special (201) and Veterinarian Song (318).

SEA LIFE

46　Gone Fishing

Maxwell the fisherman floats on the sea,
Sitting in his boat is where he really
　　loves to be. *(make boat with cupped
　　hands)*
He throws in his line and makes a
　　little wish, *(mime throwing fishing line)*
Hoping that maybe today he'll catch a
　　fish. *(cross fingers)*
When he reels it in from the water
　　cold and black, *(mime reeling in
　　fishing pole)*
He gives that little fish a little kiss,
　　(mime kissing fish)
And then he throws it back. *(mime
　　throwing it back)*

47　Octopus, Octopus

Octopus, octopus, turn around.
Octopus, octopus, touch the ground.
Octopus, octopus, reach up high.
Octopus, octopus, swimming by.

48　Dolphin Song
(to the tune of "Camptown Races")

Sign DOLPHIN as you sing this song.

DOLPHINS leaping in the sea,
Leaping, leaping,
DOLPHINS leaping in the sea,
All the livelong day.
DOLPHINS leaping high,
DOLPHINS leaping low,
DOLPHINS leaping in the sea,
All the livelong day.

49   *Take Me Out to the Ocean*
(to the tune of "Take Me Out to the Ball Game")

Take me out to the ocean,
Take me out to the sea.
There goes a starfish and sand dollar,
I'm having such fun, I've just got to holler.
Oh, it's swim, swim, swim underwater,
Catch a ride on a whale, don't fear,
For the sea animals are our friends,
Let's give a great big cheer!

50   *Five Little Fish Flannelboard*
See pattern 50.

One little fish all alone in the ocean blue,
Finds another and that makes two.
Two little fish swimming in the sea,
Find another and that makes three.
Three little fish swimming through a sunken ship's door,
Find another and that makes four.
Four little fish decide to dive,
They find another and that makes five.

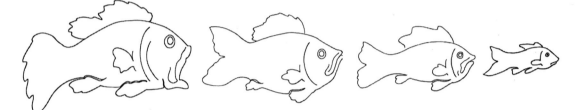

51   Blue Sea *Flannelboard*
See pattern 50 above. Based on the book by Robert Kalan (New York: Greenwillow, 1979). In this simple classic, a small fish escapes from a larger fish, the larger fish escapes from an even larger fish, and so on. Use a piece of netting to create a net and a piece of felt with various sized holes to trap the bigger fish.

52   *Jellyfish Craft*

MATERIALS: one white basket coffee filter for each child, hole punch, watercolor paints, brushes, water, markers, yarn

DIRECTIONS:
1. Fold each coffee filter in half. Punch one hole at the top of the folded edge so that two holes appear near the center of the filter when you lay it flat.
2. Punch five holes around the edges of the filter.
3. Using watercolor paints, paint the coffee filter. The wetter the paint, the more the color will spread along the filter. (For a quicker, less messy variation, use markers to decorate the coffee filter, then spritz it with water to spread the color.)
4. Once the filter is dry, thread a piece of yarn through the center holes so that the coffee filter hangs flat, making the top of the jellyfish. Add colorful yarn to the holes around the edges to make tentacles.

WOODLAND ANIMALS

53 *Animal Walk*
(traditional)

Here goes the turtle up a hill,
Creep, creep, creep.
Here goes a rabbit up a hill,
Boing, boing, boing!
Here goes an elephant up a hill,
Thud, thud, thud!
Here goes a snake up a hill,
Slither, slither, slither!

> **Quick Tip:** Animal Walk makes
> a great lap bounce for babies and
> toddlers and a great action rhyme
> for older children.

54 *Bear Rhyme*

I am a bear and I like honey. *(lumber like a bear, rub tummy)*
I live in the woods. Do you think that's funny? *(make tree shapes with hands)*
I catch fish in the river and sing a summer song. *(mime catching fish)*
Then when snow falls, I sleep all winter long. *(mime sleeping)*

55 *Little Frog*
(traditional)

A little frog in a pond am I,
Hippity-hippity-hop.
And I can jump in the air so high,
Hippity-hippity-hop!

56 *Slowly, Slowly*
(traditional)

Slowly, slowly, very slowly
Creeps the garden snail. *(creep fingers up child's arm slowly)*
Slowly, slowly, very slowly
Up the wooden rail.
But then . . .
Quickly, quickly, very quickly
Runs the little mouse. *(run fingers up child's arm quickly)*
Quickly, quickly, very quickly
Round about the house. *(tickle child)*

57 *Nocturnal Animals*

Nocturnal animals, they come out at night,
Some crawl on the land while others take flight. *(make crawling and flying motions)*
An owl soars silently, turning left and right, *(turn left and right)*
A raccoon is a sneaky bandit, trying to hide from sight. *(put hands in front of face and try to hide)*
Bats use echolocation to find even a tiny mite, *(cup ear)*
While coyotes sound an alarm before they take a bite. *(make barking coyote noise)*
Bears are foragers, lifting logs with all their might, *(pretend to lift tree)*
But beware of the stinky skunk, who lifts his tail in fright. *(wave hand in front of face)*
Although possum is not upside down, he's in the tree at quite a height, *(look up)*
While the foxes' bushy tails often delight. *(shake your tail)*

58 *Bats Are Flying*
(to the tune of "Frère Jacques")

Bats are flying, bats are flying,
In the sky, in the sky.
Only in the nighttime, only in the nighttime.
Bats fly by, bats fly by.

> **Quick Tip:** When you do tickle
> rhymes, pass out pom-poms for the
> adults to use to represent the mouse
> or other small animal.

59   Turtle, Turtle

TURTLE, TURTLE, off you go. *(sign TURTLE)*
You are small and green and slow.
(move sign slowly in front of you)
When you're scared, into your shell you go. *(tuck thumb into fist)*
We hope you'll pop out and say hello! *(poke thumb out)*

60   On the Pond
(to the tune of "The Wheels on the Bus")

The ducks on the pond go quack quack quack.
Quack quack quack, quack quack quack,
The ducks on the pond go quack quack quack
All through the day.

The frogs on the pond go ribbit ribbit ribbit,
Ribbit ribbit ribbit, ribbit ribbit ribbit.
The frogs on the pond go ribbit ribbit ribbit
All through the day.

61   In the Woods Flannelboard

See pattern 61. Hide the flannelboard pieces around the room; then say the rhyme while the children play an I Spy woodland creature game.

In the woods, I can see, so many animals looking at me!
I spy a *(name of animal)*.

62 The Mixed-Up Chameleon *Flannelboard*

See pattern 62. Based on the book by Eric Carle (New York: HarperCollins, 1984). A chameleon wishes he could be like all the other animals, but when he gets his wish, it's not exactly what he had in mind.

WEB

63 Time to Sleep *Flannelboard*

See pattern 63. Based on the book by Denise Fleming (New York: Henry Holt, 1997). Bear is ready to sleep for the winter, but first she must tell Snail, who must tell Skunk, and so on.

WEB

64 Porcupine Craft

MATERIALS: half a paper plate for each child, long spikes cut from black construction paper, one googly eye for each child, glue sticks, crayons or markers

DIRECTIONS:
1. Glue spikes onto the curved edge of the plate.
2. Glue one googly eye to one end of the plate.
3. Draw a mouth and decorate as desired.

65 Worm Finger Puppet Craft

MATERIALS: one chenille stem for each child, two googly eyes for each child, glue

DIRECTIONS:
1. Glue the googly eyes side by side on one end of the chenille stem.
2. Coil the chenille stem around your finger so that the eyes sit by your fingernail.

See also Mother, Mother, I Want Another *Flannelboard (127)*, If You Give a Moose a Muffin *Flannelboard (230)*, *Way Up High in the Maple Tree (297)*, and Moongame *Flannelboard (312)*.

ZOO ANIMALS

66 Alligator, Alligator

Alligator, alligator, swim around,
Alligator, alligator, don't make a
    sound.
Alligator, alligator, if we tap,
You open your jaws with a great big
    snap!

67 I'm a Giraffe
(traditional)

I'm a big tall giraffe stretching way up
    high, *(stretch arms up over head)*
A big tall giraffe, I almost reach the
    sky. *(stand on tiptoes)*
I eat the leaves from the tallest trees,
    (pretend to pull leaves from the trees)
And when I run, I move with ease.
    (run in place)
I'm a big tall giraffe stretching way up
    high, *(stretch arms up over head)*
A big tall giraffe, I almost reach the
    sky. *(stand on tiptoes)*

68 Kangaroo Baby

If I were a kangaroo baby,
I'd stay with my mommy all day,
Curled up in her little pouch
As we hopped along our way.
Everyone would call me joey
Until I got bigger, then they'd stop,
Because I would come out of my
    mommy's pouch
With a hop, hop, hop, hop, hop!

69 The Animals at the Zoo
(to the tune of "The Wheels on the Bus")

The lions at the zoo go roar roar roar,
Roar roar roar, roar roar roar.
The lions at the zoo go roar roar roar,
All day long!

The snakes at the zoo go hiss hiss hiss . . .
The hyenas at the zoo go ha ha ha . . .
The monkeys at the zoo go eee-eee-
    eee . . .

70   The Elephant Hokey-Pokey
(to the tune of "The Hokey-Pokey")

You put your trunk in,
You put your trunk out,
You put your trunk in,
And you shake it all about.
You stomp around on your big feet
    and turn yourself around,
That's what it's all about.

. . . right ear in . . .
. . . left ear in . . .
. . . tail in . . .
. . . tusks in . . .
. . . whole self in . . .

71   Five Little Snakes Flannelboard
Use the snake from pattern 61.

One little snake looking for something
    to do,
He finds another and that makes two.
Two little snakes wrapped around a
    tree,
Another slithers up and that makes
    three.
Three little snakes by the garden door,
They see another and that makes four.
Four little snakes notice one more arrive,
Basking in the sun, the snakes make
    five.

72   Five Little Camels Flannelboard
See pattern 72.

Five little camels letting out a snore,
They woke up, one ran away, and
    then there were four.
Four little camels, so many humps we
    see,
One ran away and then there were
    three.
Three little camels, when the day was
    new,
One ran away and then there were
    two.
Two little camels under the desert sun,
One ran away and then there was one.
One little camel climbing up a dune,
He ran away and then there were
    none.

73   Did You Ever Eat . . . ? Flannelboard
See pattern 73. As you pull out the felt animals, ask children, "Did you ever eat . . . ?"
For the ending, you can use an empty animal-cracker box or make one from the pattern.

Did you ever eat a hippo?
No? Hmph, I love to eat hippos!
Did you ever eat a zebra?
No? Hmph, I love to eat zebras!
. . . monkeys . . .
. . . elephants . . .
. . . tigers . . .
Well, I love to eat all the animals that
    come in my box of animal crackers!

74   *I Love You More Than . . . Flannelboard*
(adapted traditional)

See pattern 74.

I love you more than one bird,
Two monkeys, three lions, four giraffes, five elephants,
And all the stars in the sky.

75   *Lion Hide-and-Seek Flannelboard*

See pattern 75. For each place the cub hides, place the cub under the item on the flannelboard with its tail or nose or ear sticking out so the children can see it.

Lucy Lion was looking for her cub. But he wanted to play hide-and-seek! Can you see him? Yes, he's there behind the tree! Oh no, he's hidden again. Can you see him? Yes, there he is, behind that rock! *(Repeat with other hiding places.)*

Lucy couldn't find her cub anywhere! Finally she called "Suppertime!" and her cub popped out and said, "Here I am, Mama!"

See also Little Elephant (87), Five Little Monkeys Flannelboard (126), and Animal Opposites Flannelboard (173).

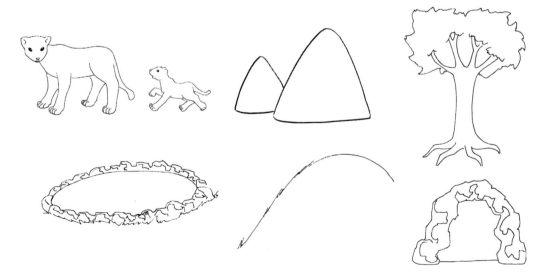

ANIMALS: TEN GREAT BOOKS FOR STORYTIME

Mommy, Carry Me Please! by Jane Cabrera. New York: Holiday House, 2006. (for all ages)
Dear Zoo by Rod Campbell. New York: Little Simon, 2007. (for all ages)
Mister Seahorse by Eric Carle. New York: Philomel, 2004. (for preschoolers)
Five Little Monkeys Sitting in a Tree by Eileen Christelow. New York: Clarion, 1991. (for preschoolers)
Peek-a-Moo by Maria Torres Cimarusti. New York: Dutton, 1998. (for toddlers)
Buster by Denise Fleming. New York: Henry Holt, 2003. (for all ages)
In the Tall, Tall Grass by Denise Fleming. New York: Henry Holt, 1991. (for toddlers)
At the Zoo by Douglas Florian. New York: Greenwillow, 1992. (for toddlers)
Down by the Station by Will Hillenbrand. New York: Gulliver, 1999. (for all ages)
Little Monkey Says Good Night by Ann Whitford Paul. New York: Farrar, Straus, and Giroux, 2003. (for all ages)

Chapter 4

Around the World

ALL AROUND THE WORLD

76 *Kids around the World Wake Up*
(to the tune of "When Ducks Wake Up in the Morning")

When French kids wake up in the
     morning, they always say good day.
But when French kids wake up in the
     morning, they say it the French way:
"Bonjour!" "Bonjour!" That is what
     they say.

When Spanish kids wake up in the
     morning, they always say good day.

But when Spanish kids wake up in the
     morning, they say it the Spanish way:
"¡Buenos días!" "¡Buenos días!" That
     is what they say.

When Chinese kids wake up in the
     morning, they always say good
     day.
But when Chinese kids wake up in the
     morning, they say it the Chinese
     way:
"Ni hao!" "Ni hao!" That is what they
     say. *(pronounced "knee how")*

77 *Map Activity*

Show a map of the world and have the children mark the country where they live and mark some of the countries you discuss during storytime.

78 *Let's Write a Rhyme Activity*

Many cultures' traditional nursery rhymes are about nature and everyday things children see and use. Work with the children to create a short rhyme about something from where they live. Have them color a picture to go with it.

79 *Around the World: Fun Facts to Share*

The country of Italy is shaped like a boot.
The capital city of Germany is Berlin.
Siberian tigers are the world's biggest tigers, and they live in Russia.
Russia is the largest country in the world.
The country of Japan is made up of a string of islands.
The giant panda lives in the mountains of China.

The Great Wall of China stretches over four thousand miles in northern China.
Brazil is the largest of twelve countries that make up the South American continent.
The Eiffel Tower is in France.
London is the capital city of England.
In Canada there are moose, seals, and polar bears.

AFRICA

From Egypt

80   *Mommy Is Coming*
(adapted traditional)

Perform using a box with animal puppets inside.

Mommy is coming,
She's almost here,
She's bringing toys and gifts.
She's got a box,
Inside is a duck
That goes
Quack quack quack,
Quack quack.
Repeat with other animals.

From Kenya

81   *The Leaf*
(traditional)

The leaf, the leaf
On the coconut tree, on the coconut tree.
When the wind blows
It shakes, shakes, shakes.

From Tunisia

82   *Teddy Bear*
(traditional)

I have a nice soft teddy bear,
His nose looks very fine.
Look at his eyes so beautiful.

ASIA

From China

83   *Red Dragonflies*
(traditional)

Red dragonflies, red dragonflies,
They gently stop.
On the rocks gently they stop.
On the water gently they stop.
In the breeze gently they stop.

From Japan

84   *Acorn*
(traditional)

An acorn rolled down and down,
He suddenly fell into a pond.
Then came the fish,
And said, "Hi! Come play with us!"

The acorn enjoyed playing with them,
But he soon began to cry,
"I want to go back to the mountain."
The fish didn't know what to do.

85   *Close Hands, Open Hands*
(traditional)

Close hands, open hands,
Clap hands, close hands.
Open hands again, clap hands,
Put those hands up.
Close hands, open hands,
Clap hands, close hands.

86   *Kite Song*
(traditional)

Kites are rising in the sky,
Catching fair winds far up high,
Rise and rise to clouds that float,
Fly high up in the sky!

Kites are neat in the sky,
Dancing, leaping way up high,
Rising to the white clouds,
Fly high up in the sky!

Falling, falling is the kite,
Run and run to keep it high,
Oh, the kite is rising now,
Hold, hold your string tight!

Quick Tip: Use the kite streamers from Let's Fly a Kite Streamer Game (343) while saying this rhyme.

87   *Little Elephant*
(traditional)

Little elephant, little elephant,
You have a long, long nose.
Yes, sir, my mother has a long nose,
    too.

Little elephant, little elephant,
Who do you like best in the world?
Well, I like my mother best in the
    world.

From South Korea

88   *Springtime Outing*
(traditional)

Lily, lily, golden bell.
Pluck it, put it in your bill.
Bunch of chickies, hop, hop, hop!
Springtime outing, off they go.

AUSTRALIA

89   *An Australian Creation Story Flannelboard*
   See pattern 89. (Full-size patterns can be found at www.ala.org/editions/extras/macmillan09775.) Adapted from the book Sun Mother Wakes the World: An Australian Creation Story *by Diane Wolkstein (New York: HarperCollins, 2004).*

In the beginning there was darkness. The earth was asleep. In the sky, Sun Mother was also asleep until she heard a soft whisper telling her to wake up. When Sun Mother opened her eyes, light appeared and Sun Mother sped to the earth. With each step that Sun Mother took, the earth awakened, and grass, plants, and trees sprouted. Sun Mother visited the dark caves and awakened the sleeping animal spirits. First the bugs and insects awakened, then the lizards, frogs, snakes, and fish.

Next birds and animals of every kind awakened. Sun Mother looked at all she had awakened and told them that she needed to return to her home in the sky.

The animals were all scared because it grew dark again, but then a little frog noticed that the Sun Mother was returning in the eastern sky. "Welcome!" all the animals cried joyously. The animals watched as the Sun Mother glided slowly across the sky to the west. And so it continued each day.

Over time the animals forgot the joy they felt when they first received the gift of life. They all became envious of what they did not have. They fought often, and their loud cries reached Sun Mother. Sun Mother sped to earth and told the animals that if they were unhappy, they could change their shape, but to choose carefully because it would be their form for a long time.

Wombat chose to have strong claws to dig tunnels. Kangaroo chose to have a pouch to keep her babies close to her. Emu chose to have long legs to run faster than any other bird. Platypus could not decide so she chose everything: a beak, fur, webbed feet, and a tail. After all the animals were done choosing their new forms, Sun Mother gave birth to a daughter and a son, the Moon and Morning Star. The Sun Mother told all the animals that when she left them in the evening, her daughter Moon and son Morning Star would be there to give them light.

Moon and Morning Star grew brighter and in time gave birth to the first woman and the first man. "Welcome!" called the Sun Mother. The Sun Mother told the woman and man that all the animals were their relations. The earth was there to take care of them, just as they were to take care of the earth.

EUROPE

From Belgium

90 **Hat**
(traditional)

One, two, three, four, paper, paper,
One, two, three, four, paper hat.
And if you have no more hat,
Make one with gift wrap.
One, two, three, four, paper hat.

From France

91 **Hello, Mrs. Monday**
(traditional)

Hello, Mrs. Monday!
How is Mrs. Tuesday?
Very fine, Mrs. Wednesday!
Tell Mrs. Thursday
To come on Friday
To dance on Saturday
In Sunday's ballroom.

92   *Kisses for Mommy*
(traditional)

On a very, very soft piece of material,
I'm drawing, I'm drawing.
On a very, very soft piece of material,
I'm drawing kisses
for Mommy's Day.
I'm drawing, I'm drawing.
For Mommy's Day
I'm drawing and doing my best.

From Italy

93   *Firefly, Firefly*
(traditional)

Firefly, firefly, yellow and bright,
Bridle the horse under your light.
The son of the king is ready to ride,
Firefly, firefly, fly by my side.

From Switzerland

94   *Spring Has Come*
(traditional)

Now spring is here and soft winds
    blow
To melt from the mountains the ice
    and the snow.
The cuckoo is calling in vales below
To say that this is so.
Yo holee-holee, hola-leeho,
Up in the mountains the cows will go.
Yo holee-holee, hola-leeho,
Up in the mountains the cows will go.

The herdsman looks up at the blue
    spring sky,
He shouts and he sings to the
    mountains high.
Good-bye little valley, good-bye,
    good-bye.
You can hear his loud cry.

Yo holee-holee, hola-leeho,
Up in the Alps where the grasses
    grow.
Yo holee-holee, hola-leeho,
Up to the Alps we'll go.

NORTH AMERICA AND THE CARIBBEAN

From the Bahamas

95   *I Went Up on the Hill*
(traditional)

I went up on the hill
With a bucket on my head, *(mime
    walking with bucket on head)*
The road so rocky,
Till my bucket fall down. *(mime bucket
    falling)*
Rock-a-my-cherry, one, two,
Rock-a-my-cherry, three, four.

From Canada

96   *Leaves Flannelboard*
(traditional)

See pattern 96.

A yellow leaf
Is falling down, falling down, falling
    down.
A yellow leaf
Is falling down to the ground.

A red leaf
Is moving, moving, moving.
A red leaf
Is moving with the wind.

A brown leaf
Is flying, flying, flying.
A brown leaf
Is flying up to the sky.

From Haiti

97 *Turtle's Flight Flannelboard Story*
(traditional)

See pattern 97. If you can find turtle and bird puppets with movable mouths, this also works well as a puppet story.

It was springtime, and the birds were all getting ready to fly north to New York City. Turtle was sad as he said good-bye to his friends. "I wish I could go north with you and see all the big buildings, but I have no wings," he said. "I even know how to say a word in English: bye-bye. Wouldn't it be lovely if I could go and meet those New York City turtles and talk to them?"

Pigeon was his special friend, and she took pity on him. "Maybe you can come," she said. "I have an idea." And she looked around until she found a sturdy stick. "I will put the stick in my beak, and you hold the other end in your mouth. Then, when I fly up into the air, you will go with me."

"Oh, thank you!" said Turtle. He was so excited.

"Just be careful to keep your mouth closed around the stick," warned Pigeon. "I can't come back and get you if you let go."

"Oh, I will," Turtle promised. "I'll hold on tight."

Soon it was time to go. Pigeon put one end of the stick in her beak, and Turtle clamped his mouth shut over the other end. Pigeon flapped her wings, and they rose high into the air. Turtle was nervous and excited. He had never seen the ocean and his island from up in the air before. He looked down and saw all the animals lined up on the shore, waving good-bye to the birds. He saw the looks of astonishment on their faces when they saw him hanging from the stick.

"Is that Turtle?" they said. "Is he really going to New York City?"

Turtle was so pleased with himself that he decided to show off. He opened his mouth to say the one word of English he knew.

"Bye-bye!" he cried, and he fell, fell, fell down into the ocean and landed with a splash.

"Turtle! Why did you let go?" called Pigeon. "I told you I wouldn't be able to come back for you! Good-bye! I will see you in the autumn!" And she flew away.

Turtle swam back to the shore, very disappointed.

And that is why you will see plenty of pigeons in New York, but Turtle is still in Haiti.

From Puerto Rico

98 *Moon*
(traditional)

Moon, little charming moon,
You are so pretty, so enchanting.
Your light comes in through my window,
And when I go to sleep I will say good night to you.

From the United States

American Sign Language

99 Sign Me Hello

Sign the words in capital letters as you say this rhyme.

Sign me HELLO,
Sign me GOOD-BYE,
Sign me a CAT,
Sign me a BUTTERFLY,
But of all the signs that you can do
My very favorite is I LOVE YOU!

100 Two Hands Signing

Sign the words in capital letters as you say this rhyme.

I have two HANDS,
I can use them to SIGN.
I can tell you HELLO,
I can ask for the TIME,
I can say you're my FRIEND,
I can ask you to PLAY,
And I can sign GOOD-BYE
At the end of the DAY.

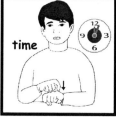

101 Friendship Sign Song

(to the tune of "Row, Row, Row Your Boat")

Sign the words in capital letters as you say this rhyme.

Here's the sign for YOU,
Here's the sign for ME.
I put my fingers together like this
'Cause FRIENDS we'll always be.

102 *Signing*

(to the tune of "A Bicycle Built for Two")

Sign the words in capital letters as you sing this song.

SIGNING, SIGNING,
It's what we LIKE to do.
We know SIGN LANGUAGE
Is a way to talk too.
You DON'T KNOW what you're missin'
Till you use your EYES to listen.
Talk with your HANDS,
We'll UNDERSTAND
'Cause we love SIGN LANGUAGE too!

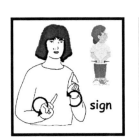

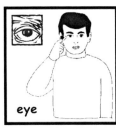

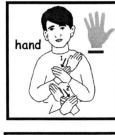

103 *I LOVE YOU Sign-Language Stick-Puppet Craft*

MATERIALS: construction paper, scissors, craft sticks, glue, decorating materials

DIRECTIONS:
1. Trace your hand onto construction paper and cut out the shape.
   (Precut hand shapes may be provided instead.)
2. Glue down the middle and ring fingers to make the sign for I LOVE YOU.
3. Attach a craft stick and decorate.

Native Americans

104 Coyote and the Laughing Butterflies *Flannelboard Story*

See pattern 104. Based on the book by Harriet Peck Taylor (New York: Macmillan, 1995). The butterflies play a trick on lazy Coyote. When you make the pieces, attach the butterfly pieces to clothespins with springs so that you can use them to lift the coyote piece when the butterflies carry him through the air.

SOUTH AMERICA

From Bolivia

105 She Dances Alone
(traditional)

I want to see her dance,
Jump and spring,
Walk in the air,
And move with much elegance.
Leave her alone, all alone and alone.

AROUND THE WORLD: TEN GREAT BOOKS FOR STORYTIME

My Granny Went to Market: A Round-the-World Counting Rhyme by Stella Blackstone. Cambridge, MA: Barefoot Books, 2005. (for all ages)
Can You Say Peace? by Karen Katz. New York: Henry Holt, 2006. (for preschoolers)
The Colors of Us by Karen Katz. New York: Henry Holt, 1999. (for preschoolers)
Dad and Me in the Morning by Patricia Lakin. New York: Whitman, 1994. (for preschoolers)
My House Has Stars by Megan McDonald. New York: Orchard, 1994. (for preschoolers)
Snug in Mama's Arms by Angela Shelf Medearis. Columbus, OH: Gingham Dog Press, 2004. (for toddlers)
Moses Goes to the Circus by Isaac Millman. New York: Farrar, Straus, and Giroux, 2003. (for all ages)
Bake You a Pie by Ellen Olson-Brown and Brian Claflin. Berkeley, CA: Tricycle, 2006. (for all ages)
How to Make an Apple Pie and See the World by Marjorie Priceman. New York: Knopf, 1994. (for all ages)
Sleep, Sleep, Sleep: A Lullaby for Little Ones around the World by Nancy Van Laan. New York: Little, Brown, 1995. (for all ages)

Chapter 5

At Home

IN THE MORNING

106 *Every Morning*

Every morning I jump out of bed
And neatly comb the hair on my head.
I brush my teeth and get dressed
In my play clothes that can get
  messed.
I run downstairs while I sing
And wonder what today will bring!

107 *Wake Up*

(to the tune of "Twinkle, Twinkle, Little Star")

Sign WAKE UP as you sing this song.

WAKE UP, WAKE UP, it's morning.
Open your eyes, the sun is shining.
First I get dressed, then I eat,
Starting my day is such a treat.
WAKE UP, WAKE UP, it's morning.
Open your eyes, the sun is shining.

108 *Good Morning Song*

(to the tune of "Happy Birthday")

Sign GOOD MORNING as you sing this song.

GOOD MORNING to you,
GOOD MORNING to you.
GOOD MORNING, everybody,
GOOD MORNING to you.

See also Kids around the World Wake Up (76), Breakfast (215), and Cereal for Breakfast (220).

SAFETY/CLEANING

109 Chores
(to the tune of "The Wheels on the Bus")

There are lots of chores around the
house, around the house, around
the house,
There are lots of chores around the
house that we will do today.
First we'll wash the windows, the
windows, the windows,
First we'll wash the windows around
the house today.
Next we'll vacuum the carpet, the
carpet, the carpet,
Next we'll vacuum the carpet around
the house today.
Last we'll mop the kitchen floor,
kitchen floor, kitchen floor,
Last we'll mop the kitchen floor in the
house today.

110 Cleanup Song
(to the tune of "Camptown Races")

Sign CLEAN as you sing this song.

Toys are scattered everywhere,
CLEAN up, CLEAN up.
Toys are scattered everywhere,
Time to CLEAN up now.
Put the toys away,
We'll play another day.
Toys are scattered everywhere,
Time to CLEAN up now.

111 Old MacDonald's Cleaning Cart
(to the tune of "Old MacDonald")

Old MacDonald had a cleaning cart,
E-I-E-I-O,
And on this cleaning cart he had a
vacuum, E-I-E-I-O.
With a vroom-vroom here and a
vroom-vroom there,
Here a vroom, there a vroom,
everywhere a vroom-vroom.
Old MacDonald had a cleaning cart,
E-I-E-I-O.

. . . duster/dust . . .
. . . rag/wipe . . .
. . . broom/sweep . . .
. . . mop/mop . . .

clean

112 Do We Touch It? Activity
See pattern 112. (Full-size patterns can be found at www.ala.org/editions/extras/
macmillan09775.) Additional props needed: teddy bear, children's book, toy car, another
toy, such as a jack-in-the-box. Hold up each item or picture and ask the children if they are
allowed to touch it or not. Ask why or why not. Pass the touchable items around.

BATH TIME

113 *Bath-Time Fun*

Wash your hair and wash your face,
Wash your neck and every place
On your arms and on your thumbs.
Wash your hands—are we almost done?
Wash your tummy, wash your knees,
Legs and ankles, if you please.
Wash your feet and each little toe.
Bath time is so much fun, you know?

114 *Bubbles, Bubbles*
(traditional)

Sign BUBBLE as you say this rhyme.

BUBBLES, BUBBLES all around.
BUBBLES, BUBBLES fat and round.
BUBBLES on my toes and on my nose.
BUBBLES way up high they go.
BUBBLES, BUBBLES all around.
BUBBLES, BUBBLES on the ground.

115 *All through Bath Time*
(to the tune of "The Wheels on the Bus")

The bubbles in the tub go
Pop, pop, pop! Pop, pop, pop! Pop, pop, pop!
The bubbles in the tub go pop, pop, pop!
All through my bath time!

The washcloth in the tub goes scrub, scrub, scrub . . .
The ducky in the tub goes squirt, squirt, squirt . . .

116 *Bath*
(to the tune of "Here We Go Round the Mulberry Bush")

This is the way to fill the bath, fill the bath, fill the bath.
This is the way to fill the bath, so early in the morning.

This is the way to wash our faces . . .
This is the way to wash ourselves . . .
This is the way to wash our hair . . .
This is the way to dry ourselves . . .
This is the way to brush our teeth . . .

117 *Bubbles*
(to the tune of "Twinkle, Twinkle, Little Star")

Bubbles, bubbles everywhere,
They are even in my hair.
First I scrub my little toes,
Then I scrub my ears and nose.
Bubbles, bubbles everywhere,
They are even in my hair.

118 *Five Rubber Ducks Flannelboard*
(to the tune of "One Elephant Went Out to Play")

See pattern 118.

Five rubber ducks came out to play,
Battling the waves in the tub today.
Along came the splash that sent one to shore,
And then he couldn't play anymore.
Four rubber ducks . . .
Three rubber ducks . . .
Two rubber ducks . . .
One rubber duck came out to play,
Battling the waves in the tub today.
Along came the splash that sent him to shore,
Now no rubber ducks can play anymore.

WEB

119 *Three Bubbles Flannelboard*
(adapted traditional)

See pattern 119.

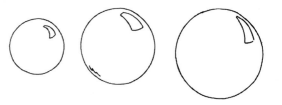

A small bubble,
A medium bubble,
A great big bubble I see! Now let's
    count them, one, two, three!
Now let's pop them, one, two, three!

See also Three Little Kittens (40) and Dog's Colorful Day Flannelboard (45).

BEDTIME

120 *Bedtime Tickle Bug*

Tickle bug, tickle bug
Hunting feet.
Creeping, creeping
Over the sheet.
One! Two!
Catch 'em like this. *(catch feet)*
Tickle-y, tickle-y, *(tickle toes)*
Tummy kiss! *(kiss tummy)*

WEB

121 *Going to Bed*

This little child is going to bed, *(point
    to self)*
Down on the pillow he lays his head.
    (rest head on hands)
He wraps himself in a blanket tight,
    (hug yourself)
And this is the way he sleeps all night.
Zzzzzzz . . . ZZZZZZZZ.

122 *Lullaby*

Lullaby and good night,
Lay your head down and rest now.
Mama loves you, Daddy too,
And everything's OK.
Good night, little one,
Close your eyes, the day's done.
Sleep well, little one,
We love you so.

WEB

123 *Sweet Dreams*

Before I go to bed each night,
My mama tucks my covers in tight.
I cuddle my teddy
While she cuddles me,
And I settle in for the sweetest
    dreams.

124 *Four Little Stars Flannelboard*
See pattern 124.

Four little stars winking at me,
One shot off, then there were three.
Three little stars with nothing to do,
One shot off, then there were two.
Two little stars afraid of the sun,
One shot off, then there was one.
One little star, alone is no fun,
It shot off, then there were none.

125 *So Many Stars Flannelboard*
See pattern 124 above.

See the stars up in the sky,
Let us count them by and by.
One, two, three, four, five!

126 *Five Little Monkeys Flannelboard*

(traditional)

See pattern 126. Use Velcro to stick the monkeys to a horizontal paint-stick bed. Bounce the paint stick while saying the rhyme and pull off each monkey at the appropriate time.

Five little monkeys jumping on the bed,
One fell off and bumped his head.
Mama called the doctor and the doctor said,
"No more monkeys jumping on the bed!"
Four little monkeys . . .
Three little monkeys . . .
Two little monkeys . . .
One little monkey jumping on the bed,
He fell off and bumped his head.
Mama called the doctor and the doctor said,
"Put those monkeys straight to bed!"

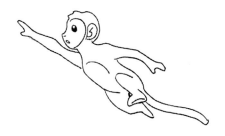

127 Mother, Mother I Want Another *Flannelboard*

See pattern 127. Based on the book by Maria Polushkin (New York: Knopf, 2005). A frantic mother mouse tries to comfort her baby with a series of animal mothers until she realizes that what he really wants is another kiss from his own mother.

128 Ready for Bed Flannelboard

See pattern 128. Ask the children to help your felt child get ready for bed. Show them the pieces and let the children tell you in what order to apply the pieces to the board.

Quick Tip: Read the poem "Wee Willie Winkie" before you do the Ready for Bed Flannelboard. Sharing classic nursery rhymes enhances children's appreciation and understanding of language. Following up with this hands-on activity will enhance the text-to-self connection by allowing children to apply the classic rhyme to their own everyday routines.

129 Wee Willie Winkie Bedtime Clock Craft

MATERIALS: Wee Willie Winkie coloring page (a good one can be found at www.tlsbooks.com/mothergooseweewilliewinkie.pdf), clock (from pattern 129), glue, crayons, and other decorating materials

DIRECTIONS:
1. Glue the clock onto the coloring sheet.
2. Draw the hands on the clock to show that it is eight o'clock.
3. Decorate as desired.

130 *Design Your Own Pajamas Craft*

MATERIALS: one copy of pajama top and bottom for each child (from pattern 130), glue, stickers, feathers, glitter, and other decorating materials

DIRECTIONS: Decorate pajamas as desired with feathers, glitter, and the like.

131 *Star Mobile Craft*

MATERIALS: one paper plate for each child, hole punch, one long piece of yarn for each child (about 12 inches), four 6-inch pieces of yarn for each child, four star shapes cut from construction paper for each child (from pattern 131), stickers, crayons, and other decorating materials

DIRECTIONS:

1. Punch four holes around the edge of the paper plate and one hole in the center.
2. Tie a knot in one end of the 12-inch piece of yarn. Pull the yarn through the hole in the center of the plate so that the knot stops on the bottom of the plate.
3. Punch a hole in the top of each star.
4. Decorate the star shapes as desired.
5. Attach the stars to the remaining holes in the plate with the shorter pieces of yarn.

See also Moon (98), Twinkling Stars (307), Five Little Stars and the Moon Too Flannelboard (309), Shhhhh! Everybody's Sleeping Flannelboard (321), and Teddy Bear, Teddy Bear (336).

AT HOME: TEN GREAT BOOKS FOR STORYTIME

Pig, Horse, or Cow, Don't Wake Me Now by Arlene Alda. New York: Doubleday, 1994. (for preschoolers)
Five Little Monkeys with Nothing to Do by Eileen Christelow. New York: Clarion, 1996. (for all ages)
Maisy Takes a Bath by Lucy Cousins. Cambridge, MA: Candlewick, 2000. (for toddlers)
Wake-Up Kisses by Pamela Duncan Edwards. New York: HarperCollins, 2002. (for toddlers)
Time for Bed by Mem Fox. New York: Gulliver, 1993. (for all ages)

Bubble Bath Pirates by Jarrett J. Krosoczka. New York: Viking, 2003. (for preschoolers)

Tom and Pippo Make a Mess by Helen Oxenbury. New York: Macmillan, 1988. (for toddlers)

King Bidgood's in the Bathtub by Audrey Wood. San Diego: Harcourt Brace Jovanovich, 1985. (for all ages)

How Do Dinosaurs Say Goodnight? by Jane Yolen. New York: Blue Sky, 2000. (for all ages)

Clara Ann Cookie, Go to Bed! by Harriet Ziefert. New York: Houghton Mifflin, 2000. (for preschoolers)

Chapter 6

Bugs and Insects

132 Bee Dance

I wiggle my belly
And I flap my wings,
I have big eyes
And a stinger that stings.
I love that pollen,
It's good stuff,
I fly around till I find enough.
Then I fly back home
To the hive,
And tell the others where it is
With a jiggle jump jive!

Quick Tip: Follow up with a bee dance. Have all the children line up and do a wiggly dance around the room to "Flight of the Bumblebee" by Nikolai Rimsky-Korsakov.

133 Firefly

Firefly, firefly, light your light.
Firefly, firefly, fly through the night.
Firefly, firefly, fly down low.
Firefly, firefly, off you go!

134 Fuzzy-Wuzzy Caterpillar
(traditional)

Fuzzy-wuzzy caterpillar
Creeping, creeping, creeping, *(crawl around floor)*
Spins herself a blanket, *(spin in circle)*
Now she's sleeping, sleeping, sleeping. *(lay head on hands)*

135 Grasshopper Hop

We're doing the grasshopper hop!
We're jumping like we're never gonna stop.
We crouch down low and spring up high
And jump! Jump! Jump!

136 Hurry-Scurry Little Spider
(traditional)

Hurry-scurry little spider
Starts down at your toes. *(touch toes)*
Hurry-scurry little spider
Past your knees he goes. *(touch knees)*
Hurry-scurry little spider
Past where your tummy is. *(touch tummy)*
Hurry-scurry little spider
Gives you a spidery kiss. *(make loud kiss noise)*

137 I Saw a Butterfly

I saw a butterfly,
I saw a bee,
I saw a grasshopper,
And they saw me.
I flew like a butterfly,
I buzzed like a bee,
I hopped like a grasshopper,
And I laughed like me.

138 All through the Summer
(to the tune of "The Wheels on the Bus")

The bees on the flowers go buzz buzz
    buzz,
Buzz buzz buzz, buzz buzz buzz.
The bees on the flowers go
Buzz buzz buzz
All through the summer.
The butterflies in the air go flutter
    flutter flutter . . .
The crickets in the grass go chirp chirp
    chirp . . .
The fireflies in the night go blink blink
    blink . . .

139 Flutter, Flutter, Butterfly
(to the tune of "Twinkle, Twinkle,
Little Star")

Sign BUTTERFLY as you sing this song.

Flutter, flutter, BUTTERFLY,
Floating in the summer sky.
Floating by for all to see,
Floating by so merrily.
Flutter, flutter, BUTTERFLY,
Floating in the summer sky.

140 A Fly Is on My Toe
(to the tune of "The Farmer in the Dell")

*Pass out fly stickers or small pom-poms to
use as flies and invite the children to place
them on the appropriate body part as you
sing the song.*

A fly is on my toe,
A fly is on my toe,
Hi-ho-the-derrio,
A fly is on my toe.
A fly is on my nose . . .
A fly is on my head . . .
A fly is on my ear . . .
A fly is on my elbow . . .
A fly is on my knee . . .

141 I'm a Little Ladybug
(to the tune of "I'm a Little Teapot")

I'm a little ladybug
Small and red.
I've got black spots and a round black
    head.
When I come out on a sunny day,
I spread my wings and fly away.

142 Five Little Ladybugs Flannelboard
(traditional)

*Use the ladybug from pattern 146. (Full-
size patterns can be found at www.ala
.org/editions/extras/macmillan09775.)*

Five little ladybugs on our front door,
One flew to (child's name), and that left
    four.
Four little ladybugs, oh so wee,
One flew to (child's name), and that left
    three.
Three little ladybugs saying howdy-do,
One flew to (child's name), and that left
    two.
Two little ladybugs snoozing in the
    sun,
One flew to (child's name), and that left
    one.
One little ladybug alone on the door,
It flew to (child's name), then there
    were no more.

143 Five Little Fireflies Flannelboard
See pattern 143.

Five little fireflies shining in the
    twilight,
One found a leaf to eat that was just
    right.
Four little fireflies shining in the
    twilight,
One got his wing stuck in a tree and
    couldn't take flight.
Three little fireflies shining in the
    twilight,
One decided he'd try to sing a new
    song tonight.
Two little fireflies shining in the
    twilight,
One flew off to look at a bright yellow
    light.
One little firefly shining in the
    twilight,
He noticed it was getting late, so he
    said good night.

**144 Five Little Caterpillars/Five Little
Butterflies Flannelboard**
See pattern 144.

Five little caterpillars and not one
    more,
One spun a cocoon and then there
    were four.
Four little caterpillars on a leafy tree,
One spun a cocoon and then there
    were three.
Three little caterpillars looking for
    something to do,
One spun a cocoon and then there
    were two.
Two little caterpillars sitting in the
    sun,
One spun a cocoon and then there was
    one.
One little caterpillar sitting all alone,
That one spun a cocoon and then there
    were none.
But . . .
One cocoon opened underneath the
    sun,
Now there's a butterfly and that
    makes one.
Another cocoon opened and we know
    what to do,
We say, "Hello, butterfly! You are
    number two!"
Another cocoon opened, we're happy
    as can be,
Another butterfly comes out and that
    makes three.
Could it be, another cocoon? Yes,
    here's one more.
Hello, Mr. Butterfly! You are number
    four.
Another cocoon opens as the
    butterflies dip and dive,
Another butterfly comes out and now
    we have five!

WEB

145 *Ant Picnic Flannelboard*

See pattern 145.

The ants came to the park today,
Hoping to find a luncheon buffet.
One ant found a basket of cherries,
The second ant found some delicious
    strawberries.
A third ant found a piece of bread,
The fourth ant found some cheese to spread.
The fifth ant was as lazy as could be,
While the others worked, he napped in a tree.

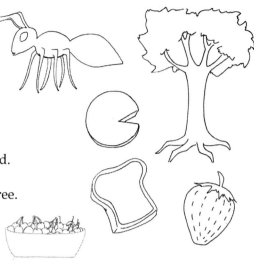

WEB

146 *Bugs in the Rug Flannelboard*

See pattern 146. Line the bugs up along the top of the flannelboard. Place a rectangle of felt in the middle to represent a rug. Ask the children to close their eyes while you hide a bug or two under the rug. While their eyes are closed, have them chant the following rhyme, then open their eyes to guess.

Bug in the rug, bug in the rug,
Who is that bug in the rug?

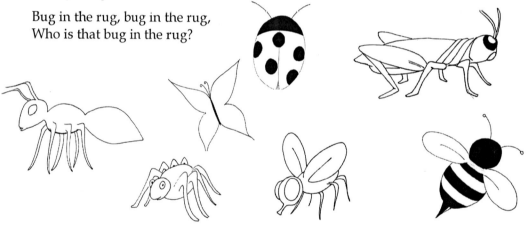

WEB

147 *Buggy Guessing Game*

Print out pictures of a grasshopper, ant, mosquito, and honeybee (from pattern 146). Give children clues; then when they guess correctly put the picture of the bug on the board. Or for a younger group, before giving the clues put the pictures on the board to give the children an idea of the possible answers.

I have super strong legs and can jump. I'm a . . . (grasshopper)!
I am super strong. I can lift thirty times my size. Sometimes I come to your picnic.
    I'm an . . . (ant)!
I buzz in your ears and have a needle on my nose. If I sting you, you'll itch. I'm a . . .
    (mosquito)!
I have baskets on my legs. I make honey. I'm a . . . (honeybee)!

148 Eensy-Weensy Spider Rainspout Craft

MATERIALS: one toilet paper roll for each child, hole punch, black yarn, black pom-poms, googly eyes, colored yarn, crayons, decorating materials

DIRECTIONS:
1. Punch a hole in one end of the toilet paper roll, about half an inch from the edge.
2. Tie an 8-inch piece of black yarn to the toilet paper roll through the hole.
3. Tie the other end of the yarn around the black pom-pom.
4. Glue the googly eyes on the pom-pom.
5. Decorate the rainspout as desired.

> **Quick Tip:** Make enough of these rainspout crafts to hand out in storytime and use them with the book *The Itsy Bitsy Spider* by Lorianne Siomades (Honesdale, PA: Boyds Mills, 1999). Using props with books and nursery rhymes enhances young children's learning by allowing them to engage multiple senses.

149 Egg-Carton Caterpillar Craft

MATERIALS: cardboard egg cartons cut into sections of three (one section of three for each child), googly eyes, glue, chenille stems, stickers, markers

DIRECTIONS:
1. Turn the egg-carton section over.
2. Glue the googly eyes to the front of the egg carton.
3. Poke two holes in the top of the front section of the egg carton. Insert the chenille stems into the holes for antennae.
4. Decorate as desired.

150 Paper-Bag Butterfly Wings Craft

MATERIALS: one large paper grocery bag for each child, hole punch, two 18-inch pieces of yarn for each child, stickers, markers, and other decorating materials

DIRECTIONS:
1. Cut the bag open and lay it flat.
2. Cut out the shape of wings.
3. Decorate the wings as desired.
4. Punch holes at the top and bottom of the base of the wings on each side.
5. Attach a piece of yarn from the top to the bottom on each side so that the children can put their arms through the yarn and wear the wings.

See also Red Dragonflies (83) and Firefly, Firefly (93).

BUGS AND INSECTS: TEN GREAT BOOKS FOR STORYTIME

The Very Lonely Firefly by Eric Carle. New York: Philomel, 1995. (for all ages)

Waiting for Wings by Lois Ehlert. San Diego: Harcourt, 2001. (for all ages)

The Very Lazy Ladybug by Isobel Finn. Wilton, CT: Tiger Tales, 2003. (for toddlers)

In the Tall, Tall Grass by Denise Fleming. New York: Henry Holt, 1991. (for toddlers)

The Eensy-Weensy Spider by Mary Ann Hoberman. New York: Little, Brown, 2000. (for all ages)

Miss Spider's Tea Party by David Kirk. New York: Scholastic, 1994. (for preschoolers)

I Love Bugs! by Philemon Sturges. New York: HarperCollins, 2005. (for toddlers)

The Itsy Bitsy Spider by Iza Trapani. Strongsville, OH: Gareth Stevens, 1996. (for all ages)

Two Bad Ants by Chris Van Allsburg. Boston: Houghton Mifflin, 1988. (for preschoolers)

Over in the Garden by Jennifer Ward. Flagstaff, AZ: Rising Moon, 2002. (for preschoolers)

Chapter 7

Concepts

ALPHABET

151 *Alphabet, Alphabet*

Alphabet, alphabet, turn around,
Alphabet, alphabet, make a sound.
Alphabet goes from A to Z,
Will you say the alphabet with me?

152 *Letters Are Hiding Game*

Hide plastic or foam letters in a bag. Invite each child to reach into the bag and guess the letter by touch only as you recite this rhyme.

Letters are hiding, hiding from me.
Reach into the bag and you will see.
Not with your eyes, just feel and guess.
What letter is it? (Child's name), tell us!

> **Quick Tip:** Using their senses to recognize the shapes of letters in Letters Are Hiding helps young children with letter recognition by engaging their senses with the alphabet in new ways.

153 *ABC Clapping Game*

Invite everyone to stand in a circle. Recite the rhyme as everyone claps in rhythm.

B, B, I like the letter B.
(Child's name), tell me a word that starts with B?
That child must say a word that begins with that letter, then recite the rhyme with another letter and choose another child. If a child can't think of a word, he or she can say "Help," and another child can volunteer a word.

154 *Alphabet Game*

Give a different foam, cardboard, or magnetic letter to each child. Discuss the sounds the letters make. Ask each child to share a word that starts with her letter.

155 Giant Pencils Activity

Give each child a rhythm stick and invite the group to draw and write in the air. Some suggested items to draw and write are simple shapes (circles, squares, triangles), letters of the alphabet, numbers zero through ten, the children's names, and simple shapes relating to the seasons (sunshine, Christmas tree, heart, Easter egg, rain cloud, etc.).

> **Quick Tip:** Giant Pencils promotes gross motor skills, visual acuity, and letter and shape recognition.

156 Name Craft

MATERIALS: one piece of construction paper for each child, one pencil for each child, crayons, clip art, or magazine pictures of items beginning with various letters of the alphabet

DIRECTIONS:
1. Write your name down one side of the paper.
2. Think of a word that starts with each letter of your name and write it, using the letter of your name as the first letter. For example, Amy would write something like this:

    Apple
    Monkey
    Yogurt

3. Find or draw a picture to go with each word.

CALENDARS AND TIME

157 Clock Stretch

I am a clock,
I have two hands.
Let us see
Just where they land.

One hand straight up,
The other too.
It's twelve noon—lunchtime
For me and you.

One hand straight up,
One out to the side.
It's three o'clock,
It can't be denied.

One hand straight up,
The other down.
It's six o'clock
All over town.

This hand up straight,
Now the other out to the side.
It's nine o'clock,
And it's bedtime.

One hand straight up,
The other too.
It's twelve midnight,
Quiet time for me and you.

158 Months
(to the tune of "One Potato")

January, February, March, April, May,
June, July, August—that's not all I'll say.
September, October, November too,
December will finish the whole year through!

159 Wiggle Week

Mondays I wiggle,
Tuesdays I giggle,
Wednesdays I jump,
Thursdays I slump,
Fridays I dance,
Saturdays I prance,
Sundays I run,
And the week is done!

160 Days of the Week

(to the tune of "Ten Little Indians")

There are seven days of the week,
There are seven days of the week,
There are seven days of the week,
Yes, indeed there are.
Sunday, Monday, Tuesday,
   Wednesday,
Thursday, Friday, Saturday,
There are seven days of the week,
And I know them all!

See also Hello, Mrs. Monday (91) and Picking Fruits and Vegetables Flannelboard (228).

COLORS

161 Color Song

(to the tune of
"Frère Jacques")

Sign the colors as you sing this song.

RED and YELLOW,
ORANGE and PURPLE,
GREEN and BLUE,
PINK and WHITE too.
There are so many
   COLORS,
Pretty, pretty COLORS,
Here for me
And for you.

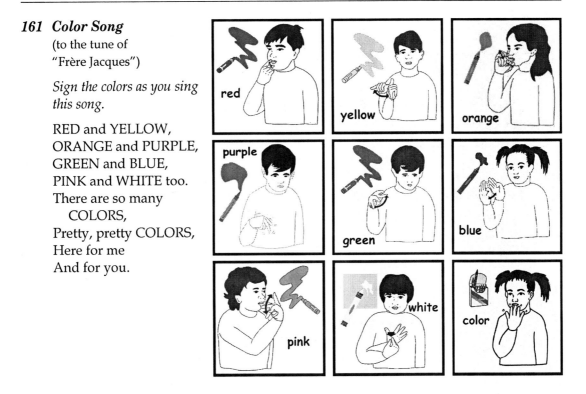

162 Rainbow Flannelboard

See pattern 162. (Full-size patterns can be found at www.ala.org/editions/extras/macmillan09775.)

With my eyes, I can see
The colors of the rainbow in front of me!
Red, orange, yellow, green, blue, indigo, and purple!

See also Rooster's Feathers Flannelboard (34) and A Blanket for the Princess Flannelboard Story (193).

163 *Mrs. Mark's Favorite Color File Folder Story*

See pattern 163. Use the pattern to place a paint-can shape on the front of a file folder. Carefully cut out the paint portion of the can so that items placed in the folder will show through. Copy the story below and tape it to the back of the folder for reference. Tape the top and bottom edges of the folder together. Arrange sheets of colored construction paper in the order the colors are mentioned in the story: white, brown, orange, blue, red, yellow, black, green, purple. The white paper should be on top of the pile. To create the last piece in the pile, tape strips of construction paper together to make a rainbow. Place the sheets of construction paper, in sequence, in the folder. Each time Mrs. Mark's favorite color changes, remove the top piece of paper.

Once upon a time there was a lady named Mrs. Mark. Her living room was white, which was her favorite color. But one day she decided she was tired of it. She looked at the beautiful brown tree trunks and decided that was the color she wanted her living room to be.

Now brown was her favorite color. But soon she saw a pretty orange flower and decided that the color she really liked best was orange.

Repeat the pattern with blue – blueberries; red – strawberries; yellow – sun; black – night sky; green – grass; purple – grapes.

Then she decided that she liked all of those colors, so she couldn't choose just one to be her favorite. And she wanted all of them in her living room. So she painted her living room with a . . . rainbow!

NUMBERS

164 *Building Rhyme*

Stack flat hands to represent bricks as you count.

One, two, three, build a building with
   me,
Four, five, six, we need more bricks,
Seven, eight, nine, this building looks
   fine,
Number ten, let's do it again!
Alternative: Number ten, that's the end!

165 *Counting Cheer*

One, two, three, four—let me hear you
   scream for more,
Five, six, seven, eight—counting is
   really great!
I can count nine and ten,
Want to hear me do it again?

166 *Pennies in My Piggy Bank Flannelboard*

See pattern 166.

Having an empty piggy bank is not
   much fun,
But my grandmother gave me a penny
   and now I have one.
One penny in my piggy bank, and I
   asked Mom what I should do,
She gave me a penny for taking out
   the trash and then I had two.
Two pennies in my piggy bank, I told
   Dad to come and see,
He gave me a penny to help him wash
   the car and then I had three.
Three pennies in my piggy bank, but I
   still wanted more,
I got one for my birthday and then I
   had four.
Four pennies in my piggy bank, I
   wished more would arrive,
I found one lying on the ground and
   then I had five.

Five pennies in my piggy bank, and I knew what they were for,
I used one to buy a flower for my mother and then there were four.
Four pennies in my piggy bank, so I went on a shopping spree,
I bought a ball for my brother and then I had three.
Three pennies in my piggy bank, and I knew what to do,
I bought some candy for my sister and then I had two.
Two pennies in my piggy bank, and I was having fun.
I bought some lemonade for my father and then I had one.
One penny in my piggy bank for a special someone,
I gave that one to you and then there were none.

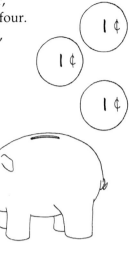

> **Quick Tip:** Pennies in My Piggy Bank also makes a great prop rhyme. Use real pennies and a real piggy bank instead of a flannelboard. Using a variety of formats in storytime adds interest and aids comprehension by allowing children to use different senses.

> **Quick Tip:** Pennies in My Piggy Bank works well as a follow-up to *Benny's Pennies* by Pat Brisson (New York: Delacorte, 1993).

167　My Number Book Craft

MATERIALS: one My Number Book for each child (assembled from pattern 167), stickers, small items that can be glued into the books (such as feathers and sequins), glue, crayons

DIRECTIONS:
1. Glue or stick the appropriate number of items on each page.
2. Decorate as desired.

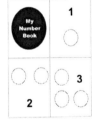

WEB

OPPOSITES

168　Here We Go
(traditional)

Here we go—up, up, up, *(stand up on toes)*
Here we go—down, down, down. *(crouch down)*
Here we go—moving forward, *(take a step forward)*
Here we go—moving backward. *(take a step backward)*
Here we go around and around and around! *(spin)*

169　Opposites
(traditional)

Roll your hands so slowly,
As slowly as can be.
Roll your hands so quickly,
As quickly as can be.
Clap your hands so softly,
As softly as can be.
Clap your hands so loudly,
As loudly as can be.
And fold your arms like me.

170 Opposites That I Know

You say stop, *(hold palm out)*
And I say go. *(motion palms toward you)*
You run fast, and I run slow. *(run in place)*
You jump high, *(jump)*
And I crawl low. *(crawl)*
These are some opposites that I know.

171 Tall as a Tree
(traditional)

Tall as a tree, *(reach for the sky)*
Wide as a house, *(stretch arms toward walls)*
Thin as a pin, *(place arms next to body)*
Small as a mouse. *(squat down)*

172 Mom's Kitchen in Contrast Flannelboard
See pattern 172.

Some days my mom's dishes are very dirty, with plates piled to the sky,
But with enough soap and bubbles, the clean dishes squeak and shine.
On winter days my mom makes soup, which can be very hot,
But in the summer a cold drink with ice really hits the spot.
I try to avoid eating anything that could be sour
And instead gobble up a tray of sweets before my mom can discover!
The best smell in the kitchen is my mom baking me a cake,
But stand around too long and dad could give me a stinky chore I hate.

173 Animal Opposites Flannelboard
See pattern 173. Use the animals to play an opposites game. For younger children, place pairs of contrasting animals on the board and discuss what makes them opposites. For older children, randomly place animals on the board and ask kids to match the opposites. Discuss why they are opposites.

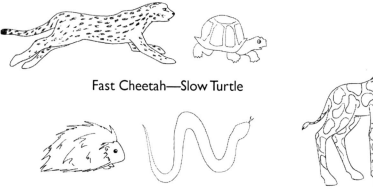

Fast Cheetah—Slow Turtle

Prickly Porcupine—Smooth Snake

Tall Giraffe—Short Monkey

Hard Crab—Soft Kitten

Fat Hippo—Skinny Flamingo

Loud Rooster—Quiet Rabbit

Big Elephant—Small Mouse

174 *Daytime/Nighttime House Picture*

MATERIALS: one daytime/nighttime house coloring sheet for each child (from pattern 174), crayons

DIRECTIONS: Decorate half of the page with things that happen in the daytime (such as children playing, someone delivering mail) and the other half with things that happen in the nighttime (an owl in a tree, Mom's and Dad's cars in the driveway, etc.).

See also Slowly, Slowly (56).

WEB

SIZE

175 *Drawing*

(to the tune of "Apples and Bananas")

Draw shapes or letters in the air as you sing the song. This song can be adapted to any theme by choosing theme-related items to draw.

I like to draw, draw, draw teeny little pictures,
I like to draw, draw, draw teeny little pictures.
I like to draw, draw, draw great big giant pictures,
I like to draw, draw, draw great big giant pictures.

Quick Tip: The song Drawing helps children develop large and fine-motor skills and practices skills they will need for writing later on.

176 Sizes Flannelboard
See pattern 176.

I am big,
My brother is bigger,
My daddy is biggest.
I am little,
My sister is littler,
My baby brother is littlest.
Sometimes I am big,
Sometimes I am little,
And sometimes I am in between.

See also Blue Sea *Flannelboard (51) and* Sandwich Shapes *Flannelboard Story (231).*

SHAPES

177 Shapes Drawing

Draw a circle,
Draw a square,
Draw a star in the air.
Draw an oval,
Draw a triangle,
Tell me, can you draw a rectangle?

178 Shape Game Flannelboard
See pattern 178. After asking each of the following questions, place the correct shape on the board.

What shape has two sides that are short and two
    sides that are long?
What shape has four sides that are all the same?
What shape has three corners and three sides?
What shape is round with no sides to be
    found?
What shape has five points?
What shape looks like a stop sign?
What shape looks like a kite?
What shape looks like an egg?

179 What Shapes Make Me?
Flannelboard
See pattern 178 above. Use the shapes to create pictures of items on the flannelboard; then say the rhyme and ask children to identify what shapes make up each picture. Picture suggestions: wagon – rectangle, wheels – circles; ice-cream cone – triangle cone, circle scoop; sandwich – square cut into triangles; book – rectangle; beach ball – circle; pizza – circle cut into triangle slices; kite – diamond.

I am a *(name of item)*, as you can see.
What shapes do you see?
What shapes make me?

180 Shapes Touch Bag Activity

Place various shapes in a bag. (Wooden shape blocks work well.) Have the children take turns putting their hands in the bag to see if they can guess which shape they're holding. After they guess, have them take the shape out to show the rest of the children.

181 Shape House Craft

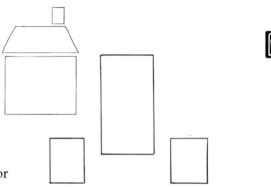

MATERIALS: one shape house coloring sheet for each child, windows (from pattern 181), glue sticks, crayons, library processing stickers in various shapes

DIRECTIONS:
1. Glue on the windows.
2. Color the shape house coloring sheet.
3. Make additional items on the picture using the library's processing stickers. For example, a circle could be the sun, and a rectangle could become a bee if you draw on wings and stripes.

182 Shapes Masterpiece Craft

MATERIALS: one piece of construction paper for each child, various shapes cut from construction paper, glue, crayons

DIRECTIONS:
1. Glue shapes onto the construction paper to create animals, machines, imaginary beasts, ice-cream cones, and so forth.
2. Decorate with crayons.

CONCEPTS: TEN GREAT BOOKS FOR STORYTIME

Little Bear's Little Boat by Eve Bunting. New York: Clarion, 2003. (for toddlers)

Cat's Colors by Jane Cabrera. New York: Dial, 1997. (for all ages)

The Turn-Around, Upside-Down Alphabet Book by Lisa Campbell Ernst. New York: Simon and Schuster, 2004. (for preschoolers)

Telling Time with Big Mama Cat by Dan Harper. San Diego: Harcourt Brace, 1998. (for all ages)

A is for . . . ? A Photographer's Alphabet of Animals by Henry Horenstein. San Diego: Harcourt Brace, 1999. (for preschoolers)

Kipper's A to Z by Mick Inkpen. San Diego: Harcourt, 2000. (for preschoolers)

Black? White! Day? Night! by Laura Vaccaro Seeger. New Milford, CT: Roaring Brook Press, 2006. (for all ages)

One Naked Baby: Counting to Ten and Back Again by Maggie Smith. New York: Knopf, 2007. (for toddlers)

One More Bunny: Adding from One to Ten by Rick Walton. New York: Lothrop, Lee, and Shepard, 2000. (for preschoolers)

Cookie's Week by Cindy Ward. New York: Putnam, 1988. (for toddlers)

Chapter 8

Fairy Tales
and Castles

183 Castle Capers

I am the king of running,
I run and run and run.
My subjects all run with me,
And we have so much fun!

I am the queen of jumping,
I jump and jump and jump.
My subjects all jump with me
And fall down with a bump.

I am the prince of turning,
I turn and turn and turn.
My subjects all turn with me,
It's an easy thing to learn!

I am the princess of dancing,
I dance and dance and dance.
My subjects all dance with me
And sit when they get the chance!

184 Cinderella Speaks

My name is Cinderella,
I am so very sad. *(make a sad face)*
My stepsisters went to the ball,
And now I'm feeling mad. *(make a mad face)*
But my fairy godmother will help me
She'll wave her wand, and see! *(wave wand)*

With a beautiful dress and glass
  slippers, *(twirl around to show dress and slippers)*
No princess is as lovely as me.
Now I'll go to the ball,
I'll dance and have some fun. *(dance)*
But when the clock strikes midnight,
  (strike index finger against opposite palm twelve times to represent a clock chiming)
It's time for me to run! *(run in place)*

185 Dragon, Dragon

Dragon, dragon, swoop and sway,
Dragon, dragon, fly away.
Dragon, dragon, fly even higher,
Dragon, dragon, breathe your fire!

186 My Castle

Four stone walls on my castle tall, *(use flat hands to show walls)*
A tower, a garden, and a garden wall.
  (mold a tower in the air and point to indicate garden)
Down goes the drawbridge over the
  moat so wide, *(move flat hands down and away from you)*
Hello, my friends! Please come inside!
  (wave and gesture friends inside)

187 *My Magic Wand*

Use a magic wand from a costume shop or make one from a straw and a tinfoil star. Let each child take a turn waving the magic wand and choosing an action for the group to perform. End by having the magic wand say "Sit down" for the next story.

I brought my magic wand to the
    library today.
And when I wave it, you must do
    what I say.
Magic wand says jump!

188 *To Win a Prince*

One sweet princess trying to win her
    prince
Slept on a bed of peas that made her
    wince.
The princess tossed and turned all
    through the night,
When she appeared for breakfast she
    was quite a sight.
Her delicate skin was black and blue,
For the peas had turned her pale skin
    an ugly hue.
But the prince knew she was fit to be
    a queen,
All because the peas had left
    something to be seen.

189 *Make a Wish: A Rhyme to Sign*

Sign the words in capital letters as you say this rhyme.

Come and make a WISH for me
I'll do some MAGIC, one, two, three!
TURN AROUND and JUMP, and then
We will make a WISH again!

190 *Crowns Everywhere*

(to the tune of "Spider on the Floor")

Make crowns from scalloped bulletin board border for this activity. Measure a length of border and staple the ends together to make a crown for each child to use as you sing the song below.

I've got a crown on my head, on my
    head.
I've got a crown on my head, on my
    head.
Did you hear what I said? I've got a
    crown on my head.
I've got a crown on my head, on my
    head.
. . . on my arm . . . it's not doing any
    harm . . .
. . . on my knee . . . oh goodness
    gracious me . . .
. . . on my bottom . . . don't think that I
    forgot 'em . . .
. . . on my head . . . did you hear what
    I said? . . .

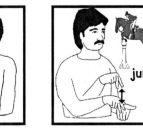

WEB

191 *Five Little Dragons Flannelboard*

See pattern 191. (Full-size patterns can be found at www.ala.org/editions/extras/macmillan09775.)

Five little dragons with great big scales,
One lost his balance and bumped his tail.
He cried "Ouch!" and breathed some fire,
And then he flew away, higher and higher.
Four little dragons . . .
Three little dragons . . .
Two little dragons . . .
One little dragon . . .

WEB

192 *Five Tiny Fairies Flannelboard*

See pattern 192.

I saw a little fairy dancing in the sun,
With a dress of red and that was one.
I saw another fairy in a dress of blue,
I counted up the fairies and that was two.
I saw another fairy in a dress of green.
Will you help me count them? That makes three.
Here comes another fairy, flying past my door,
In her dress of yellow, she makes four.
One more fairy flies in, with a soar and dip and dive,
In her pretty dress of purple, she makes five.
Five fairies in my garden on a magical sunny day,
But when the rain came, they all flew away.

WEB

193 *A Blanket for the Princess Flannelboard Story*

See pattern 193.

The king and queen had just had a beautiful baby girl. "We shall name her Princess Marigold," the king said.

"She must have a baby blanket as beautiful as she is," said the queen. She looked out the window and said, "It must be as yellow as the sun."

The king looked out and said, "It must be as yellow as the sun and blue as the sky."

The queen looked down at the garden and said, "The blanket must be as yellow as the sun and blue as the sky and orange as the beautiful flowers in my garden."

The king looked at the lawns of the palace and said, "The blanket must be as yellow as the sun and blue as the sky and orange as the beautiful flowers in my garden and green as the grass."

The queen looked at the cherry trees and said, "The blanket must be as yellow as the sun and blue as the sky and orange as the beautiful flowers and green as the grass and red as the cherries."

Night began to fall. The king looked at the darkening sky and said, "The blanket must be as yellow as the sun and blue as the sky and orange as the beautiful flowers in my garden and green as the grass and red as the cherries and purple as the twilight sky."

The moon and stars came out. The king looked at the moon and said, "The blanket must be as yellow as the sun and blue as the sky and orange as the beautiful flowers in my garden and green as the grass and red as the cherries and purple as the twilight sky and silver as the moon."

The queen looked at the stars and said, "The blanket must be as yellow as the sun and blue as the sky and orange as the beautiful flowers in my garden and green as the grass and red as the cherries and purple as the twilight sky and silver as the moon and golden as a star."

The servants looked everywhere in the palace but could not find such a blanket. They sent out a call to all the weavers and tailors in the village to find a blanket as yellow as the sun and blue as the sky and orange as the beautiful flowers in my garden and green as the grass and red as the cherries and purple as the twilight sky and silver as the moon and golden as a star. Fine tailors and weavers came from all over. The first brought a blanket as yellow as the sun, the second brought one as purple as the twilight sky, and the third brought a blanket as golden as a star. But none were what the king and queen wanted. None were as yellow as the sun and blue as the sky and orange as the beautiful flowers in my garden and green as the grass and red as the cherries and purple as the twilight sky and silver as the moon and golden as a star.

Finally an old woman shuffled forward with a faded quilt. "Your Majesties," she said, "this is the quilt I wrapped my own children in when they were babes. I made it myself from yarn as yellow as sunlight, a piece of blanket as blue as the sky, a dress as orange as the beautiful flowers in your garden, a strip of curtains as green as grass, a ribbon as red as the cherries, an apron as purple as the twilight sky, and ribbons as silver as the moon and as golden as a star. And I would be honored if you would take it now to wrap Princess Marigold in."

"No, it is we who are honored," said the king. "Yes," said the queen. "For you have given us a blanket as beautiful as our daughter but also as warm as a mother's embrace and as light as a father's kiss. Thank you." They wrapped Princess Marigold in the blanket, and they all lived happily ever after.

194 *Three Billy Goats Gruff Flannelboard*
(adapted traditional)

See pattern 194.

Once upon a time, there were three billy goats: a little billy goat, a medium-sized billy goat, and a big billy goat. Every day they grazed on a field of lovely grass. But one day, the little billy goat said, "I am tired of grazing in this same field every day. I want to see what's down the road."

"You go on," said the other two billy goats. "We will come in a while." So the little billy goat set off down the road. Well, soon he came to a bridge. And this wasn't any ordinary bridge, because there was a troll living underneath it. The little billy goat started across the bridge, trip-trap, trip-trap.

The troll was a grumpy fellow. You see, he hadn't had any breakfast that morning. So he snarled, "Who's that tripping over my bridge?"

"It's only me, the littlest Billy Goat Gruff," said the little billy goat in a tiny voice.

"Well, I am coming to gobble you up!" said the troll.

"Oh no, I would barely be a mouthful," said the clever little billy goat. "You had better wait until my big brother comes."

The troll thought about that. It seemed sensible. "Well, be off with you," he said.

And the little billy goat crossed the bridge and found a hillside full of delicious grass on the other side.

A little while later, the medium-sized billy goat set off down the road and started to cross the bridge, trip-trap, trip-trap.

"Who's that tripping over my bridge?" snarled the troll.

"It's only me, the medium Billy Goat Gruff," said the medium billy goat in a medium voice.

"Well, I am coming to gobble you up!" said the troll.

"Oh no, you'd still be hungry," said the clever medium-sized billy goat. "You had better wait until my big brother comes."

The troll thought about that. It seemed sensible. "Well, be off with you," he said.

A little while later, the big billy goat set off down the road and started to cross the bridge, trip-trap, trip-trap.

"Who's that tripping over my bridge?" snarled the troll.

"It's only me, the big Billy Goat Gruff," said the big billy goat in a big voice.

"Well, I am coming to gobble you up!" said the troll.

And the big billy goat laughed. The troll jumped up onto the bridge, and the big billy goat ran at him with his huge horns. He tossed the troll right off the bridge and into a berry bush on the other side. The troll tasted one of those berries and decided that they were much tastier than goat meat anyway.

And the big billy goat went to join his brothers in the field, and they had a wonderful time eating and playing there all day long.

195 Cinderella's Rat File Folder Story

See pattern 195. Cut a rat shape out of one side of a file folder. Copy the story below and tape it to the other outer side of the folder. Tape the top and bottom edges of the folder together. In the folder place pieces of colored construction paper in the order the colors are mentioned in the story: orange, black, white, green, gray, gold. Each time Nat changes colors, remove the top piece of paper. You could also use a magic wand each time he changes colors.

You probably know the story of Cinderella. Well, did you know that the rat her fairy godmother turned into a horse had lots of adventures too? His name was Nat. While he was at the ball, he turned back into a rat, and he had to hide, so the fairy godmother waved her magic wand. Nat said, "I'm Cinderella's rat, my name is Nat, and I can change colors just like that!" He turned orange, so he could hide in front of the pumpkin carriage. But then some of the castle servants saw him and he had to hide again, so the fairy

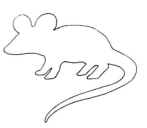

godmother waved her wand and Nat said, "I'm Cinderella's rat, my name is Nat, and I can change colors just like that!" And he turned black like the carriage wheels.

Repeat the pattern with white – walls; green – grass; gray – stone wall; gold – statue.

"I'm Cinderella's rat, my name is Nat, I'm gold now and that is that."

196 Big Bad Wolf Game

Props needed: wolf nose or mask, picture of a cheeseburger. Ask for one volunteer to play the wolf. This child should put on the wolf mask or nose and stand at the front of the room. Demonstrate the rhyme and then ask the wolf to knock on an imaginary door and repeat it. The other children can take turns standing on the other side of the door and responding No! to the wolf.

I am a wolf, hungry and thin.
Knock, knock, knock!
Will you let me in?

After everyone has had a chance to answer the wolf, have the wolf stand at the front of the room and recite the next part.

Then I will huff and I'll puff and I'll blow you all down!

Everyone pretends to fall down.

Librarian: Poor wolf! You're so hungry! Here, have a cheeseburger!

197 Bulletin Board Border Crowns

MATERIALS: wavy-edged bulletin board border cut to 22-inch lengths, crayons or markers, stickers, glue, glitter, feathers, fake gemstones and other decorating materials, stapler or tape

DIRECTIONS:
1. Decorate the crown.
2. Fit the crown to your head; then staple or tape the ends together.

198 Granny and the Wolf Puppet Craft

MATERIALS: one granny/wolf piece for each child (from pattern 198, printed or backed on card stock), one skirt piece cut from fabric for each child (use pinking shears to avoid fraying), one 1×2-inch piece of card stock for each child, glue, tape, crayons, and other decorating materials

DIRECTIONS:
1. Color the granny and the wolf as desired.
2. Glue or tape the skirt piece to the center line that divides the granny and the wolf.
3. Turn the granny/wolf piece over. Tape the small piece of card stock to the back of the puppet so that it forms a loop large enough to put one finger through.
4. Hold the puppet with the granny side up to make it a granny puppet; then turn it upside down to make it a wolf puppet.

199 Magic Wand Craft

MATERIALS: one straw for each child, one star cut from poster board for each child (from pattern 199), lengths of curling ribbon, glitter, glue, crayons, and other decorating materials

DIRECTIONS:
1. Cut two small slits in the top of the straw.
2. Place glue on the bottom edge of the star.
3. Slide the bottom edge of the star into the slit on the straw.
4. Tie lengths of ribbon around the base of the star.
5. Decorate the wand with glitter, stickers, and crayons.

FAIRY TALES AND CASTLES: TEN GREAT BOOKS FOR STORYTIME

The Little Red Hen by Byron Barton. New York: HarperCollins, 1993. (for toddlers)
Snog the Frog by Tony Bonning. Hauppauge, NY: Barron's, 2005. (for toddlers)
Dinorella: A Prehistoric Fairy Tale by Pamela Duncan Edwards. New York: Hyperion, 1997. (for preschoolers)
The Missing Tarts by B. G. Hennessy. New York: Viking, 1989. (for toddlers)
Goldilocks and the Three Bears by James Marshall. New York: Dial, 1988. (for all ages)
Good Night, Princess Pruney Toes by Lisa McCourt. Mahwah, NJ: Troll, 2001. (for all ages)
The Kiss That Missed by David Melling. Hauppauge, NY: Barron's, 2002. (for preschoolers)
Dragon Pizzeria by Mary Morgan. New York: Knopf, 2008. (for all ages)
Custard the Dragon and the Wicked Knight by Ogden Nash. New York: Little, Brown, 1961. (for preschoolers)
King Bidgood's in the Bathtub by Audrey Wood. San Diego: Harcourt Brace Jovanovich, 1985. (for all ages)

Chapter 9

Family and Friends

FAMILY

200 Some Families

Some families have a mommy,
Some families have a dad,
Some families have a grandmother,
Some have a granddad,
Some families have a sister,
Some families have a brother,
But one thing that all families have
Is lots of love for each other!

201 Someone Special

There's someone special in my family
Who doesn't talk much, but is always
    there for me.
If I am sad, I know he's always there
With a friendly hug or a listening ear.
I love my mom and my dad,
And my sister and my brother,
But the one I am talking about
Is another.
He is one I love, oh yes.
Who is it? Can you guess?
My dog!

202 Baby Song
(to the tune of "A Bicycle Built for Two")

Baby, baby, give me your hand, please
    do,
I've been waiting for kisses and hugs
    from you.

Your diaper can be stinky,
You like to suck on your binky,
But you are sweet,
With pudgy feet
And a cute little belly too.

203 Family
(to the tune of "My Darling Clementine")

There's a mother,
There's a father,
There's a sister and a brother.
Altogether they're a family,
And they all love one another.

204 The Family
(to the tune of "The Wheels on the Bus")

The sisters in the family go ha-ha-ha
    (laugh) . . . All through the day.
The brothers in the family say "Let's
    all play" . . .
The babies in the family go wah-wah-
    wah . . . (cry)
The daddy in the family says "Come
    on home" . . .
The mommy in the family says "I love
    you" . . .

205 *The Family in the Dell*
(to the tune of "The Farmer in the Dell")

The family in the dell,
The family in the dell,
Hi-ho-the-derrio,
The family in the dell.
The mother says "Hello" . . .
The father says "Good day" . . .
The baby says "Wah-wah" . . .
The sister says "Come in" . . .
The brother says "Let's play" . . .

206 *Family Portraits Craft*

MATERIALS: one sheet of construction paper for each child, craft sticks, glue, crayons
or markers, decorating materials, die-cuts or pictures of mothers, fathers, sisters,
brothers, babies, and grandparents (from pattern 206). (Full-size patterns can be
found at www.ala.org/editions/extras/macmillan09775.)

DIRECTIONS:
1. Find pictures representing the people who live in your home.
2. Glue the pictures to the construction paper.
3. Draw a frame around the edge of the paper and decorate as desired.

See also Pennies in My Piggy Bank Flannelboard (166), Sizes Flannelboard (176), D-A-D-D-Y (245),
Daddy Song (246), Mother's Day (262), M-O-M-M-Y (263), and Mommy, All through the Year (264).

FRIENDS

207 *I Went to See My Friend Call-and-Response Chant*
Have the children repeat each line after you.

I went to see my friend,
I went up to her door.
How could I let her know
I was right outside her door?

Knock!
Knock! Knock! Knock! Knock!
No answer!

I went to see my friend,
I went up to her door.
How could I let her know
I was right outside her door?
Ring the doorbell!

Ring! Ring! Ring! Ring!
No answer!

I went to see my friend,
I went up to her door.
How could I let her know
I was right outside her door?
Call her on the telephone!
Dial, dial, dial, dial.
Ring! Ring! Ring! Ring!
No answer!

I went to see my friend,
I went up to her door.
How could I let her know
I was right outside her door?
I couldn't think of any more
So I went home.
And guess who was waiting
Right outside my door?
My friend!

208 *Two Little Friends*
(traditional)

Two little friends are better than one,
*(hold up two fingers on right hand, one
on left)*
And three are better than two, *(three
on left, and two on right)*
And four are much better still. *(four on
right hand)*
Just think what four little friends can
do!

209 *Five Friends Flannelboard*
See pattern 209.

One little girl alone with nothing to do,
Decided to call a friend and then there
were two.
Two little friends sitting in a tree,
They call for another and that makes
three.
Three little friends knock on the
neighbor's door,
They invite her to come out and then
there are four.
Four little friends go for a drive,
They see another friend and that
makes five!

See also Friendship Sign Song (101).

GETTING ALONG/MANNERS

210 *Helping*
(to the tune of "A Bicycle Built for Two")

Helping, helping,
That's what we like to do.
I feel better
When I am helping you.
I might get in a pickle
And need to borrow a nickel.
But you'll help me
And I'll help you
Because that's what good friends do.

211 Manners Song

(to the tune of "If You're Happy and You Know It")

Sign the words in capital letters as you sing this song.

If we want to ask for something, we say PLEASE.
If we want to ask for something, we say PLEASE.
If we want to show good manners, then we really need to say it.
If we want to ask for something, we say PLEASE.
If someone gives us something, we say THANK YOU . . .
If we make a mistake, we say SORRY . . .
If we bump into someone, we say EXCUSE me . . .

212 My Friend Is Angry at Me

(to the tune of "On Top of Old Smoky")

My friend is angry, angry at me,
Because I pushed her and did not say sorry.
And now I am sad, as sad as can be,
Because my friend's angry and won't talk to me.
Now I tell her I'm sorry, as sorry can be,
And she says, "I forgive you, now please play with me."
So if you push your friend and she's angry at you,
You should say sorry. Yes, that's what you should do.

213 Handprint Craft

MATERIALS: construction paper, scissors, glue, crayons, and other decorating materials

DIRECTIONS:
1. Trace your hand on the construction paper and cut out the shape.
2. Trace a friend or family member's hand on the construction paper and cut out the shape.
3. Glue the hands together and decorate as desired.

214 Hug Card Craft

MATERIALS: one card (traced and cut from pattern 214) for each child, one circle (from pattern) for each child, two hands (from pattern), glue, yarn, crayons, and other decorating materials

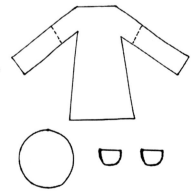

DIRECTIONS:
1. Glue the circle to the top of the card to create a head.
2. Glue the hands to the end of the arms.

3. Draw a face on the head.
4. Glue yarn to the head for hair.
5. Fold the arms on the dotted lines to create the hug.
6. Write a message on the inside and/or outside of the card.
7. Decorate as desired.

See also Thank You Rhyme (365).

FAMILY AND FRIENDS: TEN GREAT BOOKS FOR STORYTIME

Mommy, Carry Me Please! by Jane Cabrera. New York: Holiday House, 2004. (for toddlers)
Feast for Ten by Cathryn Falwell. New York: Clarion, 1993. (for all ages)
Four Friends Together by Sue Heap. Cambridge, MA: Candlewick, 2003. (for all ages)
Spot Visits His Grandparents by Eric Hill. New York: Penguin, 1996. (for toddlers)
Excuse Me: A Little Book of Manners by Karen Katz. New York: Grosset and Dunlap, 2002. (for toddlers)
Henry and Amy (Right-Way-Round and Upside-Down) by Stephen Michael King. New York: Walker, 1998. (for all ages)
Families Are Different by Nina Pellegrini. New York: Holiday House, 1991. (for preschoolers)
Truman's Aunt Farm by Jama Kim Rattigan. New York: Houghton Mifflin, 1994. (for preschoolers)
Too Close Friends by Shen Roddie. New York: Dial, 1997. (for preschoolers)
Noisy Nora by Rosemary Wells. New York: Dial, 1997. (for all ages)

Chapter 10

Food

215 Breakfast

I like breakfast,
Yes I do!
I like breakfast
For lunch and dinner too!
Eggs and bacon
And pancakes piled high,
With whipped cream
Reaching to the sky!

216 Crazy Food

Popcorn, popcorn, *(jump up and down)*
Mashed potatoes, mashed potatoes,
    (swish feet)
Boiling water, boiling water, *(run in place)*
Spaghetti, spaghetti, *(wave arms loosely)*
Fruitcake. *(sit down heavily)*

217 Five Green Peas
(adapted traditional)

Five green peas in a pea pod pressed,
    (make fist)
One, two, three, four, five. *(lift fingers one at a time)*
They grew and grew and did not stop
    (stretch fingers out)
Till one day that pea pod popped!
    (clap hands)

218 In My Garden

In my garden I can see
So many vegetables for me to eat!
Carrots, tomatoes, cucumbers, and peas,
Lettuce, potatoes—what a great treat!

219 Sandwiches

Sandwiches, sandwiches, my favorite treat.
Sometimes I have peanut butter, sometimes I have meat.
Put on some mayonnaise, or lettuce could be fun.
Now cut it in half, and eat it. Yum!

220 Cereal for Breakfast
(to the tune of "Here We Go Round the Mulberry Bush")

This is the way we pour the cereal, pour the cereal, pour the cereal,
This is the way we pour the cereal, so early in the morning.
This is the way we pour the milk . . .
This is the way we take a bite . . .
This is the way we drink the milk . . .

221 *I Like to Eat*
(to the tune of "Apples and Bananas")

Teach the children the signs for the various foods as you sing this song.

I like to EAT, EAT, EAT lots of yummy APPLES.
I like to EAT, EAT, EAT lots of yummy APPLES.
   ...ORANGES...
   ...GRAPES...
   ...COOKIES...
   ...CRACKERS...
   ...CHEESE...

222 *Making a Sandwich*
(to the tune of "Here We Go Round the Mulberry Bush")

This is the way we smash the peanuts,
   smash the peanuts, smash the
   peanuts,
This is the way we smash the peanuts
   when making peanut butter.
This is the way we crush the grapes,
   crush the grapes, crush the grapes,
This is the way we crush the grapes
   when we make some jam.
This is the way we bake the bread,
   bake the bread, bake the bread,
This is the way we bake the bread,
   bread for our sandwich.
This is the way we spread the peanut
   butter, spread the peanut butter,
   spread the peanut butter,
This is the way we spread the peanut
   butter on our sandwich.
This is the way we spread the jam,
   spread the jam, spread the jam,
This is the way we spread the jam on
   our sandwich.
This is the way we eat our sandwich,
   eat our sandwich, eat our sandwich,
This is the way we eat our sandwich,
   munch, munch, munch, munch,
   munch. Yummy!

223 *Pizza Man*
(to the tune of "Do You Know the Muffin Man?")

Oh do you know the pizza man,
The pizza man, the pizza man.
Oh do you know the pizza man,
Who makes it hot and fresh?

224 *Five Little Apples Flannelboard*
(traditional)

Use the apple from pattern 228. (Full-size patterns can be found at www.ala.org/editions/extras/macmillan09775.)

Five little apples lying on the floor.
One rolls away and that leaves four.
Four little apples hanging on a tree.
I'll pick one and that leaves three.
Three little apples, I know what to do!
I'll put one in my pocket and that
   leaves two.
Two little apples sitting in the sun.
I'll pick one up and that leaves one.
One little apple waiting in my lunch.
I'll eat it up with a crunch, crunch,
   crunch!

WEB

225 *Five Little Jelly Beans Flannelboard*

(traditional)
See pattern 225.

Five little jelly beans rolling on the
    floor,
I'll eat one and now there are four.
Four little jelly beans all just for me,
I'll eat one and now there are three.
Three little jelly beans, red, purple,
    and blue,
I'll eat one and now there are two.
Two little jelly beans having lots of
    fun,
I'll eat one and now there is one.
One little jelly bean, we're almost
    done,
I'll eat one and now there are none.

226 *Five Little Cookies in the Bakery Shop Flannelboard*

(traditional)
See pattern 226.

Five little cookies in the bakery shop,
The ones with the sugar and the icing
    on top.
Along comes a child with a nickel to
    pay,
She buys a cookie and takes it away.
Repeat for four, three, two, one.

Quick Tip: Practice money and
counting with this rhyme. Give
each child a felt nickel. Have an
assortment of flannelboard cookies
for the children to purchase.

227 *Ice-Cream Shop Flannelboard*

See pattern 227. Pass out a variety of colored scoops of ice cream to each child. Place an ice-cream cone on the bottom of the flannelboard. Say the rhyme and call a color or flavor of ice cream. Have the children add their scoops to the cone.

Let's all go to the ice-cream shop!
What type of scoop should we add on top?
. . . Strawberry!
After you've called all the children, count how many scoops make up the giant ice-cream cone.

228 *Picking Fruits and Vegetables Flannelboard*

See pattern 228.

Monday is my apple day,
I pick apples from the tree this way.
Tuesday is my blueberry day,
I pick blueberries from the bush this way.
Wednesday is my raspberry day,
I pick raspberries from the bramble this way.
Thursday is my strawberry day,
I pick strawberries from the plant this way.
Friday is my sweet potato day,
I pick sweet potatoes from the ground this way.

Saturday is my pumpkin day,
I pick pumpkins from the vine this way.
Sunday is my pie-making day,
I eat all my pies this way!

229 *Pizza Pie Flannelboard*

See pattern 229. Pass out a variety of pizza toppings to each child. Place a round pizza crust on the flannelboard. Say the rhyme and call out a topping. Have the children add their toppings to the pizza crust.

Pizza, pizza! I love to eat it while it's hot!
What type of toppings should we add on top?
. . . Anchovies!
. . . Cheese!
. . . Meat!
. . . Pineapple!
. . . Pepperoni!

230 **If You Give a Moose a Muffin** *Flannelboard*

See pattern 230. Based on the book by Laura Numeroff (New York: Laura Geringer Books, 1991). If you give a moose a muffin, it leads to all kinds of trouble. Read the book and ask the children to help retell the story on the flannelboard. Ask prompting questions like, "If you give the moose the paper, what will happen next?"

Quick Tip: *If You Give a Moose a Muffin* is a circle story. Ask the children if they noticed that the story begins and ends with the same items. Try creating a short circle story with your group.

WEB

231 *Sandwich Shapes Flannelboard Story*
See pattern 231.

Jill's mother always cut her sandwiches into fancy shapes. Sometimes she cut them into moons. Would you like to eat a moon? Sometimes she cut Jill's sandwiches to look like stars. *(Continue the story in this pattern, showing all shapes except the triangle.)* One day, her mother asked her what shape she would like best. Jill said, "Mommy, today I would like to have a sandwich shape I have never had before. I would like my sandwich to be in the shape of a sandwich." Her mother thought that was a splendid idea. And Jill thought her sandwich-shaped sandwich was the most delicious one she'd ever had!

232 *Bake Me a Cupcake Craft*

WEB

    MATERIALS: one printout of a cupcake for each child (from pattern 232), tissue paper, stickers, glue, crayons, glitter, and other decorating materials

    DIRECTIONS:
1. Squish small pieces of tissue paper and glue to make toppings for your cupcake.
2. Add stickers and other toppings, such as sequins or glitter.
3. Decorate as desired.

233 *Make a Pizza Craft*

    MATERIALS: old cardboard or brown construction paper cut into pizza slices, one slice for each child; tissue paper; circle stickers; glue; crayons; and other decorating materials

    DIRECTIONS:
1. Squish small pieces of tissue paper and glue to make toppings for your pizza.
2. Add stickers and other toppings, such as sequins or shapes cut from construction paper.
3. Decorate as desired.

234 Pea Pod Craft

MATERIALS: one printout of a pea pod for each child (from pattern 234), green tissue paper, glue, crayons, and other decorating materials

DIRECTIONS:
1. Color the pea pod.
2. Squish small pieces of green tissue into balls to make peas for your pod.
3. Decorate as desired.

See also Did You Ever Eat . . . ? Flannelboard (73), Pumpkin Pie Flannelboard (272), Sweet Potatoes Growing (291), and I Am a Grocer Flannelboard (319).

FOOD: TEN GREAT BOOKS FOR STORYTIME

Stone Soup by Marcia Brown. Little Rock, AR: August House, 1998. (for preschoolers)

The Very Hungry Caterpillar by Eric Carle. New York: Philomel, 1979. (for toddlers)

Maisy Goes to the Playground by Lucy Cousins. Cambridge, MA: Candlewick, 1992. (for all ages)

Ants at the Picnic by Michael Dahl. Minneapolis: Picture Window Books, 2006. (for preschoolers)

Jamberry by Bruce Degen. New York: Harper and Row, 1983. (for all ages)

Growing Vegetable Soup by Lois Ehlert. San Diego: Harcourt Brace Jovanovich, 1987. (for toddlers)

Lunch by Denise Fleming. New York: Henry Holt, 1992. (for toddlers)

Spot Goes to the Park by Eric Hill. New York: Putnam, 1991. (for all ages)

If You Give a Moose a Muffin by Laura Numeroff. New York: HarperCollins, 1991. (for preschoolers)

If You Give a Mouse a Cookie by Laura Numeroff. New York: Harper and Row, 1985. (for preschoolers)

Chapter 11

Holidays and Celebrations

BIRTHDAYS

235 *My Birthday*

Today is my birthday,
It's my very special day!
I'll get all my favorite foods
And a cake made any way I say!
After everyone sings
And all my candles I blow,
I'll open my presents
While my family enjoys the show.

236 *My Birthday Party*

I'm having a birthday party,
It's this Saturday.
Here is your invitation.
Will you come and play?
We will have some cake
And presents and ice cream too.
When I open my presents,
I will say thank you.
So light the candles,
Here I go!
Happy Birthday to me!
Now blow!

237 *Birthday Crown Craft*

MATERIALS: one large piece of construction paper cut with zigzag points or bulletin board border paper for each child, stickers, gems, crayons, and other decorating materials

DIRECTIONS:
1. Make a birthday crown by either cutting a large piece of construction paper with zigzag points or using bulletin board border paper.
2. Decorate with stickers, drawings, gems, and more.
3. Fit the crown to your head and staple the ends together.

CHRISTMAS

238 *Christmas Tree*

I wish I could be
A Christmas tree.
I'd have a star of red
Right on my head,
And tinsel of gold
Around me rolled.
I'd shine with lights
All through the night,
And then I'd say,
"Merry Christmas today!"

239 *Giving Presents*

(to the tune of "Frère Jacques")

Giving presents, giving presents
Is such fun, is such fun.
Let's open Christmas presents,
Let's open Christmas presents,
Everyone, everyone.

240 *The Reindeer-Pokey*

(to the tune of "The Hokey-Pokey")

You put your antlers in,
You put your antlers out,
You put your antlers in,
And you shake them all about.
You do the Reindeer-Pokey
And you dance around the room,
Christmas is coming soon!
. . . tail . . .
. . . red nose . . .
. . . hooves . . .
. . . whole self . . .

241 *Five Little Candy Canes Flannelboard*

See pattern 241. (Full-size patterns can be found at www.ala.org/editions/extras/macmillan09775.)

Five little candy canes on my
    Christmas tree.
The first one said, "Please don't eat
    me!"
The second one said, "I've got stripes
    of red and white."
The third one said, "It's Christmas Eve
    tonight."
The fourth one said, "Soon Santa
    Claus will come!"
The fifth one said, "Isn't Christmas
    fun?"
Then the tree lit up and they each
    made a wish,
And five little candy canes shouted,
    "Merry Christmas!"

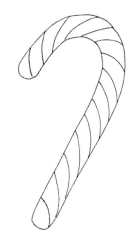

242 Celebration Streamer Craft

> MATERIALS: strips of crepe paper in green, red, and white for each child; one drinking straw for each child; stickers; tape; crayons; and other decorating materials

Quick Tip: You can make a celebration streamer for any special occasion: red, white, and pink crepe paper for Valentine's Day; pastel crepe paper for Easter; and so on.

> DIRECTIONS:
> 1. Tape crepe-paper streamers to the straw.
> 2. Decorate with stickers as desired.

EASTER

243 Five Little Easter Eggs Flannelboard
See pattern 243.

Five little Easter eggs hidden by the door,
(Child's name) found one and then there were four.
Four little Easter eggs so beautiful to see,
(Child's name) found one and then there were three.
Three little Easter eggs and we knew what to do,
(Child's name) found one, and then there were two.
Two little Easter eggs, this egg hunt is such fun!
(Child's name) found one and then there was one.
One little Easter egg sitting in the sun,
I found that one, and then there were none.

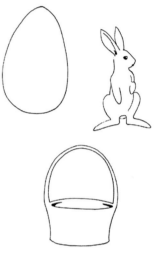

244 Bunny with a Basket Flannelboard Matching Game
See pattern 243 above. Place the bunnies and baskets on the flannelboard and pass the eggs out to the children. Use the rhyme below to invite the children to place their eggs in the basket of the same color.

Bunny with a *(name of color)* basket
Lost his eggs, I don't know how.
If you have a *(repeat name of color)* egg,
Come give it to him now.

FATHER'S DAY

245 D-A-D-D-Y
(to the tune of "B-I-N-G-O")

There is a man we celebrate,
And Daddy is his name, oh.
D-A-D-D-Y, D-A-D-D-Y, D-A-D-D-Y,
And Daddy is his name, oh.
Repeat, gradually replacing letters with claps.

246 Daddy Song
(to the tune of "Frosty the Snowman")

My dad's the greatest dad in the world,
He plays with me and lets me be
Anything I want!
Daddy loves me just the way I am,
And I love the days we get to play
Just me and him!

247 *You're Special Craft*

MATERIALS: one sheet of paper for each child, pictures cut out of magazines, glue, crayons, and other decorating materials

DIRECTIONS:
1. List the things you like to do with a special person or things that make the person special. Then make a collage about those things with pictures and words cut from a magazine.
2. Decorate as desired.

FOURTH OF JULY

248 *Fireworks*

Fireworks, fireworks, green and blue,
Fireworks, fireworks, just for you.
Fireworks, fireworks, bursting high,
Fireworks, fireworks, Happy Fourth
    of July!

250 *Marching Band*

The marching band and the music
    man
Have come to town today.
To celebrate the Fourth of July with
A good old-fashioned parade.

249 *Fourth of July*

When fireworks light up the night sky,
I know it's the Fourth of July!
The distant drums beat and I march
    along,
While I sing a patriotic song.

251 *Wave the Flag*

Wave the flag on the Fourth of July!
Wave the flag and wave it high!
We're so proud of the red, white, and
    blue.
It means freedom for me and you!

GROUNDHOG DAY

252 *Pop Up, Little Groundhog*

Pop up, little groundhog, *(crouch down and jump up)*
From the ground.
Look around, don't make a sound. *(place hand at forehead and look around)*
If there's no shadow, spring is on its way. *(spread arms)*
If you see a shadow, winter's here to stay. Brrrrr! *(shiver)*

253 *Groundhog Pop-Up Puppet Craft*

MATERIALS: one groundhog shape for each child (from pattern 253), one Styrofoam or paper cup with a hole poked in the bottom for each child, one craft stick for each child, glue, crayons or markers

WEB

DIRECTIONS:
1. Decorate the groundhog as desired.
2. Glue the groundhog to the craft stick.
3. Place the groundhog in the cup so that the stick goes through the hole in the bottom. Move the stick to make the groundhog pop up.

HALLOWEEN

254 *Trick or Treat*
(to the tune of "The Addams Family")

On every Halloween
We like to make a scene.
Our costumes are a scream
When we go trick or treat.
Trick or treat! *(knock, knock)*
Trick or treat! *(knock, knock)*
Trick or treat, trick or treat, trick or
treat! *(knock, knock)*
There are ghosts and there are bats,
Witches and black cats,
Clowns with funny hats,
When we go trick or treat.
Trick or treat! *(knock, knock)*
Trick or treat! *(knock, knock)*
Trick or treat, trick or treat, trick or
treat! *(knock, knock)*

255 *Five Little Ghosts Flannelboard*
See pattern 255.

Five little ghosts out on Halloween
night,
One runs away because he has a
fright.
Four little ghosts out on Halloween
night,
One is amazed when he takes flight!
Three little ghosts out on Halloween
night,
One left to play in the park with a kite.
Two little ghosts out on Halloween
night,
One tries to trick or treat but doesn't
get a bite.
One little ghost out on Halloween
night,
Realizes it's time for bed and says
good night.

See also Bats Are Flying (58).

HANUKKAH

256 *Festival of Lights*

Light the lights
On this Hanukkah night.
It's so great to celebrate
This festival of lights!

257 *Our Menorah*

On our menorah, we have candles
eight,
One for each night of Hanukkah we
celebrate.
We start with one, and you can be
sure
That every night we add one more.
Here we go! I can't wait!
One, two, three, four, five, six, seven,
eight!

KWANZAA

258 Seven Candles on the Kinara

Seven little candles shining on our
    kinara bright,
Help us celebrate Kwanzaa on each
    Kwanzaa night.
The first candle stands for *Umoja* —
    that means unity.
The second is for *Kujichagulia* — that
    means self-determination, you see.
The third is for *Ujima*, working
    together and taking responsibility.
The fourth is for *Ujamaa*, supporting
    businesses in our community.
The fifth is for *Nia*, to remember the
    great ones who came before.

The sixth is for *Kuumba*, creativity and
    imagination and more!
The seventh is for *Imani*, the faith our
    people possess.
We celebrate them all and wish you a
    Kwanzaa full of happiness!

259 Light the Candles
(to the tune of "Frère Jacques")

Light the candles, light the candles,
This Kwanzaa night, this Kwanzaa
    night.
We celebrate our people, we celebrate
    our people,
With their light, with their light.

MARTIN LUTHER KING JR. DAY

260 The World Is Like a Rainbow: A Rhyme to Sign
Sign the words in capital letters as you say this rhyme.

The world is like a RAINBOW
Made up of DIFFERENT colors.
But we are all BEAUTIFUL
And should RESPECT each other.
It DOESN'T MATTER if your skin
Is black or tan or white
Or purple polka dots or plaid
Or orange with yellow stripes!
Every PERSON is a PERSON,
And in the end,
Every PERSON is a PERSON
Who could be your FRIEND!

rainbow

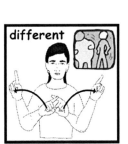
different

beautiful

respect

doesn't matter

person

friend

261 *Martin Luther King Jr. Day*
(to the tune of "Do You Know the Muffin Man?")

Do you know Martin Luther King? Martin Luther King? Martin Luther King?
Do you know Martin Luther King? We celebrate him today.
He believed everyone was equal, everyone was equal, everyone was equal,
He believed everyone was equal, and the world should be that way.
He said it doesn't matter if you're black or white, if you're black or white, if you're black or white,
He said it doesn't matter if you're black or white, we should all be friends.
Martin Luther King was a great man, a great man, a great man.
Martin Luther King was a great man, we celebrate him today.

MOTHER'S DAY

262 *Mother's Day*

Mother's Day is a special day for Mom,
But we should celebrate her all year long.
She helps you out and takes good care of you,
And kisses your knee if you get a boo-boo.
So now is the perfect time to say,
"I love you, Mom! Happy Mother's Day!"

263 *M-O-M-M-Y*
(to the tune of "B-I-N-G-O")

I have a very special friend,
And Mommy is her name, oh.
M-O-M-M-Y, M-O-M-M-Y, M-O-M-M-Y,
And Mommy is her name, oh.
Repeat, gradually replacing letters with claps.

264 *Mommy, All through the Year*
(to the tune of "The Wheels on the Bus")

My mommy plays with me, plays with me, plays with me,
My mommy plays with me all through the year.
My mommy bakes me food . . .
My mommy gives me hugs and kisses . . .

See also Kisses for Mommy (92).

NEW YEAR'S EVE / NEW YEAR'S DAY

265 *Staying Up Till Midnight*

On other nights we go to bed at eight,
But on New Year's Eve we celebrate!
Mommy says we can stay up till midnight,
We'll bang pots and pans and shout in the night.
We'll count down to zero and give a cheer,
And wish everyone a happy New Year!
It's only nine thirty and so much fun I can't take it.
I'm starting to yawn. Do you think I'll . . . ZZZZZ.

266 *Happy New Year*
(to the tune of "Good Night Ladies")

Happy New Year,
Happy New Year,
Happy New Year,
Today is New Year's Day.
Hello, new year,
Good-bye, old year,
Happy New Year,
Today is New Year's Day.

SAINT PATRICK'S DAY

267 *Saint Paddy's Day*

Dressed in green the leprechauns
   scurry through the fields,
Following the rainbows and hiding
   under clover shields.
Carrying their treasures they hatch a
   secret plot,
They bury their gold and hope the
   children can't find the spot.

268 *Shamrock Song*
(to the tune of "Ten Little Indians")

One little, two little, three little
   shamrocks,
Four little, five little, six little
   shamrocks,
Seven little, eight little, nine little
   shamrocks,
On Saint Patrick's Day.

269 *Shamrock Craft*

MATERIALS: three or four hearts cut from green paper for each child (from pattern
269), one green chenille stem for each child, glue, crayons, and other decorating
materials

DIRECTIONS:
1. Glue edges of three hearts together to make a three-leaf
   shamrock or four hearts for a four-leaf clover.
2. Decorate as desired.
3. Tape green chenille stem to decorated shamrock.

THANKSGIVING

270 *Pilgrims*

One happy pilgrim preparing for
   Thanksgiving Day,
She asked for help making sure the
   horses had hay.
Two happy pilgrims preparing for
   Thanksgiving Day,
They asked a friend to pour the water
   in the glasses on the tray.
Three happy pilgrims preparing for
   Thanksgiving Day,

They asked another to set the table in
   a special way.
Four happy pilgrims preparing for
   Thanksgiving Day,
Asked their guests to relax, sit down,
   and stay.
Five happy pilgrims preparing for
   Thanksgiving Day,
Began their meal with thanks and
   bowed their heads to pray.

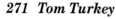

271 Tom Turkey

Little Tom Turkey, come home, come
  home,
Little Tom Turkey, why do you roam?
"I am running far, far away
For it is almost Thanksgiving Day!"

Quick Tip: Perform this rhyme with
a turkey puppet or stuffed turkey,
acting out Tom running away. Let the
children take turns making Tom run
far away.

272 Pumpkin Pie Flannelboard

*See pattern 272. Make enough felt
pumpkin pies for all of the children. Count
how many pies you have on the board
to start. As you say the rhyme, call a
child's name to come and take a pie off the
flannelboard. Continue until all the pies
are gone.*

(Number) pumpkin pies on the bakery
  shelf,
(Child's name) bought a whole one for
  herself!

VALENTINE'S DAY

273 Five Valentines

Five valentine cards outside my door,
I gave one to my sister and then there
  were four.
Four valentine cards so beautiful to see,
I gave one to my brother and then
  there were three.
Three valentine cards, lovely and new,
I gave one to my mother and then
  there were two.
Two valentine cards, isn't this fun?
I gave one to my father and then there
  was one.
One valentine card, and I will say
As I give it to you, "Happy Valentine's
  Day!"

274 Hearts and Flowers
(to the tune of "Frère Jacques")

Hearts and flowers, hearts and flowers,
Chocolates too. Chocolates too.
A day to say I love you,
A day to say I love you.
Valentine's Day. Valentine's Day.

275 Five Little Valentines Flannelboard
(traditional)

See pattern 275.

Five little valentines were having a
  race.
The first little valentine was frilly with
  lace.
The second little valentine had a
  funny face.
The third valentine said "I love you."
The fourth valentine said "I love you
  too."
The fifth valentine was sly as a fox.
She ran the fastest to your valentine
  box.

276 *Four Candy Hearts Flannelboard*
(traditional)

See pattern 276.

I had a candy heart that said "I love you,"
My mommy gave me another,
Now I have two!
Two candy hearts just for me,
My daddy gave me another,
Now I have three!
Three candy hearts — sister gave one more,
This one said "You're the best!"
Now I have four!
Four candy hearts say "You're the best,"
"I love you," and "Be mine."
It sure is sweet to be
My family's valentine!

277 *Matching Hearts Magnetboard*
(to the tune of "Happy Birthday")

See pattern 276 above. Cut out at least ten hearts from white poster board. If you will have a large group at your program, cut out two hearts for each child. Using magic markers, decorate the hearts with stripes, polka dots, and other designs. Make two hearts with each design. You may wish to laminate the hearts so you can reuse them. Place adhesive magnets on the back of each heart. In storytime, place one set of hearts on the magnetboard and distribute the other set to the children. Use the song below to invite each child to the magnetboard to find a match.

Which two hearts are the same?
Which two hearts are the same?
(Child's name), please show me,
Which two hearts are the same?

HOLIDAYS AND CELEBRATIONS: TEN GREAT BOOKS FOR STORYTIME

Maisy's Snowy Christmas Eve by Lucy Cousins. Cambridge, MA: Candlewick, 2003. (for toddlers)
Jamie O'Rourke and the Big Potato: An Irish Folktale by Tomie dePaola. New York: Putnam, 1992. (for preschoolers)
Spot's First Easter by Eric Hill. New York: Putnam, 2002. (for toddlers)
Little Bear's Valentine by Else Holmelund Minarik. New York: HarperCollins, 2003. (for all ages)
Fourth of July Mice! by Bethany Roberts. New York: Clarion, 2004. (for all ages)
Father's Day by Anne Rockwell. New York: HarperCollins, 2005. (for preschoolers)
Mother's Day by Anne Rockwell. New York: HarperCollins, 2004. (for preschoolers)
Big Pumpkin by Erica Silverman. New York: Macmillan, 1992. (for preschoolers)
John, Paul, George and Ben by Lane Smith. New York: Hyperion, 2006. (for preschoolers)
Five Little Pumpkins by Iris Van Rynbach. Honesdale, PA: Boyds Mills, 1995. (for toddlers)

Chapter 12

The Natural World

WINTER

278 Snow Day

No school today,
It's time to play,
Out in the snow so white!
We'll build a snowman,
Ride sleds all we can,
Then we'll have a snowball fight!

279 Snow, Snow

Snow, snow, falling from the sky,
Snow, snow, white before my eyes.
Pat it into a great big ball,
We will make a snowman tall!

280 I Like Snowflakes
(to the tune of "Frère Jacques")

I like snowflakes,
I like snowflakes,
In the air,
In the air.
Falling, twirling snowflakes,
Falling, twirling snowflakes,
Hit the ground,
Hit the ground.

281 I'm a Friendly Snowman
(to the tune of "I'm a Little Teapot")

I'm a friendly snowman big and fat,
(stretch arms out to sides)
Here is my tummy and here is my hat.
(point to tummy, then top of head)
I'm a happy fellow, here's my nose,
(smile, then point to nose)
I'm all snow from my head to my toes.
(point to head, then to toes)
I have two bright eyes so I can see
(point to eyes)
All the snow falling down on me.
(flutter fingers downward)
When the weather's cold I'm strong
and tall, *(stand up tall)*
But when it's warm I get very small.
(crouch down low)

282 Five Little Snowmen Flannelboard
Use the snowman from pattern 303.
(Full-size patterns can be found at www
.ala.org/editions/extras/macmillan09775.)

Five little snowmen on a Saturday
night,
One went to explore—oh what a sight!
Four little snowmen slid across the ice,
One bumped his head and it didn't
feel nice.
Three little snowmen danced with glee,
One let go—Whee!

WEB

Two little snowmen sledding down
  the hill,
One decided to sled again, it was such
  a thrill.
One little snowman noticed the
  morning sun,
He went home, but couldn't wait for
  the night's fun.

283 *Four Snowflakes Flannelboard*
See pattern 283.

One little snowflake falls on a shoe,
He calls for a friend and then there are two.
Two little snowflakes hanging in a tree,
Another drops in and then there are three.
Three little snowflakes stuck to the door,
The wind blows again and then there are four.
Four little snowflakes having lots of fun,
Playing hide-and-seek from the morning sun.

284 *Mitten Count Flannelboard*
See pattern 284.

One mitten, two mittens, three mittens, four,
Five mittens, six mittens, seven mittens, more!
Eight mittens, nine mittens, ten mittens, you see,
Can you say the colors with me?
Red, orange, yellow, green, and blue,
Purple, pink, black, white, and brown too.

285 *Cupcake-Liner Snowman Craft*

MATERIALS: one sheet of construction paper for each child, three cupcake liners for
each child, glue, crayons

DIRECTIONS:
1. Glue the three cupcake liners onto the paper to form a snowman.
2. Decorate with crayons as desired.

See also Getting Dressed from Head to Toe Flannelboard (22) and Skating Song (333).

SPRING

286 *Be a Tree*

See, see, see the trees
Sway, sway in the breeze.
Reach up high and you will see
It's easy to pretend you're a tree!

287 *Splash! Crash! Flash!*

Down comes the rain!
Splash, splash, splash!
Now comes the thunder!
Crash, crash, crash!
Lightning sizzles!
Flash! Flash! Flash!

288 What Grows

What grows?
Plants and flowers and bumblebees,
Kittens and butterflies, and don't
  forget . . . me!

289 Flowers Growing
(to the tune of "Camptown Races")

Flowers growing in our yard,
  growing, growing,
Flowers growing in our yard, growing
  in the sun.
Let the rain fall down,
Let the sunshine in,
Flowers growing in our yard, growing
  in the sun.

290 In the Spring
(to the tune of "Mary Had a Little Lamb")

In the spring the sun does shine, sun
  does shine, sun does shine,
In the spring the sun does shine.
  That's how we know it's spring.
. . . rain does fall . . .
. . . wind does blow . . .
. . . flowers grow . . .
. . . birds build nests . . .
. . . sun does shine . . .

291 Sweet Potatoes Growing

Sweet potatoes, sweet potatoes, in the
  ground,
Growing, growing, without a sound.
When you're ready, we pull you out,
"Sweet potatoes are great!" we all
  shout.

292 Growing Flower Pop-Up Puppet

MATERIALS: one Styrofoam or paper cup with a hole poked in the bottom for each
  child, one circle cut from construction paper for each child, flower petals cut from
  construction paper, one craft stick for each child, glue, crayons or markers

DIRECTIONS:
1. Glue petals around the circle to create a flower.
2. Decorate the flower as desired.
3. Glue the flower to the craft stick.
4. Place the flower in the cup so that the stick goes through the hole in the
   bottom. Move the stick to make the flower grow.

*See also Springtime Outing (88), Spring Has Come (94), Fuzzy-Wuzzy Caterpillar (134), I Saw a Butterfly
(137), Flutter, Flutter, Butterfly (139), I'm a Little Ladybug (141), Five Little Ladybugs Flannelboard (142),
Five Little Caterpillars/Five Little Butterflies Flannelboard (144), Egg-Carton Caterpillar Craft (149), Paper-
Bag Butterfly Wings Craft (150), In My Garden (218), Five Little Kites Flannelboard (337), Let's Fly a Kite
Streamer Game (343), and Kite Craft (344).*

SUMMER

293 Sand between My Toes Call-and-Response Chant

I love to feel the sand between my
  toes.
I dig in it.
I scoop it up.
Let it fall.
Pour on some water.
Mound it up.
A sand castle tall!

294 O-C-E-A-N
(to the tune of "B-I-N-G-O")

There is a place we like to swim,
The ocean is its name, oh.
O-C-E-A-N, O-C-E-A-N, O-C-E-A-N,
The ocean is its name, oh.
*Repeat, gradually replacing letters with
claps.*

295 *Sand on My Head*
(to the tune of "Spider on the Floor")

There's sand on my head, on my head,
There's sand on my head, on my head,
Oh how I dread this sand on my head,
There's sand on my head, on my head.
There's sand up my nose . . . how do
    you suppose this sand got up my
    nose . . .
There's sand in my ear . . . I really,
    really fear there's sand in my ear . . .
There's sand in my shorts . . . This
    sand in my shorts is making me out
    of sorts . . .
There's sand down my leg . . . Oh help
    me, I beg . . .
There's sand in my sandal . . . I don't
    know how to handle . . .

296 *Sand Art*

MATERIALS: coloring sheets depicting summer scenes, one for each child; glue;
    paintbrushes; sand in various colors; empty bowls (Pour the sand into condiment
    bottles for easier use.)

DIRECTIONS:
1. Paint each area of the picture with a think layer of glue.
2. Spread the desired color of sand over the area.
3. Slide the excess sand into an empty bowl.

See also Firefly, Firefly (93), Firefly (133), All through the Summer (138), Five Little Fireflies Flannelboard
(143), and Five Little Baseballs Flannelboard (334).

FALL

297 *Way Up High in the Maple Tree*

Way up high in the maple tree
A little gray squirrel smiled at me.
I said, "Little squirrel, those nuts sure
    look good,"
And he shared them with me, like
    good friends should.

298 *Autumn Leaves*
(to the tune of "London Bridge")

Autumn leaves are falling down,
Falling down, falling down.
Autumn leaves are falling down,
Red, yellow, orange, and brown.

299 *Leaves Are Falling*
(to the tune of "Frère Jacques")

Leaves are falling, leaves are falling,
On the ground, on the ground.
Rake them in a pile,
Rake them in a pile,
Then jump in,
Then jump in.

300 *Leaf Man Craft*

> **MATERIALS:** one sheet of paper for each child, a variety of leaves, glue, crayons, and other decorating materials
>
> **DIRECTIONS:**
> 1. Glue leaves on paper to create a new shape, animal, or object of choice.
> 2. Decorate as desired.

> **Quick Tip:** This craft is a great tie-in to *Leaf Man* by Lois Ehlert (Orlando, FL: Harcourt, 2005). Check out the book for great leaf shapes to create.

301 *Leaf Rubbing Craft*

> **MATERIALS:** one printout of leaves for each child (from pattern 301), crayons, variety of textured surfaces such as sidewalk, tree bark, and carpet
>
> **DIRECTIONS:** Use a crayon to color/rub the leaf. Be sure to have a textured surface under the printout.

See also Five Little Geese Flannelboard (29), Time to Sleep Flannelboard (63), Leaves Flannelboard (96), and Five Little Apples Flannelboard (224).

GENERAL SEASONAL

302 *Seasons*

> I love the seasons for so many reasons!
> Autumn's air is crisp and the leaves are too,
> Listen to them crunch when you squish them with your shoe.
> Winter is cold, with holidays and cheer,
> It's the best time of all when the snow is here.
> Spring is beautiful, with all the flowers blooming,
> Kids are outside playing, their voices booming.
> Summer is fun, even with the heat,
> The pool is great and so are icy treats!

303 *Seasons Game*

See pattern 303. Put up pictures of various seasonal activities and ask the children if they are done in the winter, spring, summer, or fall. To add challenge, include activities that can be enjoyed all year long, like playing with a ball.

304 *Season Wheel Craft*

MATERIALS: paper plates divided into quarters by one horizontal line and one vertical line, one plate for each child; seasonal pictures cut from magazines (sun, pool, leaves, snowflake, snowmen, flowers, rain, etc.); glue, crayons, and other decorating materials

DIRECTIONS:

1. In each quarter of the plate write a season: winter, spring, summer, and fall.
2. Draw a picture that represents each season, or glue on pictures from a magazine.
3. Decorate as desired.

SPACE

305 *Four Little Stars*
(traditional)

Four little stars winking at me,
One shot off, then there were three.
Three little stars with nothing to do,
One shot off, then there were two.
Two little stars, afraid of the sun,
One shot off, then there was one.
One little star, not having any fun,
It shot off, then there were none.

306 *Galaxy Bend and Stretch*

Bend and stretch, reach for the stars,
There goes Jupiter, here comes Mars.
Bend and stretch, reach for the sky,
Stand on tiptoe, oh so high!

307 *Twinkling Stars*
(traditional)

At night I see the twinkling stars
(wiggle fingers)
And the great big shining moon. *(circle arms overhead)*
My mama tucks me into bed *(fists under chin)*
And sings this good-night tune. *(sing "Twinkle, Twinkle, Little Star")*

308 *Planets Song*
(to the tune of "Ten Little Indians")

One little, two little, three little planets,
Four little, five little, six little planets,
Seven little, eight little, nine little planets
Orbiting the sun.
Mercury, Venus, and the Earth,
Mars, Jupiter, and Saturn,
Uranus, Neptune, and Pluto
Orbiting the sun.

309 *Five Little Stars and the Moon Too Flannelboard*
(traditional)

See pattern 309.

Five little stars shine and shine some more,
One fell to the earth and then there were four.
Four little stars, happy as can be,
One fell to the earth and then there were three.
Three little stars in a sky so blue,
One fell to the earth and then there were two.
Two little stars, having lots of fun,
One fell to the earth and then there was one.
One little star left all alone,
That one fell to earth and then there were none.
The moon came out—what a pretty sight!
He waved to the stars and he said good night.

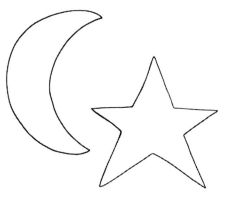

310 *Look Out into Space Flannelboard*

See pattern 310. Hand a colored star or planet to each child. Place the moon on the flannelboard and invite the children to place their planets on the flannelboard when you call their colors.

The moon is sad and all alone out in space.
But if you have a *(name of color)* star *(or planet)*,
Put it in the sky and make the moon happy!

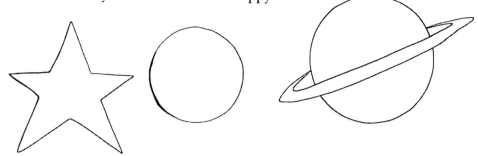

311 **There Was a Bold Lady Who Wanted a Star** *Flannelboard*

See pattern 311. Based on the book by Charise Mericle Harper (New York: Little, Brown, 2002). A bold lady uses various means of transportation to capture a star in this variation on "There Was an Old Lady Who Swallowed a Fly."

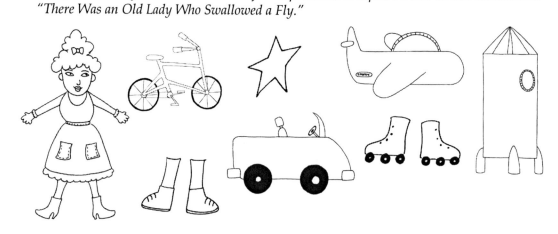

312 Moongame *Flannelboard*

See pattern 312. Based on the book by Frank Asch (New York: Aladdin, 2000). Bear plays hide-and-seek with his friend the moon.

> **Quick Tip:** Read the book first; then use the flannelboard to retell the story with the children's help. Ask prompting questions such as, "Where did the bear think the moon was hiding next?" Retelling a story builds comprehension skills in young listeners.

THE NATURAL WORLD: TEN GREAT BOOKS FOR STORYTIME

Snowmen at Night by Caralyn Buehner. New York: Dial, 2004. (for preschoolers)
Maisy's Pool by Lucy Cousins. Cambridge, MA: Candlewick, 1999. (for toddlers)
Leaf Man by Lois Ehlert. Orlando, FL: Harcourt, 2005. (for all ages)
Snowballs by Lois Ehlert. San Diego: Harcourt Brace, 1995. (for all ages)
The Biggest Snowman Ever by Steven Kroll. New York: Scholastic, 2005. (for toddlers)
Roaring Rockets by Tony Mitton. New York: Kingfisher, 1997. (for preschoolers)
Apples, Apples, Apples by Nancy Elizabeth Wallace. Delray Beach, FL: Winslow Press, 2000. (for preschoolers)
Leaves! Leaves! Leaves! by Nancy Elizabeth Wallace. New York: Marshall Cavendish, 2003. (for toddlers)
Zoom! Zoom! Zoom! I'm Off to the Moon by Dan Yaccarino. New York: Scholastic, 1997. (for all ages)
Beach Party by Harriet Ziefert. Maplewood, NJ: Blue Apple Books, 2005. (for all ages)

Chapter 13

People in My Neighborhood

313 *The Firefighter*

The firefighter wears a big yellow coat
(mime putting on coat)
And a hard hat. *(touch head)*
He pulls on one boot, and then the
other, *(mime putting on boots)*
And sprays his fire hose like that.
(mime spraying fire hose)

314 *Garbage Collector Song*
(to the tune of "The Farmer in the Dell")

We're picking up the trash,
We're picking up the trash.
The garbage truck is coming soon,
We're picking up the trash.
We put it in the trash can . . .
We're bagging up the trash . . .
We're putting out the trash . . .
Thank you, garbage collectors!

315 *Going to the Doctor*
(to the tune of "For He's a Jolly Good Fellow")

We're going to the doctor,
We're going to the doctor,
We're going to the doctor,
Because we don't feel well.
We're stepping on the scale . . . to see
how much we weigh.
The doctor looks in our ears . . . to see
what she can see.
The doctor looks in our mouths . . .
and so we all say ah.

The doctor uses a stethoscope . . . to
listen to our hearts.
Now we get a shot . . . to help us stay
well.
Now we take some medicine . . . to
help us get all better.

Quick Tip: Mine the resources of your patrons! Do you know a regular patron who is a doctor, dentist, or other community helper? Invite him or her to be a special guest at a storytime featuring his or her profession.

316 *In My Neighborhood*
(to the tune of "The Wheels on the Bus")

The people in my neighborhood help
me out, help me out, help me out,
The people in my neighborhood help
me out all throughout my life.
The doctor in my neighborhood takes
care of me, takes care of me, takes
care of me,
The doctor in my neighborhood takes
care of me every time I'm sick.
The firefighters in the neighborhood
put out fires, put out fires, put out
fires,
The firefighters in the neighborhood
put out fires anytime there's need.
The police in the neighborhood
protect me, protect me, protect me,

The police in the neighborhood
    protect me every single day.
The librarian in the neighborhood
    finds me books, finds me books,
    finds me books,
The librarian in the neighborhood
    finds me books anytime I ask.

317 *My Teacher*

(to the tune of "Mary Had a Little Lamb")

At school I learn to read and write,
    read and write, read and write,
At school I learn to read and write
    because my teacher helps me.
We learn math and ABCs, ABCs,
    ABCs,
We learn math and ABCs because my
    teacher helps us.
We learn science and history, history,
    history,
We learn science and history because
    my teacher helps us.

318 *Veterinarian Song*

(to the tune of "Happy Birthday")

My cat had a cold,
And so I was told
To take her to the vet.
Good-bye, runny nose!
My dog had the flu.
I knew what to do.
I took him to the vet.
Now he's better too.
My snake's throat was sore,
So I went once more.
I took him to the vet,
Now he's better, that's for sure!

319 *I Am a Grocer Flannelboard*

See patterns 228 and 319. (Full-size patterns can be found at www.ala.org/editions/extras/ macmillan09775.) Give out items to the children; then ask for categories by color or food type to be brought up and placed in the basket.

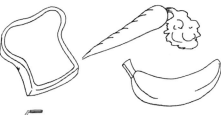

I am a grocer at the food store.
Every day I set out more food and more.
Do you like peaches and apples so sweet?
Bread and ice cream and broccoli and meat?
Whatever you want, go ahead and ask it,
And I will put it in your basket!

WEB

320 *Milo's Hats Flannelboard*

See pattern 320. Begin with Milo on the flannelboard.

Milo is trying to decide what he wants to be when he grows up. He likes to cook, so maybe he should be a chef. *(Place chef's hat on Milo's head.)* But then he thinks, "Maybe I would like to be a firefighter and ride in a big red fire truck." *(Repeat pattern until all hats have been used.)* Then Milo thinks, "Maybe I will be everything!" *(Place all hats on Milo.)*

321 **Shhhhh! Everybody's Sleeping** *Flannelboard*

See pattern 321. Based on the book by Julie Markes (New York: HarperCollins, 2004). After a hard day at work, everyone is tired, and all the community helpers are tucked into bed.

Quick Tip: Don't miss the wonderful illustrations by David Parkins in *Shhhhh! Everybody's Sleeping*. Use this flannelboard to bolster comprehension by having the children help you retell the story. As you put each community helper to bed, discuss his or her job.

322 Sorting the Mail Game

See pattern 322. Make three baskets or mailboxes labeled "Zoo," "School," and "Jones Family." Copy the pictures from the pattern and attach them to fifteen envelopes. Invite the children to sort the mail into the appropriate baskets or mailboxes.

Mr. Mailman has to sort the mail! Will you help him?

323 Make a Doctor's Kit Craft

MATERIALS: sheets of construction paper, U-shaped handles cut from construction paper, paper fasteners, Band-Aids, cotton swabs, and tissue, one of each for each child; tape; glue; crayons; and other decorating materials

DIRECTIONS:
1. Fold the piece of construction paper in half.
2. Glue the U-shaped handle to the inside of one side of the paper.
3. Decorate as desired.
4. Inside the kit tape a Band-Aid, a cotton swab, and tissue; then fold the kit shut.
5. Secure the kit shut with a paper fastener.

324 Badge Craft

MATERIALS: one badge for each child (from pattern 324), star stickers, crayons, and other decorating materials

DIRECTIONS:
1. Decorate badge as desired.
2. Place star sticker in center of badge.
3. Cut out badge if desired and tape it on your shirt.

325 *What Hat Should I Wear? Craft*

WEB

MATERIALS: one printout of community helpers for each child (from pattern 325), one set of hats (from pattern) for each child, glue, crayons, and other decorating materials

DIRECTIONS:
1. Match the hats with the appropriate community helpers and glue each hat in place.
2. Color and decorate as desired.

See also I Went to the Dentist (7), Teeth (8), The People in the School (356), and Five Little Fire Trucks (390).

PEOPLE IN MY NEIGHBORHOOD: TEN GREAT BOOKS FOR STORYTIME

Going to the Dentist by Cindy Bailey. New York: DRL Books, 2002. (for all ages)

Garbage Collectors by Paulette Bourgeois. Buffalo, NY: Kids Can Press, 1998. (for preschoolers)

Police Officers by Paulette Bourgeois. Buffalo, NY: Kids Can Press, 1999. (for preschoolers)

On the Town: A Community Adventure by Judith Caseley. New York: Greenwillow, 2002. (for preschoolers)

Going to the Doctor by Anne Civardi. Tulsa, OK: EDC, 2000. (for toddlers)

Stormy's Hat by Eric Kimmel. New York: Farrar, Straus, and Giroux, 2008. (for preschoolers)

Just Going to the Dentist by Mercer Mayer. Racine, WI: Western, 1990. (for toddlers)

My Teacher Can Teach Anyone! by W. Nikola-Lisa. New York: Lee and Low Books, 2004. (for preschoolers)

Caillou: A Visit to the Doctor by Joceline Sanschagrin. Montreal: Chouette, 2001. (for all ages)

Fireman Small by Wong Herbert Yee. Boston: Houghton Mifflin, 1994. (for all ages)

Chapter 14

Play

326 *Ahoy!*

Ahoy, mateys! Climb on board!
My pirate ship is leaving shore.
Swab the decks and raise the mast,
We're heading out to sea at last!

327 *Basketball*

I love the beat, beat, beat
That my ball bouncing makes on the
    court,
Dribble, dribble—until I can shoot.
Beat, beat, beat, swoosh!

328 *Dribble, Dribble, Basketball*

Dribble, dribble, basketball,
Pass, pass, basketball,
Dribble, dribble, basketball,
Bounce, bounce, basketball,
Dribble, dribble, basketball,
Shoot! Two points!

329 *Jack-in-the-Box*
(adapted traditional)

Jack-in-the-box,
You sit so still. *(make fist with thumb
    inside)*
Won't you come out?
Yes, I will! *(pop out thumb)*

330 *Let's Play Outside*

I like to jump,
I like to skip,
I like to run,
And then I sit.
I stand up straight,
and take a breath,
then I start the race again!

331 *What Is It?*

You can kick it,
You can bounce it,
You can dribble it like that.
You can pass it,
You can hit it
With a club or with a bat.
You can roll it,
You can spin it,
And that's not all.
What is it? Can you guess?
It's a ball!

332 *Roll, Roll, Roll the Ball*
(to the tune of "Row, Row, Row Your Boat")

*Ask the children to sit in a circle and take
turns rolling the ball to one another as
you sing this song. This is a good activity
for children to learn one another's names.*

Roll, roll, roll the ball,
Happy as can be.
(Child's name) rolls it back to me,
Quick as one, two, three!

333 Skating Song
(to the tune of "A Bicycle Built for Two")

Skating, skating, out on the ice so cold.
Spinning, twirling, when we are
    feeling bold.
It's hard to keep our balance
When we show off our talents.
We love to skate,
It is first-rate
To twirl and slide in the cold.

334 Five Little Baseballs Flannelboard
(traditional)

Use the baseball from pattern 341.

Five little baseballs, look at them soar!
One went over the fence and now
    there are four.
Four little baseballs, look and see,
One rolled into a pond and now there
    are three.
Three little baseballs, over the hill one
    flew,
I can't find it, now there are two.
Two little baseballs, Spot wants some
    fun,
He picked one up and now there is
    one.
One little baseball flying in the sun,
Johnny hit a homer,
Look at him run!

335 Soccer Song
(to the tune of "Row, Row, Row Your Boat")

Kick, kick, kick the ball,
Soccer is such fun.
Pass the ball and kick the ball,
And run, run, run, run, run!

336 Teddy Bear, Teddy Bear
(to the tune of "Edelweiss")

Teddy bear, teddy bear,
Every evening I hug you.
Teddy bear, teddy bear,
There is no one above you.

337 Five Little Kites Flannelboard
See pattern 337.

One little kite in the sky so blue,
Along came another, then there were
    two.
Two little kites flying high above me,
Along came another, then there were
    three.
Three little kites, just watch them soar,
Along came another, then there were
    four.
Four little kites, so high and alive,
Along came another, then there were
    five.
Five little kites dancing across the sky,
What a sight to see, way up so high!

338 Color Balloons Flannelboard
Use pattern 312 to make colorful balloon shapes. (Full-size patterns can be found at www.ala.org/editions/extras/macmillan09775.) Pass out the balloons for the children to put on the flannelboard. As you say the rhyme, make windy sounds and call out a balloon color!

On a windy day, way up in the sky,
Look for the colored balloons as they fly!
I see a red balloon, wow—look at all those red balloons flying.
Continue with other colors.

WEB

339 A Little Ball Flannelboard
(traditional)

See pattern 339.

A little ball,
A bigger ball,
A great big ball I see.
Now let's count the balls.
One . . . two . . . three!

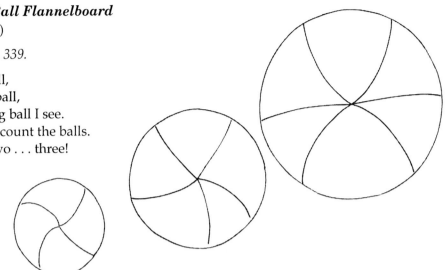

WEB

340 Silly Sally Flannelboard
See pattern 340. Based on the book by Audrey Wood (San Diego: Harcourt Brace Jovanovich, 1992). Silly Sally walks to town backward and upside down and meets silly new friends along the way.

WEB

341 Ball Flannelboard Game
See pattern 341. Ask the following questions and place the ball on the board.

I'm black and white. I often get kicked around! What sport do you play with me?

I'm orange. I get bounced up and down the court and thrown through a hoop! What sport do you play with me?

I'm small and white. After a hard hit I fly through the air! What sport do you play with me?

I'm brown. I get thrown around a lot! What sport do you play with me?

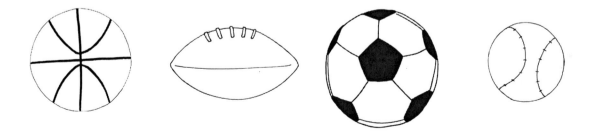

342 Baby's Favorite Toys Prop Story

Place a doll, a ball, a toy train, a teddy bear, a drum, a rubber duck, a toy car, and a board book in a bag. Pull each toy out in turn as you tell the story.

Baby has a doll. That doll is Baby's favorite toy, except for Baby's ball. That ball is Baby's favorite toy, except for Baby's train. *(Repeat with other toys.)* You know what? Baby has lots of favorite toys. Which one is your favorite?

343 Let's Fly a Kite Streamer Game

Make kite streamers by cutting out diamonds from construction paper and taping a length of curling ribbon to the back of each. Hold the end of the ribbon and swish the kite through the air as you say the rhyme below.

I took my kite to the park
And flew it in the air.
I flew it high,
I flew it low,
I flew it everywhere.
I flew it in a great big circle,
I flew it in a square,
I flew it in a squiggly line,
And tossed it in the air.

344 Kite Craft

MATERIALS: one large piece of paper or newspaper or brown grocery bag for each child, yarn, tape, crayons, stickers, streamers, and other decorating materials

DIRECTIONS:
1. Create a diamond shape from a large piece of paper, grocery bag, or newspaper.
2. In the center of the diamond punch two small holes about 6 inches apart.
3. Thread yarn through each hole, knot the ends, and secure them with tape so that you create a handle to hold on to on one side of the diamond.
4. Decorate the kite as desired and tape streamer tails to the bottom end.
5. Fly the kites through the room.

345 Toy Box Craft

MATERIALS: one old shoe box or envelope or piece of white paper folded in half and glued along side edges for each child, pictures of toys or games cut from a magazine or store ad, paper, crayons, glue, and other decorating materials

DIRECTIONS:
1. Decorate a shoe box, envelope, or folded piece of paper as desired to create your own special toy box.
2. Color your own pictures of favorite toys or use pictures of toys cut out of a magazine.
3. Place your pictures inside your toy box.

See also Fancy Me *(18),* Gone Fishing *(46),* Teddy Bear *(82),* Kite Song *(86),* Drawing *(175),* Two Little Friends *(208),* Five Friends Flannelboard *(209),* Seasons Game *(303),* There Was a Bold Lady Who Wanted a Star *Flannelboard (311), and* I Can *(371).*

PLAY: TEN GREAT BOOKS FOR STORYTIME

Pickle and the Ball by Lynn Breeze. New York: Kingfisher, 1998. (for all ages)

Maisy Plays by Lucy Cousins. Cambridge, MA: Candlewick, 2001. (for all ages)

Farmer Will by Jane Cowen-Fletcher. Cambridge, MA: Candlewick, 2001. (for all ages)

Cowboy Kid by Max Eilenberg. Cambridge, MA: Candlewick, 2000. (for toddlers)

Olivia and the Missing Toy by Ian Falconer. New York: Atheneum, 2003. (for preschoolers)

Traction Man by Mini Grey. New York: Knopf, 2005. (for preschoolers)

Fancy Nancy by Jane O'Connor. New York: HarperCollins, 2006. (for preschoolers)

The Little Engine That Could by Watty Piper. New York: Platt and Munk, 1999. (for toddlers)

Plaidypus Lost by Janet Stevens and Susan Stevens Crummel. New York: Holiday House, 2004. (for toddlers)

Knuffle Bunny by Mo Willems. New York: Hyperion, 2004. (for toddlers)

Chapter 15

School and Library

346 *Back to School*
(traditional)

Two little houses all closed up tight,
(make fists)
Open up the window and let in the
light. *(open fists)*
Ten little children tall and straight,
(show ten fingers)
Ready for school at half past eight.
(walk with fingers)

347 *Field Trip*

Teacher says we are going somewhere
special today,
Maybe it will be a place where we can
play!
It will have really neat people and
stories in books,
And lots of neat things so we can take
a look.
All of our favorite friends will be
there —
Hey! We have that at school! We don't
have to go anywhere!

348 *Here Is My Book*
(traditional)

Here is my book. *(hold hands together)*
I open it wide *(open hands like a book)*
To see all the pictures that are inside.

349 *I Like Books*
(traditional)

I like books, I really do,
Books with stories and pictures too,
Books of birds and things that grow,
Books of people we should know,
Books of animals and places too,
I like books, yes I do.

350 *Library Storytime*

When I am going to storytime *(point
to self)*
I jump right out of bed. *(jump)*
I wash my face, *(scrub face)*
And brush my teeth, *(brush teeth)*
And pull on clothes over my head.
(arms up and down)
I run downstairs, *(run in place)*
And drink my milk, *(pretend to drink)*
And eat my breakfast just so. *(pretend
to chew)*
I wave good-bye as I go out the door,
(wave)
I'm so happy that I can go! *(smile)*

351 *Story Hour*
(traditional)

When the sun lights up the sky,
I sit right up and rub my eyes.
I dress myself with greatest care,
and brush my teeth and comb my hair.
Then off to story hour I go,
To hear the stories that I love so!

352 We're Going to the Library

We're going to the library,
We're leaving right away!
If we could, we would stay all day!
We might see a book on castles or
    maybe one on dragons,
We might see a book on dinosaurs or
    how to build wagons.
The best thing about the library is that
    every time you go,
You can check out a new book and
    start an adventure, you know?

353 Bumpin' Up and Down in My Yellow School Bus

(to the tune of "Bumpin' Up and Down in
My Little Red Wagon")

Bumpin' up and down in my yellow
    school bus,
Bumpin' up and down in my yellow
    school bus,
Bumpin' up and down in my yellow
    school bus,
Won't you be my darling?
One wheel's off and the axle's broken,
One wheel's off and the axle's broken,
One wheel's off and the axle's broken,
Won't you be my darling?

354 Going to School

(to the tune of "Twinkle, Twinkle, Little
Star")

Going to school is so great,
I know you can hardly wait.
First you'll learn your ABCs,
Then you'll count your 123s.
Going to school is so great,
I know you can hardly wait.

355 Hi-Ho-Librario

(to the tune of "The Farmer in the Dell")

The author writes a book, the author
    writes a book,
Hi-ho-librario, the author writes a
    book.
The illustrator draws a picture, the
    illustrator draws a picture,
Hi-ho-librario, the illustrator draws a
    picture.

The publisher puts it together, the
    publisher puts it together,
Hi-ho-librario, the publisher puts it
    together.
The patron checks it out, the patron
    checks it out,
Hi-ho-librario, the patron checks it
    out.

356 The People in the School

(to the tune of "The Wheels on the Bus")

The teacher in the school says, "Time
    to learn," "Time to learn," "Time to
    learn."
The teacher in the school says, "Time
    to learn," all through the day.
The librarian says, "Let's read a book"
    . . .
The cafeteria lady says, "Time to eat"
    . . .
The gym teacher says, "Let's run, run,
    run" . . .
The art teacher says, "Let's draw a
    picture" . . .
The students in the school say, "We
    love school" . . .

357 The School Bus Went Down the Road

(to the tune of "The Bear Went Over the
Mountain")

The school bus went down the road,
The school bus went down the road,
The school bus went down the road,
To pick up all the children.
It picked up all the children . . . so they
    could go to school.
The school bus drove them to school
    . . . so they could start their day.
The children learned to read and write
    . . . while they were at school.

358   *This Is the Way We Get to School*
(to the tune of "Here We Go Round the Mulberry Bush")

This is the way we get to school,
Get to school, get to school.
This is the way we get to school, so
   early in the morning.
Some of us walk to school . . .
Some of us are car riders . . .
Some of us ride the bus . . .

359   *This Is the Way We Go to the Library*
(to the tune of "Here We Go Round the Mulberry Bush")

This is the way we go to the library,
Go to the library, go to the library.
This is the way we go to the library, all
   through the day.
This is the way we read our books . . .
This is the way we turn the pages . . .
This is the way we look at pictures . . .
This is the way we listen to stories . . .

360   *Ten Little Books Flannelboard*
(to the tune of "Ten Little Indians")

[WEB]

See pattern 360. (Full-size patterns can be found at www.ala.org/editions/extras/macmillan09775.)

One little, two little, three little books,
Four little, five little, six little books,
Seven little, eight little, nine little books,
Ten little books on the library shelf!

361   The Bus for Us *Flannelboard*

[WEB]

See pattern 361. Based on the book by Suzanne Bloom (Honesdale, PA: Boyds Mills, 2001). A little girl sees a variety of vehicles as she waits eagerly for the bus on the first day of school.

362 My Book Craft

MATERIALS: paper cut in half and folded to create a four-page booklet for each child, pictures cut out of magazines, glue, crayons, stickers, and other decorating materials

DIRECTIONS:
1. Glue on pictures of things you like, pictures that create a story you would like to tell, or even pictures to remind you of a favorite book you can find in the library.
2. Draw additional pictures as needed to complete your story.
3. Decorate as desired.
4. Make sure you share your book with a special person!

363 School Bus Craft

MATERIALS: one school bus (from pattern 363) on yellow construction paper for each child, rectangle and circle stickers or those shapes cut from construction paper, glue, crayons, and other decorating materials

DIRECTIONS:
1. Place rectangle stickers where windows would be, or glue on rectangle shapes.
2. Place circle stickers where wheels would be, or glue on circle shapes.
3. Decorate bus as desired.

Encourage children to write their names and bus numbers (if they have a number) on their buses.

See also My Teacher (317).

SCHOOL AND LIBRARY: TEN GREAT BOOKS FOR STORYTIME

Book! Book! Book! by Deborah Bruss. New York: Arthur A. Levine, 2001. (for toddlers)
Maisy Goes to the Library by Lucy Cousins. Cambridge, MA: Candlewick, 2005. (for all ages)
The Seals on the Bus by Lenny Hort. New York: Henry Holt, 2000. (for all ages)
I Took My Frog to the Library by Eric Kimmel. New York: Viking, 1990. (for toddlers)
If You Take a Mouse to School by Laura Numeroff. New York: Laura Geringer Books, 2002. (for toddlers)
The Kissing Hand by Audrey Penn. Washington, DC: Child Welfare League of America, 1993. (for preschoolers)
Wild about Books by Judy Sierra. New York: Knopf, 2004. (for preschoolers)
I Love School! by Philemon Sturges. New York: HarperCollins, 2004. (for all ages)
Library Lil by Suzanne Williams. New York: Dial, 1997. (for preschoolers)
Baby Bear's Books by Jane Yolen. Orlando, FL: Harcourt, 2006. (for toddlers)

Chapter 16

Sing and Dance

HELLO AND GOOD-BYE

364 *Hello You!*

Hello eyes! Hello toes!
Hello mouth! Hello nose!
Hello shirt! Hello shoe!
Hello tummy! Hello you!

365 *Thank You Rhyme*
(adapted traditional)

Sign THANK YOU as you say this rhyme.

Our hands say THANK YOU with a
clap clap clap.
Our feet say THANK YOU with a tap
tap tap.
Clap clap clap, tap tap tap.
THANK YOU, everyone!

366 *Wave Good-bye*

We had so much fun at the library today,
We came to read and sing and play,
We did a craft and said some rhymes,
Now let's wave good-bye until next
time!

367 *Hello/Good-bye, Friends*
(to the tune of "Good Night Ladies")

Hello, friends, hello, friends,
Hello, friends, it's time to say hello!

*Repeat, replacing "friends" with each child's
name until everyone has been greeted.*

Good-bye, friends, good-bye, friends,
Good-bye, friends, it's time to say good-
bye!

368 *Hello, My Friends*
(to the tune of "Skip to My Lou")

*Sign HELLO and HOW ARE YOU as you
sing this song.*

HELLO, my friends, and HOW ARE YOU?
HELLO, my friends, and HOW ARE YOU?
HELLO, my friends, and HOW ARE YOU?
HELLO, my friends, HOW ARE YOU?
HELLO, (child's name), and HOW ARE
YOU . . . (continue until all children have
been greeted)

369 *Storytime Hello and Good-bye Song*
(to the tune of "Mary Had a Little Lamb")

Hello, hello, all my friends,
All my friends, all my friends.
I am glad to see my friends
At storytime today.

Good-bye, good-bye, all my friends,
All my friends, all my friends.
I was glad to see my friends
At storytime today.

370 *What Is Your Name?*
(to the tune of "Happy Birthday")

Please tell me your name,
Please tell me your name.
What is your name? (*get name*)
Hello, (*child's name*).

TRANSITIONS

371 *I Can*

I can run, run, run.
I can walk, walk, walk.
I can reach, reach, reach.
I can talk, talk, talk.
I can smile, smile, smile.
I can frown, frown, frown.
I can jump, jump, jump.
I can sit right down.

372 *My Fingers Can*

My fingers can wiggle.
My fingers can tickle.
My fingers can clap.
My fingers can tap.
My fingers can count.
My fingers can bounce.
My fingers can wave—through the air
　they go.
My fingers can fold gently in my lap
　just so.

373 *Reach and Wiggle*

Lift your arms way up high,
Wave them, wave them in the sky.
Reach way down and touch your toes.
Wiggle your eyebrows, wiggle your
　nose.
Put your bottom on the floor,
Count with me: one, two, three, four.
Clap your hands now: one, two, three,
Then fold them in your lap like me.

374 *Wiggles*

Put a wiggle in your head,
Put a wiggle in your toes.
Put a wiggle in your arms,
Put a wiggle in your nose.
Put a wiggle in your bottom,
Put a wiggle in your knee.
Put a wiggle in your whole body,
　Now sit quiet as can be.

See also I Wiggle My Fingers (2), All about You (4), Opposites (169), Castle Capers (183), My Magic Wand (187), Crazy Food (216), and Galaxy Bend and Stretch (306).

MUSIC AND DANCE

375 *That's a Dance*

If you jump up and down and you make a silly sound,
That's a dance! Toodly-doo, toodly-doo.
If you reach for your toes and you wrinkle up your nose,
That's a dance! Toodly-doo, toodly-doo.
If you stretch your hands up high and flap like you can fly,

That's a dance! Toodly-doo, toodly-doo.
If you swing your arms loose and you shake your caboose,
That's a dance! Toodly-doo, toodly-doo.
If you shake your hair like you just don't care,
That's a dance! Toodly-doo, toodly-doo.

376 *Admission Ticket Craft*

MATERIALS: a half sheet of paper with the written words "Admit One" for each child, glue, crayons, stickers

DIRECTIONS:

1. Write your name on your ticket so your parents and friends know that you are having the show.
2. Decorate as desired.

Encourage children to put on a show for their parents after dinner and collect tickets.

377 *Microphone Craft*

MATERIALS: one toilet paper roll for each child, decorating paper cut to fit tubes, one foam ball for each child, glue, crayons, and other decorating materials

DIRECTIONS:

1. Glue paper around toilet paper roll.
2. Decorate roll as desired.
3. Glue foam ball on top, then allow to dry.

Encourage children to put on a show for their parents after dinner and use their microphones.

378 *Show Off Your Talent Craft*

MATERIALS: one sheet of paper for each child, glue, crayons, stickers

DIRECTIONS:

1. Draw a microphone, dance shoes, or an instrument on the poster, or glue on pictures cut from magazines.
2. Decorate as desired.

Encourage children to put on a show for their parents after dinner, using the poster as an announcement. Children who made tickets (376) and microphones (377) may also incorporate those props into the show.

379 *Dancing Shoes Craft*

MATERIALS: one printout of dancing shoes page for each
child (from pattern 379), crayons, stickers, and other
decorating materials (Full-size patterns can be found
at www.ala.org/editions/extras/macmillan09775.)

DIRECTIONS:
1. Color the dancing shoes.
2. Decorate as desired.

See also She Dances Alone (105) and Bee Dance (132).

> **Quick Tip:** Ask the children if they can match each type of shoe to the appropriate
> activity: tap shoes for tap dancing, ballet shoes for ballet dancing, bunny slippers for
> nighttime fun, and so forth.

SING AND DANCE: TEN GREAT BOOKS FOR STORYTIME

Song and Dance Man by Karen Ackerman. New York: Knopf, 1988. (for preschoolers)
Giraffes Can't Dance by Giles Andreae. New York: Orchard, 2001. (for toddlers)
Barnyard Dance by Sandra Boynton. New York: Workman, 1993. (for all ages)
Gabriella's Song by Candace Fleming. New York: Atheneum, 1997. (for preschoolers)
When Uncle Took the Fiddle by Libba Moore Gray. New York: Orchard, 1999. (for all ages)
Got to Dance by Mary-Claire Helldorfer. New York: Doubleday, 2004. (for preschoolers)
Barn Dance by Pat Hutchins. New York: Greenwillow, 2007. (for toddlers)
Zin! Zin! Zin! A Violin by Lloyd Moss. New York: Simon and Schuster, 1995. (for
    preschoolers)
Skip to My Lou by Nadine Bernard Westcott. New York: Little, Brown, 1989. (for toddlers)
Belinda the Ballerina by Amy Young. New York: Viking, 2002. (for preschoolers)

Chapter 17

Transportation

380 *Choo-Choo Rhyme*

Choo-choo, choo-choo, riding on the
   train,
Choo-choo, choo-choo, riding on the
   train.
Conductor yells, "All aboard!"
Then the engine starts to roar.
I'll take your ticket, hop on board,
Riding on the train.
Whistle blows, toot-toot!
Riding on the train.

381 *Helicopter*
*Sign HELICOPTER as you say this
rhyme.*

HELICOPTER going up,
HELICOPTER going down,
HELICOPTER turning, turning all
   around.
HELICOPTER going left,
HELICOPTER going right,
HELICOPTER going up, out of sight.

helicopter

382 *In the Car*

Riding, riding, in the car, *(mime driving)*
Driving near and driving far.
We always buckle our seat belts just
   so, *(mime buckling seat belt)*
Start the engine and off we go! *(mime
   turning key and driving)*

383 *Red Light Game*

Red light, green light, stop and go,
Sometimes fast and sometimes slow.
   (mime driving)
Step on the gas and we speed up,
Step on the brake and we come to a
   stop!

384 *Vehicle Guessing Game*

I have headlights and a steering wheel,
I take you near and far.
My horn says honk! And my engine
   says vroom!
Hop in! I am a *(car)*.

I pull my cars along the rails,
I chug through sun or rain.
My smokestack lets out a woo-woo!
Hop aboard! I am a *(train)*.

I'll take you soaring in the sky,
We'll reach the clouds and soon!
I come in bright colors, with a basket
   for you.
Hop in! I am a *(balloon)*.

I have two wheels and a handlebar,
And pedals you will like.
You can ride me down the road.
Hop on! I am a *(bike).*

I have wings and an engine that roars.
My comfy cabins contain
Lots of seats where passengers sit.
Hop aboard! I am a *(plane).*

I have a great big cab and a loud horn,
And big wheels so I won't get stuck,
A giant trailer to carry big loads.
Hop aboard! I am a *(truck).*

385 *Zoom!*
(traditional)

Zoom!
Let's go to the moon!
Let's take a trip
In my rocket ship!
Get ready for the countdown!
Ten-nine-eight-seven-six-five-four-
    three-two-one!
Blastoff!

386 *Airplane*
(to the tune of "A Bicycle Built for Two")

Airplane, airplane,
Spread out your wings for me.
We'll go flying
Over mountains and sea.
Your cabin is cozy and comfy,
Your pilot is never grumpy,
And we will fly
Up in the sky
And away into the clouds.

387 *At the Construction Site*
(to the tune of "The Wheels on the Bus")

The hook on the crane goes up and
    down, up and down, up and down,
The hook on the crane goes up and
    down at the construction site.
The shovel on the digger goes dig, dig,
    dig . . .
The barrel on the mixer goes round
    and round . . .
The dumper on the dump truck goes
    dump, dump, dump . . .

388 *Drive the Car*
(to the tune of "Row, Row, Row Your
Boat")

Drive, drive, drive the car,
Driving to and fro.
When the light is green we know
That now it's time to go.
Drive, drive, drive the car,
Driving through the town.
When the light is yellow we know
That it's time to slow down.
Drive, drive, drive the car,
Driving to the shop.
When the light is red we know
That now it's time to stop.

389 *Farmer's Riding on the Tractor*
(to the tune of "I've Been Working on the
Railroad")

Farmer's riding on the tractor
All the live long day.
Farmer's riding on the tractor
Just to pass the time away.
Can't you hear the engine turning?
Rise up so early in the morn.
Can't you hear the soil churning?
Tractor, blow your horn.
Tractor won't you pull,
Tractor won't you pull,
Tractor won't you pull
Your load?
Tractor won't you pull,
Tractor won't you pull,
Tractor won't you pull
Your load?
The farmer is riding the tractor,
He's riding the tractor right now.
The farmer is riding the tractor,
And the tractor is pulling the plow.

390 *Five Little Fire Trucks*
(to the tune of "Down by the Station")

Five little fire trucks at the fire station.
See the engines gleaming all in a row.
When the fire chief sounds the
    alarm—
Nee-naw! Nee-naw! Off they go!

391 *Found a Tractor*

(to the tune of "Found a Peanut")

Found a tractor, found a tractor,
Found a tractor just now.
Just now I found a tractor,
Found a tractor just now.
Turned it on . . .
It was broken . . .
Turned it off . . .

Fixed the tractor . . .
Turned it on . . .
Rode the tractor . . .
Cut the grass . . .
Swept the grass . . .
Parked the tractor . . .
Turned it off . . .

392 *Five Big Boats Flannelboard*

See pattern 392. (Full-size patterns can be found at www.ala.org/editions/extras/ macmillan09775.)

Five big boats sailing from the shore,
One stopped to catch some fish and then there were four.
Four big boats sailing out to sea,
One stopped to look around and then there were three.
Three big boats with so much to do,
One stopped at an island and then there were two.
Two big boats sailing under the sun,
One pulled into a port and then there was one.
One big boat sailing all alone,
That one turned around and sailed for home.

393 *Five Hot-Air Balloons Flannelboard*

See pattern 393.

Five hot-air balloons, up they soar,
One floats north and then there are four.
Four hot-air balloons, so pretty to see,
One floats south and then there are three.
Three hot-air balloons in the sky so blue,
One floats east and then there are two.
Two hot-air balloons having so much fun,
One floats west and then there is one.
One hot-air balloon when the day is done,
That one floats home and then there are none.

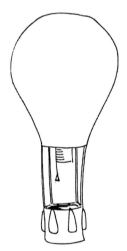

394 *Five Little Trucks Flannelboard*

(to the tune of "Five Little Ducks")

See pattern 394.

Five little trucks drove out one day,
Over the hills and far away.
Mother truck said, "Beep-beep-beep,"
Four little trucks drove home to sleep.
Four little trucks . . .
Three little trucks . . .
Two little trucks . . .
One little truck . . .
Mother truck said, "Beep! Beep! Beep!"
Five little trucks drove home to sleep.

395 Rocket Ships Flannelboard
See pattern 395.

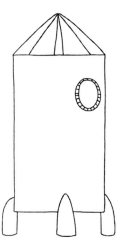

Five shiny rocket ships exploring outer space,
One saw aliens and set off on a chase.
Four shiny rocket ships exploring outer space,
One bumped into an asteroid and was knocked out of place.
Three shiny rocket ships exploring outer space,
One found Jupiter first and thought he was an ace.
Two shiny rocket ships exploring outer space,
One caught a shooting star and took off in a race.
One shiny rocket ship left in outer space,
He wanted to go home so he headed for Earth's base.

396 Grandma Rabbitty's Visit *Flannelboard*
See pattern 396. Based on the book by Barry Smith (New York: DK, 1999). Two little bunnies see a series of vehicles as they wait for their grandmother to arrive.

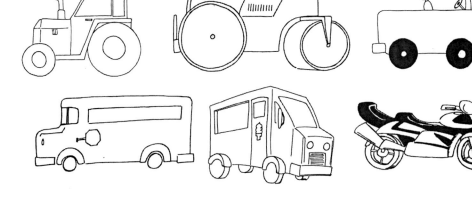

397 My Dump Truck Fred Flannelboard Story
See pattern 397.

If I had a dump truck, I would name it Fred. Fred and I would go everywhere together, and everyone would get out of the way when they saw us coming! Fred would eat dinner with my family every night, and I would teach him good table manners. I'd make sure he brushed his teeth every night, and put his nightcap on, and then I'd tuck him into bed right next to me. In the morning I would make sure he ate a healthy breakfast of gravel cereal. I'd even hang a stocking up for him on Christmas Eve, but it would have to be pretty big! In the winter I would make sure Fred bundled up warm and wore his scarf, and in the summer I would remind him to wear his sunglasses and hat. But no matter what, I would know that I loved Fred and that Fred loved me!

398 Helicopter Craft

MATERIALS: one helicopter coloring sheet for each child (from pattern 398), one cotton ball for each child, glue, crayons, stickers, and other decorating materials

DIRECTIONS:
1. Stretch out the cotton ball to look like clouds in the sky. Glue it in the sky.
2. Decorate as desired.

399 Tractor Craft

MATERIALS: one printout of tractor for each child (from pattern 399), hay bales cut from brown construction paper, vegetable shapes cut from construction paper, glue, crayons, stickers, and other decorating materials

DIRECTIONS:
1. Glue hay bales and vegetables in the fields around the tractor.
2. Decorate as desired.

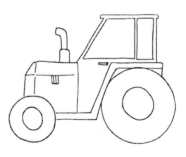

400 Train Craft

MATERIALS: one printout of a train for each child (from pattern 400), one ½ x 11 inch strip of black construction paper for each child, one cotton ball for each child, glue, crayons, stickers, and other decorating materials

DIRECTIONS:
1. Glue the black strip of construction paper under the train to make the track.
2. Stretch out the cotton ball to look like a puff of smoke. Glue it on the smokestack.
3. Decorate as desired.

401 Outer Space Craft

MATERIALS: one printout of a rocket ship for each child (from pattern 401), planet circles cut from construction paper, glue, crayons, stars cut from construction paper or star stickers, and other decorating materials

DIRECTIONS:
1. Glue planets and stars around the rocket ship.
2. Decorate as desired.

See also Bumpin' Up and Down in My Yellow School Bus (353), The Bus for Us *Flannelboard (361), and School Bus Craft (363).*

TRANSPORTATION: TEN GREAT BOOKS FOR STORYTIME

Airplanes by Byron Barton. New York: T. Y. Crowell, 1986. (for all ages)
The Bridge Is Up! by Bab Bell. New York: HarperCollins, 2004. (for toddlers)
Freight Train by Donald Crews. New York: Tupelo Books, 1996. (for all ages)
Truck by Donald Crews. New York: Tupelo Books, 1997. (for all ages)
The Journey Home from Grandpa's by Jemima Lumley. Cambridge, MA: Barefoot Books, 2006. (for toddlers)
All Aboard the Dinotrain by Deb Lund. Orlando, FL: Harcourt, 2006. (for preschoolers)
Choo Choo Clickety-Clack! by Margaret Mayo. Minneapolis: Carolrhoda Books, 2005. (for preschoolers)
Dig Dig Digging by Margaret Mayo. New York: Henry Holt, 2002. (for preschoolers)
Roaring Rockets by Tony Mitton. New York: Kingfisher, 1997. (for all ages)
Zoom! Zoom! Zoom! I'm Off to the Moon! by Dan Yaccarino. New York: Scholastic, 1997. (for all ages)

Further Resources for Storytime Planning

RESOURCE BOOKS

Baltuck, Naomi. *Crazy Gibberish and Other Story Hour Stretches*. Hamden, CT: Linnet Books, 1993.

Benton, Gail, and Tricia Waichulaitis. *Ready-to-Go Storytimes: Fingerplays, Scripts, Patterns, Music, and More*. New York: Neal-Schuman, 2003.

Briggs, Diane. *52 Programs for Preschoolers: The Librarian's Year-Round Planner*. Chicago: American Library Association, 1997.

_____. *101 Fingerplays, Stories, and Songs to Use with Finger Puppets*. Chicago: American Library Association, 1999.

_____. *Preschool Favorites: 35 Storytimes Kids Love*. Chicago: American Library Association, 2007.

Castellano, Marie. *Simply Super Storytimes: Programming Ideas for Ages 3–6*. Fort Atkinson, WI: Upstart Books, 2003.

Chupela, Dolores C. *Once Upon a Childhood: Fingerplays, Action Rhymes, and Fun Times for the Very Young*. Lanham, MD: Scarecrow Press, 1998.

Cobb, Jane. *I'm a Little Teapot! Presenting Preschool Storytime*. Vancouver, BC: Black Sheep Press, 1996.

Cooper, Cathie Hilterbran. *The Storyteller's Cornucopia*. Fort Atkinson, WI: Alleyside Press, 1998.

Cullum, Carolyn N. *The Storytime Sourcebook: A Compendium of Ideas and Resources for Storytellers*. New York: Neal-Schuman, 1999.

_____. *The Storytime Sourcebook II: A Compendium of 3,500+ New Ideas and Resources for Storytellers*. Neal-Schuman, 2007.

Davis, Robin Works. *Toddle on Over: Developing Infant and Toddler Literature Programs*. Fort Atkinson, WI: Alleyside Press, 1998.

Dowell, Ruth E. *Move Over, Mother Goose! Finger Plays, Action Verses, and Funny Rhymes*. Mt. Rainier, MD: Gryphon House, 1987.

Esche, Maria Bonfanti, and Clare Bonfanti Braham. *Kids Celebrate! Activities for Special Days throughout the Year*. Chicago: Chicago Review Press, 1998.

Faurot, Kimberly K. *Books in Bloom: Creative Patterns and Props That Bring Stories to Life*. Chicago: American Library Association, 2003.

Frey, Yvonne Awar. *One-Person Puppetry Streamlined and Simplified*. Chicago: American Library Association, 2005.

Fujita, Hiroko. *Stories to Play With: Kids' Tales Told with Puppets, Paper, Toys, and Imagination.* Little Rock, AR: August House, 1999.

Ghoting, Saroj Nadkarni, and Pamela Martin-Diaz. *Early Literacy Storytimes @ your library: Partnering with Caregivers for Success.* Chicago: American Library Association, 2006.

Hamilton, Leslie. *Child's Play: 200 Instant Crafts and Activities for Preschoolers.* New York: Crown, 1989.

———. *Child's Play around the World: 170 Crafts, Games, and Projects for Two- to Six-Year-Olds.* New York: Perigee, 1996.

Lima, Carolyn and John. *A to Zoo: Subject Access to Children's Picture Books.* Westport, CT: Libraries Unlimited, 2001.

MacDonald, Margaret Read. *Bookplay: 101 Creative Themes to Share with Young Children.* North Haven, CT: Library Professional Publications, 1995.

———. *Twenty Tellable Tales.* Chicago: American Library Association, 2005.

MacMillan, Kathy. *A Box Full of Tales: Easy Ways to Share Library Resources through Story Boxes.* Chicago: American Library Association, 2008.

———. *Try Your Hand at This: Easy Ways to Incorporate Sign Language into Your Programs.* Lanham, MD: Scarecrow Press, 2006.

Nichols, Judy. *Storytimes for Two-Year-Olds.* Chicago: American Library Association, 1998.

Reid, Rob. *Children's Jukebox: The Select Subject Guide to Children's Musical Recording.* 2nd ed. Chicago: American Library Association, 2007.

———. *Family Storytime: Twenty-four Creative Programs for All Ages.* Chicago: American Library Association, 1999.

———. *Storytime Slam! 15 Lesson Plans for Preschool and Primary Story Programs.* Fort Atkinson, WI: Upstart Books, 2006.

Ring a Ring o' Roses. Flint, MI: Flint Public Library, 2000. (810) 232-7111.

Roberts, Lynda. *Mitt Magic.* Beltsville, MD: Gryphon House, 1985.

Schiller, Pam, and Jackie Silberg. *The Complete Book of Activities, Games, Stories, Props, Recipes, and Dances for Young Children.* Beltsville, MD: Gryphon House, 2003.

Schiller, Pamela Byrne. *The Complete Resource Book for Toddlers and Twos.* Beltsville, MD: Gryphon House, 2003.

Sierra, Judy. *The Flannelboard Storytelling Book.* New York: H. W. Wilson, 1997.

Silberg, Jackie, and Pam Schiller. *The Complete Book of Rhymes, Songs, Poems, Fingerplays, and Chants.* Beltsville, MD: Gryphon House, 2002.

Stangle, Jean. *Is Your Storytale Dragging?* Belmont, CA: Fearon Teacher Aids, 1989.

Story-Hoffman, Ru. *Nursery Rhyme Time.* Fort Atkinson, WI: Alleyside Press, 1996.

Warren, Jean, ed. *Nursery Rhyme Theme-a-Saurus.* Torrance, CA: Totline Publications, 1993.

———. *Storytime Theme-a-Saurus.* Everett, WA: Warren Publishing House, 1993.

Wilmes, Liz and Dick. *Felt Board Fingerplays with Patterns and Activities.* Elgin, IL: Building Blocks, 1997.

———. *2's Experience Felt Board Fun.* Elgin, IL: Building Blocks, 1994.

———. *2's Experience Fingerplays.* Elgin, IL: Building Blocks, 1994.

SOFTWARE

American Sign Language Clip and Create 4. Institute for Disabilities Research and Training Inc. (www.idrt.com), 2003.

WEBSITES

ASL Pro (American Sign Language Video Dictionary): www.aslpro.com
The Best Kids Book Site (Thematic Book Recommendations, Crafts, Fingerplays):
    www.thebestkidsbooksite.com/storytimes.htm
Child Care Lounge (Fingerplays): www.childcarelounge.com/Caregivers/main.htm
ChildFun (Fingerplays, Crafts, and Activities): www.childfun.com
DLTK Kids (Crafts and Fingerplays): www.dltk-kids.com
Enchanted Learning (Crafts and Fingerplays): www.enchantedlearning.com
    (Paid subscription required to print craft templates and coloring pages.)
First School (Crafts and Fingerplays): www.first-school.ms
The Idea Box (Activities and Crafts): www.theideabox.com
Kids' Chalkboard (Crafts and Fingerplays): www.kidschalkboard.com
Let's Create a Flannelboard! http://members.aol.com/Ivinsart/handbook.html
Miss Lisa's Theme Sharing (Crafts and Fingerplays): www.geocities.com/Heartland/
    Acres/7875/themes.html
Nuttin' But Kids (Crafts and Fingerplays): www.nuttinbutkids.com
Preschool Rainbow (Crafts and Fingerplays): www.preschoolrainbow.org
Songs for Teaching (Fingerplays and Songs): www.songsforteaching.com

VENDORS OF PREPACKAGED FLANNELBOARDS, BIG BOOKS, AND OTHER PROPS

Book Props, LLC: www.bookprops.com
Brodart: www.shopbrodart.com
Demco: www.demco.com
The Felt Source: www.thefeltsource.com
Folkmanis Puppets: www.folkmanis.com
Highsmith: www.highsmith.com
Holcomb's Education Resource: www.holcombscatalog.com
Lakeshore Learning: www.lakeshorelearning.com
The Library Store: www.thelibrarystore.com
Merry Makers Inc.: www.merrymakersinc.com
School Specialty: www.schoolspecialtyonline.net
Teacher's Paradise: www.teachersparadise.com

Making Flannelboards, Stick Puppets, and More

FLANNELBOARDS/MAGNETBOARDS

Every theme in this book features flannelboard rhymes or stories. Flannelboards are a wonderful addition to all storytimes. If you don't own a large flannelboard, you can make your own flannelboard by taking a metal cookie sheet and covering the inside (where cookies normally go) with felt. This homemade flannelboard can travel anywhere with you and can also serve as a magnetboard. Any metal surface can be made into a magnetboard, and magnetboard story pieces are easy to make using adhesive magnets.

You can buy premade art for flannelboards, or you can make your own. There are several easy ways to make your own. If you don't feel you are artistic, clip art is readily available online or on many common computer packages such as Microsoft Word. Print out the pictures you need, trim, and mount on construction paper. Laminate the clip art for durability. If you don't have a laminating machine, use self-sealing laminated pouches or contact paper. Then glue a piece of felt or a magnet to the back of each picture, and you're done.

When making your own flannelboard with felt, you can use any of the patterns included in this book or one of your own creations. Patterns can be enlarged or reduced on a copy machine to fit your specific needs. When tracing a pattern on felt, use a Sharpie or other marker. Use a good pair of scissors to cut the felt. Be creative! Decorate the felt pieces with fabric paint, feathers, sequins, and the like. Googly eyes can be used on animals and people to give a more animated appearance.

If you have a scanner, you can scan characters and items directly from books and magazines and then print them on fusible fabric. The fusible fabric can then be mounted on felt. When creating a flannelboard based on a book, remember to cite the book title and author.

STICK PUPPETS

Stick puppets are a fun addition to storytimes. Most of the flannelboards and rhymes in this book can be converted for use with stick puppets, and stories often lend themselves to being told with stick puppets. You can make stick puppets with clip art, hand-drawn illustrations, or pictures cut from books or magazines. Laminate the pictures and glue them to craft sticks. When using stick puppets with a lap theater, attach a square of Velcro about an inch from the bottom of each stick and strips of Velcro around the inside top edges of the theater.

This will allow you to secure your stick puppets to the lap theater. If you are dealing with a large audience, use large images glued to paint sticks so the entire crowd can see.

Paint sticks can also be used as props. With Velcro attached to the paint stick, you can attach and detach various clip art pieces and tell many rhymes and stories. An example would be to attach five monkeys to the paint stick with Velcro. While chanting the Five Little Monkeys rhyme (126), bounce the stick up and down. Every time one monkey falls off, remove a monkey from the stick.

LAP THEATER

Lap theaters are a wonderful way to tell your stick-puppet stories. They provide a concealed storage spot for your puppet pieces and thus add an element of surprise to the unveiling of the story. To create a lap theater, find a box that is big enough to accommodate a puppet show but small enough to fit easily on your lap. Cut off the top of the box as well as one of the longer sides. Decorate the remaining three sides as desired or create a curtain. The curtain need not be fancy; you could just glue a piece of fabric to the walls of the box. Along the inside top edges of the walls add a Velcro strip. This will give you the option of securing your stick puppets to the walls during your show and free your hands to introduce and move other characters.

GLOVE PUPPETS

Glove puppets are a great way to tell a story or rhyme. Inexpensive cotton garden gloves work well. Create the main characters or objects with felt, pom-poms, or clip art and use Velcro to attach the pieces to the glove's fingers. Rhymes and stories with five characters or objects are ideal, but greater numbers can be accommodated if you attach more than one item to each finger of the glove. If the story has a constant, such as the bed in the Five Little Monkeys rhyme (126), you can attach that piece to the center of the glove.

STORYCARDS

Storycards are a nice alternative to a traditional book and are easy to make. They are ideal to use when you have a large audience because they allow you to show the pictures to the crowd while reading the story text pasted on the backs of the cards. If you have a scanner, you can make storycards by scanning each page of the book and printing it. Mount each picture onto construction paper and glue the text for that page onto the back of the card. Don't forget to number the cards so they don't get out of order! Laminate the cards or seal them with contact paper so they will last for many storytimes. If you do not have a scanner but have two copies of a book, carefully cut the book apart and glue the pages to construction paper. Withdrawn books are a great source for storycard materials! Remember, when using storycards, do not edit the book and make sure to cite the title and author.

READ-ALONGS

A wonderful way to involve your audience in storytime is with a read-along. Pass out a copy of the book you are reading to each participant so that all can follow along while you read. This works really well if you read from an oversized book that has simple text.

COSTUMED STORIES

Have fun telling your stories and show your multiple personalities. When a new character is introduced, put on a headband or other identifying item. Each time that character speaks, make sure to put on the item. Animal stories and rhymes are easy to do this with because there are inexpensive, premade animal headbands for purchase. You could also invite audience members to participate by wearing the costumes and playing the parts in the story.

MANIPULATIVES FOR STORYTIME

Bubbles

Invest in a bubble gun; they are a great source of fun and will save you from trying to blow bubbles manually for an entire song. Pop on a bath or summer fun song and blow bubbles around the area while encouraging the children to clap and stomp them.

Rhythm Sticks

Rhythm sticks can be made by cutting wooden dowels and sanding the rough edges. They really help you keep the beat while the group marches around, they make excellent spider legs during rhymes, and they can be drummed to demonstrate the different sounds made by things in the room.

Scarves

Scarves are inexpensive to buy. Purchase them in a rainbow of colors. They make great kites, wonderful dancing partners, and appealing props for playing peek-a-boo.

Shakers

Shakers can be made using old plastic eggs filled with beans or rice and sealed with tape. They are fantastic background instruments for any rockin' song.

Streamers

Streamers can be made with crepe paper, old plastic bags, wrapping paper, or wide ribbon cut into strips. Streamers are fun to dance with, can be used with rhymes to represent wind, and make great ticklers.

Index of Titles and First Lines

Note: Titles of books are in italics.
First lines are in quotation marks.

G

Index of Craft Ideas

the perfect *party* planner

**Hints, tips, advice and recipes to guarantee
success at every event – from birthday parties
and buffets to weddings and special celebrations**

bridget jones

southwater

This edition is published by Southwater

Southwater is an imprint of Anness Publishing Ltd
Hermes House, 88–89 Blackfriars Road, London SE1 8HA
tel. 020 7401 2077; fax 020 7633 9499
www.southwaterbooks.com; info@anness.com

© Anness Publishing Ltd 2004

UK agent: The Manning Partnership Ltd
6 The Old Dairy, Melcombe Road, Bath BA2 3LR
tel. 01225 478444; fax 01225 478440
sales@manning-partnership.co.uk

UK distributor: Grantham Book Services Ltd
Isaac Newton Way, Alma Park Industrial Estate,
Grantham, Lincs NG31 9SD
tel. 01476 541080; fax 01476 541061
orders@gbs.tbs-ltd.co.uk

North American agent/distributor: National Book Network
4501 Forbes Boulevard, Suite 200, Lanham, MD 20706
tel. 301 459 3366; fax 301 429 5746; www.nbnbooks.com

Australian agent/distributor: Pan Macmillan Australia
Level 18, St Martins Tower, 31 Market St, Sydney, NSW 2000
tel. 1300 135 113; fax 1300 135 103
customer.service@macmillan.com.au

New Zealand agent/distributor: David Bateman Ltd
30 Tarndale Grove, Off Bush Road, Albany, Auckland
tel. (09) 415 7664; fax (09) 415 8892

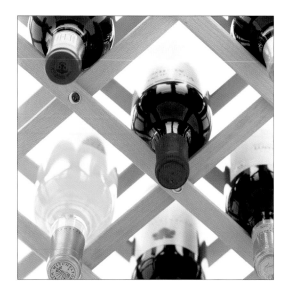

A CIP catalogue record for this book is available from the British Library.

Publisher: Joanna Lorenz
Senior Editors: Doreen Palamartschuk and Sarah Uttridge
Copy Editors: Jan Cutler, Jane Bamforth
Project Editor: Elizabeth Woodland
Production Controller: Claire Rae
Designer: Nigel Partridge
Jacket Design: Balley Design Associates
Photographers: Karl Adamson, Caroline Arber, Steve Baxter, Martin
Brigdale, Nicki Dowey, Gus Filgate, Michelle Garrett, Amanda Heywood,
Janine Hosegood, William Lingwood, Roisin Neild, Thomas Odulate, Spike
Powell, Craig Robertson, Simon Smith, Sam Stowell and Polly Wreford

Previously published as part of a larger volume, *Party Food*

13579108642

Notes

Bracketed terms are intended for American readers. For all recipes,
quantities are given in both metric and imperial measures and, where
appropriate, measures are also given in standard cups and spoons.
Follow one set, but not a mixture, because they are not interchangeable.
Standard spoon and cup measures are level.
1 tsp = 5ml, 1 tbsp = 15ml, 1 cup = 250ml/8fl oz
Australian standard tablespoons are 20ml. Australian readers should
use 3 tsp in place of 1 tbsp for measuring small quantities of gelatine,
flour, salt, etc. Medium (US large) eggs are used unless otherwise stated.

Contents

Introduction

Party-giving should above all be enjoyable, and timely planning ensures that any event is as relaxed for the organizer as for the guests. This book aims to provide all the advice, guidelines and reminders you need to ensure that the planning is easy, the organizing smooth and problem-free, and the occasion a complete success – whether it's casual drinks party or a grand, formal wedding celebration.

Getting started

The process of deciding on dates, times, venues and occasion style often starts the roller-coaster task of putting

Below *To create a sophisticated look, choose one colour for napkins and table linen, and mix different textures such as linen and organdie.*

Above *Pure linen napkins add style and elegance to any dining table.*

together once-in-a-lifetime gatherings. It can often be a stressful time when you are making decisions such as whether traditional ceremonies take precedence over a relaxed celebration or how to assemble different groups of family and friends. Side-stepping a

frantic start helps to avoid dips in enthusiasm later on. Often the initial problems are not as complicated as they appear. Enthusiasm and energy are the first requirements for over-coming any uncertainties, backed up by making useful lists such as key dates, numbers of guests, types of food and drink. It is important to do this before any celebration, large or small, in advance of getting down to the practicalities of invitation writing, room clearing, cooking and greeting.

Enlisting support

There is no point in playing the party hero and trying to juggle every last item alongside a normal busy life – it is far more sensible and fun to share the load and satisfaction with at least one helper, if not a team of supporters.

Hand pick a reliable and hard-working friend who shares your aims, ethos and humour to join in the process – most people are flattered to be asked for their support, especially on important occasions. Then be thoughtful about who to add to the team. For children's parties, unless the occasion is a surprise, involve the child whose party it is and allow one special friend to be included in the pre-party organization.

Getting together a round-table of enthusiastic organizers is best avoided unless there are specific, separate tasks that are ideal for distributing among several contributors. Finally, there are times when coordinating a committee of people is an essential part of putting together a group event, such as for a club or school, and adopting the same approach to selecting one or two main helpers while ensuring everyone else is usefully involved is an excellent ploy.

Mix and match

If the occasion is very formal, such as a wedding or christening, or the approach so traditional that there is little room for changing the style and form, it is best to follow the rules of etiquette. For all parties adopt a sensible attitude to all numbers, catering, ambience and entertainment and use tried and tested approaches to ensure success.

Below Add atmosphere to a party with floating candles in a glass bowl.

When the occasion allows for flexibility, do not take yourself too seriously but aim for enjoyment rather than perfection. Mixing and matching can be an inspiring approach to party planning, especially for informal events. Adopt the "do it with a good will or not at all" approach and loosen up on the rules. Concentrate on the aspects you most enjoy. Those who are not keen on cooking for crowds often do best by selecting just one or two practical one-pot dishes and complementing them with well-chosen bought foods. There is plenty of advice on making the most of bought ingredients in the following chapters.

The same goes for party drinks: while all the experts may dictate offering chilled champagne or certain wines and liqueurs to go with individual courses during a meal, or an eclectic array of drinks, if you – or your budget – dictate otherwise, then do so with conviction and without apology. And if you want guests to make a contribution by bringing a

Above *Classic cocktail glasses will impress your guests at drinks parties.*

bottle, do not be afraid to make the occasion a "bring a bottle party" by spelling it out on the party invitations.

Enjoy!

Great atmosphere is the most important feature of any party or celebration – and that does not mean ambience alone. Whether you are entertaining in a palace or on a building site, remember to do so with a genuine and warm welcome. Make your guests aware of the type, context and style of the party so that they all come suitably dressed and in the right frame of mind to enjoy themselves. Greet everyone and be sure to encourage them to mingle, making them feel relaxed, at home and with a certain responsibility to participate. At the end of the day, no matter how brilliant the tables, food and decorations, it is the people who make the party.

party
planning

Approach successful entertaining with a clear sense of occasion and a few concise, practical lists. Once you know what you are doing, involve others in the fun and share the planning with friends or family.

Grand Design or Simple Style?

A clear picture of the party style and size is the secret of success every time. Before planning venues, invitations, settings, entertainment and food and drink, decide on exactly the right type of party. Energy and enthusiasm are essential for getting things moving but it is best to sort out guidelines within which to plan before ideas snowball and practicalities are forgotten in an initial wave of excitement.

There are established routines and etiquette for many occasions and utilizing these is often sensible. They range from formal dinner parties, society drinks gatherings or balls to weddings, anniversaries and seasonal gatherings. There are also just as many small or substantially large gatherings that are organized for no particular reason other than meeting up and socializing, for example overcoming winter blues, making the most of the summer sun or catching up with a group of friends.

Below *An attractive buffet table with plates and napkins piled high.*

Who's who?

Start with an outline guest plan: is this a gathering for six or sixty, under fives or over fifties, family or friends, bosom pals or business associates? If you are inviting a complete mix of family, friends, colleagues and neighbours a proper plan would be a sensible starting point. Identify the different types and ages; by fitting individuals into groups you will be sure to include something for everyone. This eases the role of host or hostess, which can involve looking after small groups or couples – or worse – individuals drifting about on the fringes of the party.

Time of day

The party may be to celebrate a marriage, baby naming or christening, or it may be a social event. It may not be a particularly jolly occasion, for example a post-funeral wake. Double-check arrangements that cannot be changed later, for example timings for ceremonies, photography or performances and estimated travelling time between event and party venue.

Above *Summer barbecues can be day or early evening social events.*

Consider the different ages of, or relationship between, guests before fixing times. A two-phase celebration is popular for very different groups; it would typically comprise a formal meal, low-key lunch or early evening drinks party followed by a lively gathering later for younger guests or close friends. This solution works as well for informal occasions – a house warming, open house for a summer barbecue or an annual family gathering – as for weddings. Plan the transition between day and evening, and decide whether those invited to the first part will also stay late.

Formal gatherings for early evening drinks preceding a late supper for a few friends or pre-lunch gatherings must be well orchestrated. Invitations should indicate the time when guests are expected to leave: "Pre-dinner drinks between 6 p.m. and 7.30 p.m." A verbal or informal note to join family or weekend guests for "a drink before lunch" should include the expected time of arrival and departure. Be clear to avoid any confusion.

Smarten up or dress down?

Once you know who and when, make a decision on how you want your guests to dress and behave, and follow this through in invitations, food and entertainment. Be clear on invitations if you expect formal dress (white tie and ball gowns; black tie and evening wear; morning wear, or top hats and tails, and hats), lounge suits or smart daywear. For an informal occasion dress will not need to be stipulated. Indicate any special requirements, such as bathing costumes and towels for poolside parties, sun hats and picnic blankets to sit on, and sweaters or shawls for evenings outdoors.

Before and after

Guests may need accommodation for the night before and/or after the party. After a long journey, house guests will usually want to arrive early enough to freshen up. Include the preparation of guests' rooms in your plans and timings, remembering the little things that make people feel welcome and relaxed – flowers, magazines, drinks, biscuits (cookies) or chocolates as well as towels, soap, shampoo and tissues. Keeping a few disposable, travel-size miniatures, or spare small toothbrushes, toothpaste, small packs of anti-perspirant and sachets of moisturizer in stock is a good idea for party guests who stay unexpectedly.

Pay attention to detail when entertaining youngsters, especially if they may be too shy to ask for forgotten essentials. For a special occasion sleepover you could prepare fun sleepover packs including novelty toothbrushes, fruit-flavoured toothpaste, wacky toiletries, expanding face cloths, reading material such as comics, mini torches, tasty midnight snacks and fruit, and small packs of drinks or bottles of water.

Above Add romantic touches to a table dressed in white for a wedding.

For large gatherings, check out local hotels and provide guests with details on price, location and availability when sending out invitations. Remember breakfast on the morning after the party and make flexible arrangements.

Party price

As each name is added to the guest list and every idea mulled and jotted bear in mind the cost. Decide on the type of party to suit the funds available, then work out a realistic budget in more detail before progressing from idea to plan. This is just as important for small, homely events as for once-in-a-lifetime occasions if you want to avoid overspending.

Sorting an outline budget at this stage is essential and easy: make a list of every aspect of the party, adding a realistic (generous rather than mean) cost and contacting suppliers to check special prices. For extravagant occasions involving hotels, venues, caterers, entertainers and so on, make specific enquiries at this first stage. Divide the costs into fixed amounts for the occasion and variable prices that increase with the number of guests – refreshments in particular – remember that the venue size may change if the guest list grows too much. Spreading the cost by paying for some items, such as wine, spirits or beer, completely or partly in advance is one way of easing an overstretched budget, especially when planning a party at home.

Below Simple snacks, drinks and bright decorations are good basics for a party.

Have List, Will Organize

dinner parties and drinks parties are good Friday affairs, as are after-theatre or post-exhibition suppers.

Weekends are popular for group events for families and for activity club get-togethers or excursions. While weekend brunches are generally great for those without young children, Saturday brunch can also start family activities on a high note and the afternoon is a good choice for children's parties. If Saturday lunch is difficult for working hosts and guests who have to juggle family commitments, the evening is good

Lists are essential when planning for a special occasion. Suggesting that there should be a system for making them may sound like overkill but even the most super-efficient lists can become so mottled with additions that they become uninterpretable. The answer is to have separate lists with different information. Using a computer or a spiral-bound notepad is brilliant for keeping lists on separate pages but together in one place. Jot the date on each page and include notes of discussions with suppliers, orders placed and ideas as well as the guest list, special requirements, shopping and so on. Using this system it is easy to flip through to check details, and it is a good idea to sticker significant pages you refer to frequently, such as the invitation list where you will tick or

Above *Make lists for organizing all aspects of party planning.*

cross off guests' names as replies come in. Start with a list of the usual requirements for different occasions and then personalize it to your style.

Which day?
Work functions are best from midweek onwards. Friday can be a good day for lunch or an evening party if partners are invited; Wednesday or Thursday are more convenient for "colleague only" events (especially for a comparatively early finish).

Weekday dinner parties can be inconvenient but midweek evenings can be a good choice for drinks gatherings or supper parties designed to end early. Relaxed and informal

Above *Champagne is generally served at weddings and formal occasions.*

Below *One-pot feasts, such as moussaka, are good for supper parties.*

for large and/or formal dinner parties. Saturday is popular for weddings, allowing time for guests to travel; Friday is ideal when the marriage is witnessed by a small number of relations and followed by a party for friends and associates.

Sunday lunch is extremely versatile: it allows plenty of time for preparation and is suitable for informal or smart arrangements for family, couples, singles or a mixture.

Parties and celebrations for clubs and classes are usually planned for the day and time when the meetings are normally held. Annual dinners tend to be organized for Friday or Saturday evenings, depending on the work commitments of members.

Scheduling an important celebration

Lists should include all the details, whereas a schedule will set dates and deadlines for the tasks. Draw up a master schedule of key dates, tasks and reminders with references back to the lists for details where necessary. Lists can then be updated as time passes.

A few months may be enough time for organizing simple weddings but one to two years is usually allowed

Above *A stylishly dressed table for a Thanksgiving celebration.*

for extravagant affairs. Timing often depends on the booking requirements of venues and officials; check these carefully. Find out about caterers, entertainment and transport, and check the availability of all related aspects before booking the main event.

Put dates to the lists and check that they are all possible. Then draw up the outline schedule – the master guide to sourcing, booking, confirming and checking every aspect of the celebration. Schedule key dates for everything. Adding minor aspects may seem picky, particularly when coping with a big party, but they can easily be forgotten later. Use a familiar means of layout, if possible, be that a year planner, kitchen calendar, chart on a noticeboard or computer program.

Scrutinize your schedule for bottlenecks and potential problems. If too many tasks coincide make alternative arrangements by moving jobs to different dates or delegate them to helpers. When you are happy that you have not missed anything, make sure the schedule looks neat, tidy and is easy to follow.

Schedule checks

Below are items to add to the schedule according to the needs of the occasion, placing each against a date when it has to be done.

Formalities: legal/paperwork requirements, booking all officials, confirmation
Venue: viewing, booking, and confirmation, checking facilities, preparation
Entertainment: booking, venue preparation/layout requirements, details of repertoire
Accommodation: source details
Caterers: references/assessing, booking, menu decisions and/or tasting session, confirmation of numbers, caterer's advance visit
Special catering: special diets, finalizing details of presentation
Food preparation: ordering, shopping, key dates for advance cooking, days for final preparation
Bar: delivery/collection of drinks and glasses, return of items
Professional help at home: gardening, cleaning, kitchen help (before or after), butler, waiting staff, bar staff
Flowers: booking, venue visit and design liaison
Guest list: invitations out, give a date for replies back
Gifts: buy, pack

Choosing a Venue

The occasion, type and size of party, budget, convenience and availability all influence the choice of venue.

Home options

Entertaining at home can be stylish if there is suitable space. While clearing furniture to the edges of one or two small rooms and allowing everyone to spill into the hall and kitchen may be fine for an informal party, it is not necessarily the answer for a special celebration. Unless there is ample floor and table space plus kitchen facilities sufficient to cater for a sit-down meal, a buffet is most practical. When serving a fork buffet, remember that some guests may prefer to sit down to eat. When finger buffets or snacks are served, guests do not need as much space, especially if the refreshments are handed around.

Make use of outdoor areas and consider hiring an awning or marquee. Tables, chairs and barbecues can be arranged on firm areas; rugs and cushions can be laid on lawns. Be prepared for poor weather and consider erecting large umbrellas.

Above Put extra tables on patios and courtyards for home entertaining.

Below With attention to detail, dressing a table at home can be very stylish.

Hotels and restaurants

Select a venue by recommendation, reputation and personal experience if possible. Visit the restaurant for a meal to assess general quality and ambience. When comparing establishments, prepare a standard checklist and do not be embarrassed to make notes while you are there. The following are points to consider:
• How many guests can be catered for and in which room/bar. Check the maximum number of covers usually catered for; point out, if necessary, that you do not want their capabilities to be overstretched. Will a bar adjoining a function room be exclusively for the use of your party or will it also be open to the public? Check bar closing times.

• What types of menus are offered and at what price per head? What is included in the price per head? Are children's portions provided at reduced cost (prudent when a wedding guest list includes many children)?
• Do the regular kitchen staff prepare special functions, or are outside caterers or temporary chefs employed?
• Check wine lists and bar prices. Ask whether you will be able to supply your own wine or champagne and what corkage charge is applied?
• Check arrangements for overseeing the smooth running of the occasion and whether a master of ceremonies

is available. Ask about the suitability of spaces for speeches or if amplification equipment is available.

• Accommodation-wise, assess the number and type of rooms, and price per room/person, with or without breakfast. Ask if favourable rates will be offered for a block booking.

• Does the business have existing links with entertainers? At what time in the evening must music end? Are there particular florists who know the hotel/restaurant? Similarly, there may be a useful link with photographers who are familiar with the setting.

• Is the venue easily accessible by car or rail? Is there ample parking?

Hired hall or rooms

Community, sports, arts, social and religious venues often have rooms for hire. Some may have links with caterers, entertainers and dressers to prepare the venue (and you may be obliged to use bar facilities or caterers);

Below *Always visit hotel or restaurant venues to check the space and facilities before you book.*

accommodation may even be provided in some clubs. Less expensive venues are economical for self-catering. Points to check include:

• Heating (is this included in the cost?).

• Lighting and how it can be adapted to improve the ambience.

• Kitchen facilities for food preparation and storage, heating and clearing up.

• Tables and chairs – check how many there are, the table sizes and ensure they provide enough space for the number of guests.

• Bar facilities and whether alcohol is allowed; entertainment permits.

• Cloakroom facilities.

• Cleaning and preparation of venue – will the space be clear and clean? How far in advance will you have access for setting out tables, decorating the space, laying out food? Clearing up afterwards – will this have to be completed on the evening or next day?

Marquee hire

This may be a practical solution to gaining all-weather space if you have a large, flat garden. Hire companies provide guidance on size, numbers

Above *Brighten up hired tables with table linen and ribbons.*

accommodated and access required for erection. Erected sample marquees or a portfolio of examples should be available. Check the lining is intact, the flooring is solid, and there is provision for power, heating and lighting.

Picnics

These may be informal and fun, or formal social occasions attached to sporting or entertainment events. Follow custom and etiquette for society occasions, such as the serving of stylish hampers, or candlelit picnics in a country-house garden. When obtaining tickets for events, check details of times and facilities, parking (and distance from car park to picnic area), dress and conduct code.

Parties afloat

Boats range from floating restaurants and bars to those with facilities for extensive parties. Smaller vessels can be hired for small groups with or without professional staff, and entertaining up to a dozen friends with a champagne lunch or early supper is fun. Check that the company rigidly applies safety regulations – if in doubt seek advice from relevant local authorities. Inspect the vessel's facilities thoroughly. Check the duration and route of the trip and access and parking at or transport to the point of departure.

By Invitation Only

Common sense and consideration are vital for informal invitations while rules of etiquette apply to formal invitations. A note can sometimes follow informal verbal invitations or a telephone call of confirmation a couple of days in advance – typically when organizing dinner parties with friends. The timing for informal invitations depends entirely on how busy and flexible everyone is.

Invitation information

It may seem like a statement of the obvious but it is surprisingly easy to miss details or to include incorrect (conflicting) dates and days. Invitations need to include the following:

- Guest names, with correct titles.
- Host and/or hostess names.
- Occasion or reason for party.
- Venue.
- Day and date.
- Time: this may be approximate or precise. Before a formal meal, it is usual to indicate a period of about 30 minutes

Below Simple themes work best when making your own invitations.

The right time

- Breakfast may be arranged from early until mid morning.
- Coffee mornings are usually scheduled for 11 a.m.
- Brunch can be planned for any time from mid morning to early lunch, between usual breakfast and lunch times.
- Lunch is usually arranged at 12.30 p.m. or 1 p.m. but invitations may be for an early or late lunch.
- Afternoon tea invitations are often scheduled for 3 p.m. or slightly later. Children's tea usually follows the end of afternoon school, usually about 4 p.m.
- Supper is often early or late evening, indicating a light menu rather than dinner.

during which guests are expected (within the first 15 minutes). The time may include the expected duration of the gathering or a time when an evening will end – expressed as "carriages at …" on formal dinner invitations.

- Cocktails and drinks are served from 6 p.m. to 8 p.m.
- Dinner is usually served from 7.30 p.m. until 8.30 p.m., with invitations requesting the arrival of guests about 30 minutes beforehand for pre-dinner drinks.
- "At home" indicates a period of time during which guests may arrive and depart. This is informal and usually includes light nibbles and refreshments rather than a substantial or formal meal.
- "Open house" is the contemporary and particularly informal version of "At home", often extending from lunch (or mid-morning brunch) through to the evening and intended for a mix of families, friends and colleagues of all ages.

- RSVP (*répondez s'il vous plaît*), sometimes with a date, is a polite way of reminding guests that a reply is required.
- Address, telephone and other contact details for replying.
- Dress code and any other information: white tie indicating wing collars, white ties and tails for men, ball gowns for women; black tie and dinner jacket is standard evening wear for men, when women may wear long or short dresses. Notes on a party theme or other special dress requirements should be included.

Formal invitations

Written requests for the company of guests at a notable occasion are sent at least a month in advance. This is typical of family celebrations, such as weddings, when four to six weeks' notice is practical. (Key guests should be aware of the date well in advance.) Parties organized around public events may be arranged three to six months

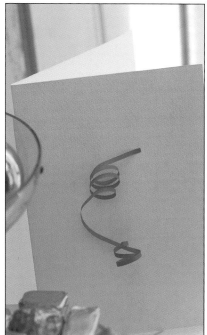

Above *Stationery for formal occasions comes in many different styles.*

in advance. Check the closing date for confirming numbers when booking a venue, confirm with suppliers and ensure invitations are sent out in good time in order for replies to be returned by the required date.

The right title

Addressing guests by an incorrect title may cause offence. Check with the households or offices of those in public or official roles. There are reference books detailing all contemporary and traditionally correct forms of address and greeting, including academic qualifications, religious orders and positions, military ranks, titled persons and those of any office requiring recognition. When in doubt about how acquaintances and relatives prefer to be addressed, check with them, if possible. Otherwise, close family or friends may be able to advise.

Traditionally, a married woman takes the name or initials of her husband when addressed singly or as a couple, for example Mr and Mrs John Smith, Mrs John Smith or Mrs J. Smith. However, some object to this,

preferring to use their first name, and women may retain their own family name after marriage, choosing the title Ms instead of Miss or Mrs. Addressing unmarried couples as "Mr and Mrs" is usually unacceptable to them and both names should be used.

Inventive invitations

Dress the message up according to the type of party. Concentrate on style and quality for all invitations, from heavy flat cards with fine lettering and discreet decorative edging to bright folded cards that may be fun but fall short of becoming garish.

When using professional designers and printers ask to see samples and prices per quantity and remember that selecting from their usual repertoire may be more convenient and more successful than asking them to create something different and complicated. Craft techniques, art skills or calligraphy can be used to make invitations and party stationery. Involve the children when preparing fun invitations for junior events.

A personal computer can be used to design and print stationery to professional standards. If the printer is not likely to deliver the required quality

Above *Good quality paper and simple decorations make pretty invitations.*

in terms of colour and graphics, ready-printed paper, cards and matching envelopes can be used as a base for black-and-white printing.

Finally, creative flair and technology are by no means essential, as ready-printed party stationery is available from quality stationers and general stores. Neat handwriting is all that is required to add individual details.

Below *For formal occasions, take care to use the correct titles for guests.*

Equipment and Materials Lists

Make lists of all equipment needed at the outset to ensure that everything is readily available, budgeted and scheduled. This applies when entertaining at home, particularly for self-catering. When caterers are commissioned they will usually source all equipment related to preparing and serving the food, often including tables and chairs. If you have particular ideas let them be known in advance.

Buying or hiring?

Hiring is often the only practical option for large celebrations. However, if you regularly entertain medium-size gatherings at home it may be worth buying a basic kit. For example, good quality white china, plain glassware and dishwasher-safe standard cutlery are often available from factory outlets. Plain white flat sheets are an alternative to table linen and perfectly presentable when dressed up for the occasion. For informal, family and children's parties it is worth buying rigid plastic plates and

Above *Table linen, napkins and glassware can all be hired.*

dishes that can be stacked in the dishwasher rather than spending almost as much on disposable ware that will be used just once. Sort out stackable, covered storage boxes at the same time so that "the kit" can be packed away afterwards for use next time.

Large items

Tables and chairs are usually included in the hire fee for halls. Check numbers and condition when booking, making sure that they all stand securely when opened. For parties at home, it is usually possible to utilize or borrow spare household or garden tables but chairs can be more of a problem. Hiring folding or stacking plastic chairs may be the answer.

Remember protective floor coverings for pale or precious carpets, especially when planning an indoor–outdoor party with guests of all ages. Specialist non-slip coverings can be useful in hallways or over areas of carpet by the patio or French doors.

When planning a large barbecue party, consider hiring large gas or charcoal barbecues from caterers' suppliers. They will make cooking lots of food easier than coping on the minimum of space on the home barbecue. Outdoor gas heaters can also be hired.

Left *Plain white linen napkins can be decorated with fresh flowers.*

Below *Make sure the barbecue is large enough to cater for all your guests.*

Check availability of entertainment equipment, such as inflatable play centres or bouncy castles, when fixing the party date, to avoid disappointment. Ask if the equipment will be assembled or inflated on delivery or left for you to erect, in which case make sure the necessary tools are also provided.

Food preparation and serving equipment

Catering hire specialists provide everything from disposable items to starched table linen and napkins, china and cutlery and serving equipment, including folding tables and chairs. When making your lists, sort requirements by category and then check outstanding queries with the hire store. Count and check equipment when taking delivery to make sure that it is all clean, present and undamaged. If there is anything dirty, missing or damaged, let the company know immediately otherwise you may be held responsible and charged for the problem at the end of the hire period. Most of the following items can be easily hired:

Below *Check in advance that you have all the cooking equipment you need.*

Above *Champagne flutes, ice buckets and cruets can all be hired for parties.*

• Cooking pans, trays and dishes – make sure your oven and burners are large enough to accommodate them.
• Coffee makers and water boilers.
• Serving bowls, trays and dishes – compare the cost of high-quality disposable items with hire charges.
• Table crockery – make a list from the menu, remembering cruets and sauceboats, if necessary, and cups, pots and spoons for coffee. Water jugs (pitchers) and glasses may be included with table crockery.
• Glassware may be hired or borrowed free of charge from wine suppliers or supermarkets – this may include spirit and beer glasses.
• Table linen, napkins and cutlery, plus serving cutlery.

All the trimmings

List all the decorative trimmings and finishing touches:
• Room decorations and streamers; garden decorations.
• Plants and/or decorations for patio and garden.
• Decorative indoor or outdoor lighting; candles or garden flares.
• Outdoor fireworks.

Above *Bright streamers and party hooters jazz up a birthday party table.*

• Table decorations, separated into fresh or silk flowers and others, such as coloured strings, confetti, candles, party poppers, whistles, bubbles, table crackers, indoor sparklers and other mini indoor fireworks.
• Balloons or balloon decorations.
• Guest gifts or children's goodie bags to take away and party-game prizes.
• Small cake boxes.

Below *Children love brightly coloured goodie bags to take home.*

Table Etiquette, Settings and Style

For formal occasions the host and hostess take their places at the ends of the table, with the most important male and female guests on their right (male to host, female to hostess). The remaining guests are seated in order of rank alternating male and female. When there is a master or top table, the most important guests take centre place. This arrangement is adopted for weddings, with the bride and groom in the middle, flanked by their parents and in-laws, with chief bridesmaid and best man at the ends.

Couples are usually seated opposite each other, the idea being that conversation flows around the table, not across it. When the numbers of men and women are equal, they are seated alternately around the table.

Above *Make sure there is ample elbow-room between each table setting.*

Below *Coloured modern cutlery mixed with elegant antique silver pieces.*

Seat people who are likely to have something in common next to each other. It is considerate to avoid pairing individuals whose opinions clash dramatically. When placing guests among several tables, try to achieve a compatible but interesting mix on each table. When there are children at formal occasions, it is sensible to put them on tables near the entrance, for easy cloakroom access. Guests with babies or small children may need space for prams or high chairs.

Make sure the writing on place cards is large enough to be legible by guests as they walk around the table. Display a seating plan on a board near the entrance to dining areas at large formal gatherings.

Formal table settings

The simple rule for formal settings is to lay cutlery for opening courses on the outside, starting from the right, and work in towards the plate.

• Use a large dinner plate to check the space for each setting and leave plenty of elbow-room between settings.

Above *Use traditional etiquette to avoid confusion: cutlery is placed on either side of the plates in order of courses.*

• Working from the right, lay the bread knife, soup spoon, fish knife or small side knife for the first course, large knife for the main course and dessert-spoon. Working in from the left, lay the fish fork or small fork for first course, fork for main course and dessert fork.
• For slightly less formal arrangements, the dessertspoon and fork may be laid across the top of the setting, spoon at the top (on the outside), with its handle to the right and fork below (on the inside), with its handle to the left.
• Cheese knives and utensils, such as a lobster pick or escargot tongs, may be brought in with the appropriate course. The cheese knife may be laid across the top, below the dessertspoon and fork.
• Arrange glasses at the top right above the setting in the order in which they are used. Include a water goblet or tumbler, white and red wine glasses.
• Distribute serving cutlery, cruets and butter dishes evenly around the table.

Above *Chevrons are just one way of folding linen napkins.*

Below *Cutlery can be bound together to add interest to an empty bowl.*

Contemporary style

Flaunt convention to make a design statement. The civilized rule when exploring new table-laying territory is to be practical and avoid confusing diners or causing embarrassment. If the cutlery is not laid in conventional positions it should be clear for which course it is intended. Bread knives can be laid on side plates, cutlery for the first course can be laid on a base platter with a napkin or brought in with the food, leaving the main course cutlery on the table. For stark effect leave the table bare, laying perfectly starched linen napkins at each place and bring out cutlery as courses are

served. Go for graphic lines and clean textures on table decorations, including any flowers and candles.

Base platters that remain in position under plates for first course and main course look attractive. They should be significantly larger than, and comfortably hold, the main-course plate so that it does not rattle. Glass, metal, wood or china in bold colours look especially dramatic under white or black plates. Match napkins to the base platter, arranging them on top as part of the setting.

Fun and lively

Strew the table with streamers and fun decorations in carefully coordinated colours. Bold flower petals and succulent leaves make a change from the usual floral decorations. Crystals, beads and glass baubles can be used to good effect in centrepieces or corner decorations. Use low or very tall candles to create pools of light. Make sure they do not block the view. Add crackers and indoor table fireworks for lively intervals between courses.

Below *Outdoor entertaining can be formal and stylish.*

Above *A wide selection of novelty items are available for children's parties.*

Mix and match

Ultimately, the best parties and meals are those where good food and entertaining company are shared in a relaxed atmosphere.

Mixing and matching food, table style and room setting can result in a wonderfully eclectic party. There is no reason why all the china, glassware, cutlery and linen should match; picking out one colour to use for decorations will transform a complete muddle of equipment into a lively style.

Presentation and Buffets

Reflect the style in atmosphere and presentation, from the first impression on entering the house to the lingering memories of an enjoyable party.

Formal sit-down meals

Give guests something to dress up for, balancing a sense of occasion and ceremony with a formal but relaxed atmosphere.

• The home or hired venue should be sparkling clean, sweet smelling and attractive with flowers or appropriate decorations. Aim for understated sophistication. Every area that guests will notice must be pristine.

• The table is the centrepiece, so devote time to planning it. Coordinate colour, shape and texture in decorations and presentation. Lay the table well in advance rather than as an afterthought. Lighting should be flattering, rather than bright, but never gloomy. Candlelight is perfect, so use candles around the room and set fairly low on the table or well above eye level of seated diners.

• The dining area should be pleasantly warm rather than uncomfortably hot. Be ready to reduce heating discreetly or provide ventilation as everyone warms

up over a meal, then to warm the room again later, if necessary.

• If possible, allow a beautiful table to be appreciated before everyone sits down. Leave the door to the prepared dining room open so that guests catch a tantalizing glimpse as they arrive. Allow time for seating guests at the table rather than rushing them.

Buffet basics

You can decorate the edge of a buffet table with flowers, garlands, bows or other trimmings. Table coverings and

Above *Highly decorative floral displays look good on buffets.*

edges can be flowing but they must not be so long that they become a hazard as people pass close by.

A fork buffet should include food that is easily eaten with just a fork. Plates should be arranged at one end of the table so that guests move along and help themselves. Displaying forks, napkins and any accompaniments on a small table slightly away from the end of the buffet will encourage guests to move away from the food. Buffet tables are often placed against a wall but moving the table into the room is better, encouraging guests to walk around and serve themselves without having to stretch over dishes.

If the buffet is self-service, all the food should be easy to serve with a spoon, tongs or slice using one hand. Try to arrange food in dishes of different heights, and display one or more large dishes as centrepieces.

Arrange food in a logical order rather than randomly on the table. Moving guests from main dishes on to

Left *A silver and white theme creates a classy dining table.*

accompaniments is logical if the menu takes that form. Replenish or replace dishes as necessary.

When the food takes the form of a main course, rather than a collection of complementary dishes, the savouries are usually cleared away before sweet dishes are brought out. This can be awkward in large gatherings if some guests are ready for dessert before others have finished the main course, so setting out cheese and desserts on a separate table is better.

Fabulously simple

Instead of setting out one large buffet table, you can distribute dishes individually among several occasional tables, adding a stack of small plates, forks and paper or linen napkins in each case. This is a brilliant way of presenting an eclectic collection of dishes, each to be sampled and savoured alone. Reflect the stylish approach by serving beautifully displayed food on plain white plates and keep decorative room trimmings uncluttered, just one step on from minimalism.

For this approach, the trick is to keep "waves" of prepared foods in reserve in the kitchen. Instead of laying them all out at once, replace empty platters as the food is consumed. Moving from one style of food to another is easy – rather like serving different courses of a meal – and it is a good idea to allow a palate-clearing pause between one variety and the next. For example, a range of marinated seafood may be followed

Above *Decorate a table for an autumnal lunch with fruits of the season.*

by a selection of roasted miniature vegetables and accompanying dips, and finally by the finest home-made chocolate truffles. Remember the rule: less is more.

Informal and fun

It is easy to lose a sense of style when casually decorating a home and displaying an informal buffet. Focus on a limited choice of fun decorations and controlled use of colour to avoid overdoing it with garish clutter.

Presenting just a small number of seriously delicious dishes or one or two types of the finest-quality ingredients is much more sophisticated than laying out an ill-matched mix of home-made and bought bits and pieces. For example, perfect seafood paella, a tureen of superlative soup and glorious platters of charcuterie and cheese will each make a fabulous meal when served with lots of fresh home-made bread and a herb-filled leafy salad.

Left *Bright table linen and plates complemented by colourful utensils add up to informal Mediterranean style.*

organizing your party food

Food with flair is the result of calm forethought rather than frantic kitchen activity. Take time out to consider all options to avoid being overwhelmed by choice when leafing through recipes or shopping for ingredients.

Planning Points

The easiest way to ensure a successful party is by tailoring your requirements to a suitable list of key points. Consider the following planning points:

• The occasion and type of meal are good starting points. Is the celebration formal or informal? Is it for adults or children, or both? Are you serving nibbles and finger food, a fork supper or a sit-down meal? A mixture of dishes can come together successfully as refreshment without fitting into accepted menu courses and this is true for seated eating as well as stand-up situations.

• Numbers and special requirements are important. Thinking up a menu that is over-ambitious to cook for a large number of guests can lead to disaster. An extravagant spread of many courses that is suitable for a dozen guests to sample in small quantities may be difficult to prepare and leave some guests embarrassed not to have done

Above Lobster Thermidor and fillets of turbot with oysters are stylish dishes for special occasions.

justice to the food. You should plan to accommodate special diets right from the beginning, for example, include vegetarian, vegan, or low-fat dishes on the menu. If guests have specific needs – such as gluten-free food – it is easier to plan suitable dishes as part of the main menu rather than preparing a set of alternatives at the last minute.

• Facilities should come high on the list of considerations. When finishing or serving food away from home, at a hired venue, or a picnic for example, make sure that every dish can be transported, reheated or cooked at the venue as appropriate. Check out facilities available at the venue, if necessary. At home, the danger is overstretching facilities, so avoid planning too many dishes requiring

last-minute cooking or heating to fit in the oven or for the top of the stove. Some recipes cooked at different temperatures cannot be adapted for cooking in the same oven. Also make sure you have enough crockery and cutlery for the menu.

• Food options are endless, so cost and capabilities are vital. When buying ready-made or commissioning caterers be aware of prices before dreaming up a menu to blow the budget. When planning to cook, work within your capabilities; being adventurous is fun within reasonable limitations but beyond this it can become a problem. Enlist the help of others or combine bought and home-made to be practical when there is a lot to be done.

Money can evaporate when using expensive ingredients and it is easy to isolate a pricey shopping list and get carried away, forgetting that it all adds up with drinks and other party costs.

Match courses or dishes

For formal menus, plan courses that complement each other and balance substantial and light dishes. The same criteria apply to finger or fork buffets, but there is more flexibility when guests don't have to eat dishes in order.

Below Tarts and quiches are popular choices for a buffet or brunch.

Selecting recipes

Confident cooks who entertain often and enjoy providing culinary theatre for guests may opt for lots of last-minute cooking, especially when they have kitchen space to accommodate spectators. Otherwise it is sensible to plan the menu around cook-ahead dishes, with last-minute cooking limited according to ability and the occasion. Being with your guests at a dinner party is important, while doing whirling dervish impressions between stove and buffet table can be stressful for both partygoers and you. Consider the following points:

• Balance hot and cold dishes to minimize last-minute work. One or two hot dishes are usually sufficient for a formal, main-meal buffet.

Above *Cut the first slice of cakes so guests can then easily help themselves.*

• Go for recipes based on familiar techniques.
• Select dishes that are practical to serve as well as prepare.
• For stand-up buffets, avoid dishes that are difficult to eat with only a fork.
• When arranging a finger buffet, select foods that are bitesize or easy to handle and bite without being messy.
• Leafy salads fill plates and can be difficult to eat when standing up, so guests tend to take less from buffets. Serve dressings separately from salads

that are likely to wilt so that they can be added to taste when served; this prevents the salad from become soggy.
• Creamy salads and dishes that can be piled neatly on plates or in which ingredients cling together are popular.

Increasing quantities

Recipes that can be increased in quantity successfully include soups, casseroles, sauces for pasta and recipes for individual portions (such as a specific number of chicken portions).
• When increasing the volume of stews and casseroles by more than three times, re-assess the volume of liquid as the proportion can be reduced slightly.
• Pies with pre-cooked fillings and a lid can be made in larger portions and cooked in larger dishes without vastly increasing the cooking time.
• Baked pasta dishes (such as lasagne or cannelloni) are excellent candidates for cooking in quantity.
• It is easier to boil large quantities of pasta in separate batches than to try to overfill a pan. Undercook it very slightly, drain and rinse, then toss with a little olive oil and reheat briefly in a suitable covered dish in the microwave.
• When increasing quantities by more than double, do not multiply up the herbs, spices and garlic several times as they may become overpowering.

Above *Baked dishes, such as lasagne, are good choices for supper parties.*

• Accompanying sauces for hot dishes and dressings for salads do not have to be increased by as much as the main ingredients when increasing the recipe by more than two or three times.

Menu cards

Displaying a menu card is an excellent way of letting everyone know what they will be eating or identifying dishes on a buffet. Arrange several menus on a large buffet table and remember to identify those dishes that are suitable for vegetarians or special diets.

Below *Use bought or home-made menu cards to identify buffet dishes.*

Cooking Plans, Shopping and Storage

With the menu organized it is time to get down to practicalities and, yet again, making the right lists eases everything along.

Cooking plan

Make a list of all the cooking. It is a good idea to copy the recipes and keep them together in a plastic folder in the kitchen when preparing them.

Divide the list into those recipes to cook well in advance and freeze, adding notes on when to remove them from the freezer, with likely thawing time and any finishing touches or reheating time. Note down any seasonings or enriching ingredients that have to be added at the last minute and include this on the checklist of things to do.

List the dishes that have to be cooked just before the party, that is the day before or on the same day. Note any advance preparation next to each dish. For example, salad dressings can be made a day or two ahead and chilled; some salad ingredients can be trimmed or peeled and washed the

day before, then chilled ready for use – spring onions (scallions), celery sticks and tomatoes are good examples.

When all the dishes are listed, with the days on which they have to be made, it is then easier to draw up a cooking plan. Order the recipes according to the day on which they have to be made, then go through this list to make sure it is all possible. If you have far too much work for any one day, check whether any can be made in advance. If you have chosen too many last-minute dishes, adjust the menu before embarking on a shopping spree.

On your cooking plan, list different items to be prepared separately – this way you are less likely to underestimate the work involved. As well as volume of work, make sure that you have enough containers, work surfaces and note the cooking appliance needed for each dish.

Shopping lists

Working from numbers and menu, check the recipes and increase the quantities if necessary. Then work out

Above *Use good quality meat cuts and poultry from the butcher's.*

Below *Keep fresh fish and shellfish chilled until ready to cook.*

the shopping list, checking storecupboard ingredients. Rather than having one mammoth list, divide it according to type of food, items that can be bought in advance and perishable last-minute purchases. Include any notes, reminders or alternatives on the lists to make shopping as efficient as possible.

Orders and deliveries

Scrutinize the list for items that should or can be ordered: meat cuts from a local butcher; fish to be prepared by the fishmonger; bread to be reserved at the supermarket or ordered from the baker and so on. Take advantage of delivery services offered by super-

Left *Local greengrocers may deliver fresh fruit and vegetables to your door.*

Above *Use temporary containers as colourful ice buckets.*

Below *Defrost frozen items slowly and then keep them cool.*

markets and organic produce that can be bought over the Internet. Do not be shy about asking for a delivery from local suppliers if you are placing an exceptionally large order.

Seek out mail-order suppliers for specialist or fine quality ingredients. Virtually all foods are available by this method and it is a particularly good option for specialist items, such as excellent raw or baked hams or high quality fish and shellfish.

Keeping cool and safe

Check refrigerator and freezer space well in advance. If you are cooking and freezing dishes ahead, make sure you have plenty of storage space. Sort and clean the refrigerator. Assess the amount of storage space you need and sort out practical options – a helpful neighbour

may have refrigerator space or, in cold weather, an unheated utility room or a suitable clean, dry outside area can be useful for less perishable items.

• Chill bottles of wine, beers and soft drinks in a large, clean plastic bin or several buckets part-filled with water and ice.

• Use chiller boxes and ice packs when the refrigerator is full – borrow or buy these in advance.

• Make temporary chiller boxes by lining rigid plastic stacking boxes with double-thick, heavy bubble wrap and covering the bottom with ice packs or ice in sealed plastic bags. Place on the floor in a clean, safe and cool area to hold ingredients or less-delicate dishes. Cover the top with more ice packs to keep the cold in.

• Prioritize your refrigerator space for highly perishable food such as fish, meat, poultry and dairy products. Fish should be kept in the coldest section of the refrigerator.

• Cool cooked dishes as quickly as possible. Cover them securely and chill them promptly.

• Leave items to be served cold in the refrigerator until the last minute.

• Thaw frozen items properly, keeping them cool.

Above *Some kinds of vegetables can be prepared and chopped in advance.*

Coping with leftovers

There are inevitably leftovers after a large party. Being prepared for coping with them makes clearing up far easier. Buy plenty of large plastic bags and clear film (plastic wrap). Some foods, such as cheese, should be wrapped and chilled promptly. Transfer leftovers to suitably small containers, cover and chill. Leftover cooked vegetables or green salads can be transformed into delicious soup with a minimum of fuss.

Below *Wrap leftovers promptly after a meal and transfer to a refrigerator.*

Cook Ahead, Stay Calm

Meat and poultry sauces and casseroles

Hearty meat and game casseroles freeze well, for 3–6 months. Poultry casseroles using portions do not have as good a texture as when they are freshly cooked, but diced poultry casseroles and sauces freeze well. Mushrooms and crisp vegetables are not as good after thawing as when freshly cooked. Add some finely diced vegetables for flavouring the casserole during the cooking, then add more sautéed vegetables when reheating for a good texture. Fine-textured or minced (ground) meat sauces – bolognese, chilli con carne – are successful when frozen and thawed.

Left *Stocks, sauces and casserole dishes can often be cooked ahead.*

It may be possible to cook the majority of a meal or buffet in advance, spreading the work load over a period of time. You will then have it all ready in the freezer, leaving accompaniments and side dishes for last-minute preparation. Select the right type of dishes for success. Try some of the following ideas remembering that the freezer life depends on the ingredients used in the dishes more than the type of dish.

Soups

Smooth soups freeze well for up to three months. Do not add cream, yogurt, fromage frais or egg yolks before freezing. Reheat gently, then add the dairy ingredients before serving.

Pâtés

Smooth, rich pâtés freeze well for up to one month. They are best served sliced or scooped, as they can look slightly tired when served from the dishes in which they were frozen. Home-made pâtés and spreads (fish, poultry or meat) are excellent for topping canapés.

Above *Most soups and some types of sauces can be cooked in advance.*

Above *Cook meat sauces in advance and freeze until needed.*

Above *Make stocks and freeze in ice cube trays until ready to use.*

Above *Make curry pastes and sauces ahead of schedule.*

Stuffings

Breadcrumb, meat or fruit stuffings can all be frozen up to one month ahead. Rice is not so good as the grains soften and become slightly granular.

Sauces, gravies and dips

Reduced cooking juices and flour-thickened sauces and gravies freeze well for up to 3 months. However, those based on eggs and oils are not suitable, as they curdle. Finely chopped or puréed vegetable salsas are excellent freezer candidates. Home-made dips also freeze well – try avocado dips (guacamole), chickpeas and tahini (hummus), or roasted vegetables puréed with cream cheese. Light, mayonnaise-based dips do not freeze well as they tend to curdle.

Vegetable dishes

Although the majority should be freshly cooked, there are some useful dishes to freeze ahead. Creamy mashed potatoes and vegetable purées freeze well for up to 6 months – great for decorative gratin edges, pie toppings or reheated in the microwave and stirred before serving. (You will be amazed at how quickly fabulous mash disappears from a buffet – with butter, chopped fresh herbs and a little grated lemon rind mash is a delicious accompaniment and easy to eat.) Grated potato pancakes are also excellent: lay them out on a baking tray ready for rapid reheating and crisping in a hot oven. Firm vegetable terrines also freeze well for up to 1 month.

Pastries

Filled pastries should be frozen raw, then cooked at the last minute. Puff or filo pastries that are time-consuming to prepare but quick to cook are ideal. Buy chilled rather than frozen pastry. Brush shaped filo pastry with a little butter or olive oil (or a mixture) before

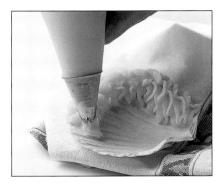

Above *Pipe mashed potato into scallop shells for Coquille St. Jacques.*

Above *Make samosas or small pastries in advance and freeze.*

freezing to prevent it from cracking. Cook small pastries from frozen. Large pastry items – pies, tarts, and pastry-wrapped fish – should be frozen raw and thawed before cooking. They will keep well for 1–3 months, depending on the ingredients in the filling.

Cooked choux pastries, such as profiteroles, freeze well unfilled. Crisp the pastries very briefly in a hot oven when thawed, then cool and fill. If serving savoury buns hot, fill then reheat them; depending on the filling, they may be filled before freezing and, if small, reheated from frozen.

Batters and baked goods

Pancakes are versatile; interleave them with clear freezer film (plastic wrap), then pack in a freezer bag. They keep well for a few months and are excellent filled with savoury or sweet mixtures, and baked. Baked sponge cakes, meringues, muffins and breads freeze

Above *Fish cakes can be made in advance and frozen individually.*

Above *Brush small savouries with a little melted butter before freezing.*

well also. Protect delicate items by packing them in rigid containers. Fill gâteaux and desserts when they are part-thawed.

Ices

You can prepare iced desserts up to a week or two in advance, but any longer and they can become "icy" with ice crystals. Richer mixtures keep better than lighter recipes: cream-rich parfaits frozen in moulds are a good choice.

Safe thawing

Thaw cooked dishes overnight in the refrigerator or a cool place and reheat to their original temperature. This is important for meat and poultry sauces.
• Defrost frozen items to be served chilled (pâtés, sponge cakes, gâteaux) in the refrigerator for up to 24 hours. Transfer delicate items to serving platters while frozen, cover and thaw in the refrigerator.

Simple Presentation

Anticipation of good food is an enjoyable part of the dining process, so creating a visual feast is as important as making food taste terrific. Getting the look just right for a smart dinner party is less daunting than creating a buffet that does not look messy or ridiculously over-elaborate. Achieving food that is easy to serve as well as appealing and delicious is the ultimate aim, and it is not difficult.

Appetizing presentation

Here are a few simple rules for food presentation – they apply to individual or large portions, fork suppers, dinner parties or buffets:
• Drips and drizzles should be wiped off dishes, especially cooking dishes.
• One or more folded clean dishtowels can be wrapped around hot dishes.

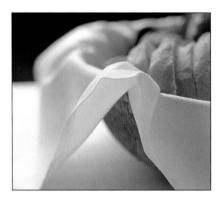

Above *Line bread baskets with crisp linen napkins.*

Below *Present hot serving dishes wrapped in clean napkins.*

• The serving dish should suit the food: neither too small nor too large, it should be deep enough to hold liquids without slopping, and large enough for items to be cut, scooped or spooned out without overflowing.
• Select dishes to complement the colour, shape and pattern of the food. Plain foods can be served on patterned crockery but fussy, bitty ingredients look best on plain designs or simple white crockery.

Appropriate garnishes

Any garnish should complement the food in style, flavour, texture, colour and shape. These finishing touches should enhance not mask the dish and they must not clash with the main ingredients.

Herb, vegetable and salad garnishes should complement the flavours of the dish or cooking style. For example, salad garnishes go well with pan-fried main courses and fairly dry bakes or pastries, but they are ghastly floating in a delicious hot sauce or gravy, where

Above *Serve appropriate sauces and accompaniments with each dish.*

they do nothing other than become limp and wreck the temperature, flavour and texture of the food.

Crisp croûtons, puff pastry shapes (*fleuron*) and shreds or shapes of pancake or omelette are all excellent for introducing contrasting shapes and textures. Nuts, roasted seeds and crisp-fried noodles or pasta shapes contribute texture. Diced or coarsely shredded potatoes, carrots and beetroot (beet) can be deep-fried to make delicious garnishes.

Divine decorations

Some good-looking sweet dishes are best left to make their own perfect statements with perhaps little more than a dusting of icing (confectioners') sugar – fabulous fruit salads, creamy roulades, whirly meringues, sparkling jellies and feather-light baked soufflés, for example. Others will benefit from a little decoration.

Sweet decorations should complement the main dish in colour, texture, flavour, style and form. The decoration should not overpower or clash with the dessert in any way. Be aware that it is easy to overdo the decoration on desserts, so avoid a cheap-looking concoction.

Many desserts are inherently decorative – set or baked in moulds, using decorative ingredients, topped with swirled cream, or served with colourful fruit sauces. A minimalist hint at decoration is often all that is needed – a single strawberry leaf with a part-sliced fruit; a cluster of perfect red currants; the smallest mound of chocolate curls; a simple dusting of dark cocoa powder; or a tiny sprinkling of golden-toasted flaked (sliced) almonds.

Elaborate piped decorations may not make a contemporary fashion statement but they can be lusciously alluring when applied with style. The fatal mistake is adding one swirl too many. Instead of using a decorative nozzle, try a plain one or use a medium-size spoon to apply cream and a fork to swirl it lightly.

Buffet sense

When adding finishing touches to buffet food, keep individual dishes simple, remembering that they will make a mosaic of colour and form when they are together on the buffet. Make the food look approachable and easy to serve when you expect guests to help themselves, otherwise elaborate or awkward-looking creations will be avoided by all but the most confident.

• So that food is easy to reach, stagger the arrangement of dishes and do not overfill the table. Instead, top up plates or dishes or remove and replace empty dishes occasionally.
• Do not overfill dishes or platters.

• When possible, present individual portions of food that are easier to serve and make them smaller than you would for a sit-down meal as diners usually prefer to sample a range of foods from a buffet than to take a full-size portion of one dish.
• Cut large items into small portions and remove the first piece, resting it on a serving spatula or laying it on the first guest's plate. This applies to items such as quiches, pies, pizzas and gâteaux.
• When serving whole hams, roasted poultry or large pieces of meat, the best solution is to present the whole item, then make a display of carving the first batch as an invitation to guests to eat. Encourage everyone to cut as much as they require, check occasionally and enlist the help of a friend to check that enough is carved.

Food centrepieces

Buffet tables will benefit from some form of centrepiece, which is usually a large main dish or an elaborate dessert. Alternatively, a fabulous display of fruit

Above *Stunning cakes and tortes make good buffet centrepieces.*

or a superb cheese board arranged on a raised stand, with splendid breads and crackers in a huge basket all look good towards the back of a buffet table. These form a focal point and backdrop, and are ready to bring forward when the main course has been consumed; they also help to keep the buffet looking neat, whole and appealing.

Below *Raised dishes or platters save space on a buffet table.*

Garnishing and Decorating

The possibilities are endless, and much creative use can be made of the main ingredients in the dish, presenting them with a slightly different twist. These classic, simple ideas are versatile and effective.

Herbs

Sturdy sprigs sit well alongside main food, while fine, feathery sprigs can be placed on top. Tiny sprigs are best for small or delicate items.

• Chopped herbs bring fresh colour to soups, casseroles, sauces, rice, pasta and vegetables. As they also add flavour, they should be used with discretion. Neat lines of finely chopped herbs, applied from a large chef's knife, add dimension to large areas of pale and creamy mixtures.

• Fried parsley is delicious with fish and shellfish, and it brings crunchy texture to creamy sauced dishes. Wash and thoroughly dry small tender sprigs of curly parsley, then drop into hot deep oil and deep-fry for a few seconds until bright green and crisp. Drain well on kitchen paper.

Vegetables

Finely sliced vegetables, such as cucumber, (bell) peppers, carrots or tomatoes, can be overlapped in threes or arranged in groups.

• Julienne, or fine matchstick strips,

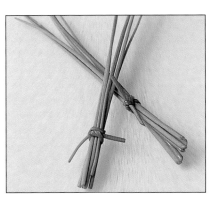

Above *Cut four lengths of chives and use another chive to tie them together.*

look good in neat little heaps or criss-cross rows. Root vegetables – carrots, beetroot (beet), potatoes or swede (rutabaga) – are good raw or cooked as appropriate. Other suitable vegetables include celery, courgettes (zucchini), fennel, peppers or cucumber.

• Fine dice of raw or cooked vegetables look good in rows or heaps. Adjacent rows of contrasting coloured vegetables look very smart.

• Ribbons pared using a potato peeler can be used raw or cooked, depending on the vegetables. Carrots and courgettes are ideal.

• Grated or shredded raw carrots, white radish or cooked beetroot look good heaped in tiny mounds or other neat arrangements.

• Decorative shapes can be cut from lightly cooked sliced root vegetables,

Above *Chopped fresh parsley sprinkled on savoury dishes is an effective garnish.*

sliced courgettes, blanched peppers, pared cucumber peel or the outer flesh and skin of quartered tomatoes. Use tiny aspic cutters or a small, very sharp knife.

Citrus shapes

Slices and wedges are easy and effective. Wedges are easier to squeeze if the juice is required to sharpen the food. Slices – whole, halved or cut into sections – are useful for sweet dishes.

• Twists are fine slices with a single cut from centre to edge and the cut edges separated in opposite directions.

• Shreds of citrus rind can be cut using a cannelle knife (zester). Simmer them in boiling water until tender, and then drain. For sweet dishes, quickly roll the shreds in caster (superfine) sugar and leave them on a board to dry.

Below *Bundles of herbs tied together can be used to garnish savoury dishes.*

Below *Chillies can be arranged as garnishes for hot and spicy dishes.*

Below *Cut vegetables into fine strips to add a splash of colour.*

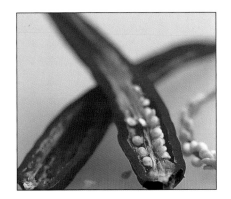

Above *Cut small chillies with scissors or a sharp knife to make chilli flowers.*

Below *Make cucumber flowers by folding alternate cut slices inwards.*

Salad ingredients

A chiffonade of bright salad leaves makes an extremely fresh garnish. Roll one or two leaves together fairly tightly and use a sharp knife to cut the finest slices, then shake these out into shreds.

• Curls are highly decorative and slightly oriental. Shred spring onions (scallions), leaving the shreds attached at the root end. Pare short, thin, curly strips off carrots using a vegetable peeler. Cut fine julienne of celery. Place the prepared vegetables in a bowl of iced water and leave for at least 30 minutes, or until they curl.

• Tomatoes and red radishes can be decoratively cut to resemble flowers. Use a small, sharp, pointed knife and, starting at the base, make small "V"-shaped cuts with the points at the top. Make sure the flesh is still attached at

the wide base. Make another row of cuts around the base, and then continue making successive neat rows of cuts up to the top of the vegetable. Always curve the knife around the shape of the vegetable to keep the section of cut flesh evenly thin. Place in a bowl of iced water until the cuts open out to create a flower shape.

Vandyke is the name given to a zigzag cut used to divide radishes and tomatoes decoratively in half. Use a small, fine, pointed knife to make zigzag cuts around the middle, cutting in as far as the centre. Carefully pull the two halves apart. This technique is also useful for citrus fruit and apples; eating apples can be sprinkled with lemon juice and sugar and placed under a preheated grill (broiler) until the sugar turns golden and caramelizes.

Above *Individual twists of sliced lemon look good grouped together.*

Above *Tomato flowers are made by peeling back the skin of cut tomatoes.*

Breads

Croûtons, croûtes and croustades are all crisp and browned bread garnishes. Croûtons may be small, neat dice or hearty chunks; croûtes are thin or thick but fairly small slices served on the side or used as a base for serving main ingredients; croustades are small containers that can be filled with a variety of savoury mixtures.

Croûtons and croûtes are fried in a mixture of oil and butter. However, if the slices of bread are brushed with a little oil before being cut up they can be spread out on an ovenproof dish and baked until crisp and golden.

• To make croustades, cut thick slices of bread, then cut them into cubes or rounds and hollow these out neatly. Brush sparingly all over with a little oil and bake until crisp and golden.

Above *Brush croûtons with a little oil before baking.*

Above *Use a sharp knife to make ridges in avocados and then slice thinly.*

Pastries

Puff pastry shapes can be savoury or sweet: glaze savoury shapes with beaten egg before baking or brush sweet ones with a little egg white and sprinkle with sugar. Use aspic cutters or large pastry cutters to stamp out suitable shapes.

• Filo pastry shreds are decorative, crisp and delicious with savoury or sweet dishes that have a soft texture. Roll up the pastry, then cut it into 1cm/½in wide slices. Shake these out on to a greased baking sheet and brush with a little oil before baking until golden. Dust with caster (superfine) sugar for sweet decorations.

The shreds can be sliced more finely and arranged in neat nests to be filled with savoury or sweet ingredients.

Pancakes

Thin crêpes or pancakes make excellent garnishes for clear soups and leafy green salads. To cut shreds, tightly roll up one or two pancakes and with a sharp knife slice them into very fine or thin slices, then shake them out. Alternatively, use aspic or pastry cutters to stamp out shapes.

Below *Toasted coconut is a delicious decoration for many desserts.*

For sweet decorations, melt some unsalted (sweet) butter in a frying pan and cook the shreds or shapes, turning once or twice, for a few minutes, until crisp. Transfer to a board or plate and sprinkle with sugar.

Nuts, seeds and grains

Dry-fry nuts, seeds or grains in a heavy frying pan until they are lightly browned. Stir them constantly so that they brown evenly. Remove from the pan immediately. Use the nuts, seeds or grains to garnish soups, salads (savoury or sweet) or creamy desserts.

• Lightly toast nuts on a piece of foil under a medium-hot grill (broiler), turning them frequently so that they brown evenly. Use to garnish soups, salads, vegetables or sauced dishes. They are also good on desserts, gâteaux and ices. For sugary nuts, lightly toast halved blanched almonds, then immediately toss them with sugar and transfer to a plate to cool.

• Praline is made by tossing lightly roasted nuts, usually almonds, in caramel. Toast blanched almonds or hazelnuts under a grill or in a heavy, dry pan. Make a caramel sauce and stir in the nuts, then pour the mixture on to an oiled baking sheet. Leave to cool completely and set. Crush the praline with a rolling pin and use to decorate creamy desserts, gâteaux or ices.

Jelly garnishes and decorations

Aspic is the savoury jelly used to glaze chilled cold dishes or make attractive garnishes. Available in packet form, for either fish or poultry, or made by adding dissolved gelatine to clarified fish or chicken stock, set the jelly in a thin layer in an oblong container. Use aspic cutters to stamp out tiny shapes or turn the jelly out on to a board and chop it neatly. Aspic can also be set on sliced black or stuffed green olives,

Above *Fresh seasonal fruits look stunning on this Genoese sponge cake.*

herb sprigs or tiny colourful vegetable shapes in ice cube trays.

• Fruit jelly, home-made or from a packet, can be set and cut into shapes or chopped as for aspic. It can also be set over pieces of fruit in ice cube trays.

Creamy finishes

Whipped cream can be swirled or piped over desserts using a decorative or plain nozzle. Small swirls make decorative edging while large and luscious whirls are good toppings for individual desserts. For a looser feel, drop spoonfuls of cream on to the dessert and sprinkle with chopped toasted nuts.

Below *Boston Banoffee pie decorated with piped whipped cream.*

Above *Iced Christmas torte with sugared leaves.*

Use double (heavy) or whipping cream. When whipping cream, make sure it is well chilled and use cold utensils, then whip it until it stands up in soft peaks – slightly softer than you need as it firms when piped or spooned. Swirled cream provides contrast and interest in savoury or sweet dishes, such as smooth soups and fruit or chocolate sauces. Trickle a little single (light) cream into the dish, then drag it slightly with a cocktail stick (toothpick).

Feathered cream is attractive in sauces. Drop small dots of cream into the sauce, then drag them with a cocktail stick into feather shapes.

Sugared decorations
These are effective as decorations on all sorts of sweet dishes. Select tiny bunches of currants, small whole fruit or edible flowers, such as rose petals, and small leaves from mint, scented geraniums or blackcurrants. Make sure the fruit or flowers are clean and dry.

Lightly whisk a little egg white and brush over the fruit or flowers, then dust generously with caster (superfine) sugar. Transfer to a wire rack and leave until crisp and dry.

Chocolate shapes
Melted plain (semisweet), milk or white chocolate can be used to make a variety of shapes. Melt the chocolate in a bowl over a pan of hot, not boiling, water. Pour the chocolate on to a board covered with baking parchment, then spread it out evenly and thinly using a metal spatula. Leave until just set but not brittle.

Use cutters to stamp out shapes, and use a ruler and sharp knife to cut geometric shapes. Use a large, sharp cook's knife to make chocolate caraque or long curls: hold the knife at an acute angle and scrape off the surface of the chocolate in large curls. Transfer each curl to a separate board and leave until they are firm. To make chocolate leaves, instead of pouring the chocolate on to a board, brush it over the back of washed and dried perfect rose leaves. Apply two or three coats, then set the leaves aside to dry. Ease the leaves away from the chocolate once it has set.

Ice bowls
An ice bowl makes an impressive serving dish for ice creams and sorbets (sherbets). Make the bowl well in advance and store it in the freezer. Fill it with scoops of ice cream a few hours before dinner, return to the freezer and dessert is ready to serve at once!

Below *Serve ice cream or sorbets in a spectacular ice bowl.*

Making an ice bowl

1 Select two bowls, one about 5cm/2in smaller than the other. Stand a few ice cubes in the bottom of the larger bowl and place the smaller bowl on top so that the rims of both bowls are level. Tape the bowls at intervals at the edge. Slide slices of fruit or flowers between the bowls and pour in cold water to fill the gap.

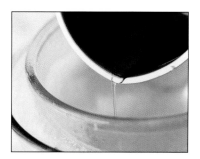

2 Freeze the bowls. Use a skewer to push the fruit or flowers down between the bowls if they float during freezing. To release the ice bowl, remove the tape and pour a little hot water into the small bowl and stand the bottom bowl in hot water. As soon as the ice bowl is released place it in the freezer.

party themes

Make the most of every party opportunity by focusing

on a particular approach. Whether the occasion

demands etiquette and sophistication or

relaxation of the rules, there are plenty of

options to consider. Once the style is set,

follow it through with enthusiasm.

Shaken and **Stirred:** the **Drinks Party**

Today's drinks party is a celebration of relaxed sophistication. From easy evenings with friends to an opportunity for semi-formal pre- or post-wedding congratulations, sharing drinks and nibbles is sociable. Plan carefully to ensure the occasion flows smoothly.

Setting the scene
Try the following checklist for straightforward drinks party planning. Make lists of all your ideas while you write shopping lists and notes on aspects to organize.
• Define the occasion precisely.
• Focus on the ambience.
• Decide on the type of drinks.
• Select the style of finger food.

Occasion
Drinks party invitations range from "stylishly casual" to "lounge suit and tie" – a balance of relaxed formality in varying proportions. Within this context, define your occasion before making precise plans. For example, a wedding may provide the opportunity for a gathering of friends not invited to the ceremony and main meal, or a celebration with colleagues and

Below *Colourful drinks add to the thrill of the cocktail hour.*

business clients, neighbours or other associates outside your immediate circle of personal friends.

Whatever the occasion, the number of guests and whether you intend inviting one or more groups of people are important. There is no reason why a drinks party should be connected to any particular event – this is precisely the sort of opportunity to catch up with friends or meet and greet acquaintances. The party may be short – lunchtime or pre-dinner – or an open-ended evening. So there is plenty of scope for setting subtle differences in ambience once you have clear aims.

Drinks
Decide on the type of drinks: cocktails, champagne, wine or an open bar. Cocktails are classic pre-dinner drinks. Champagne is always acceptable and perfect when there is a special toast to raise. Red and white wines are a popular choice. Providing an open bar (that is, offering a selection of shorts and mixers, wine or beer) is the most difficult and expensive, but this can be successful for a limited number of guests, especially if you know them well. Always provide mineral water and a good choice of soft drinks as alternatives to alcohol.

Food style
The food should fit the occasion, ambience and drinks. A plentiful supply of chunky and satisfying finger food is ideal for the sort of relaxed drinks party that drifts into late evening. Dainty canapés and cocktail nibbles are sufficient for a short pre-dinner party. Generous quantities of extra-special, stylish finger food go down well on special occasions. Among the myriad of food options, remember bread and cheese; hot fondues and dips; or international savouries, such as Japanese sushi or Spanish tapas.

Above *Arrange nibbles on platters so that guests can easily help themselves.*

Serving snacks
Distribute plates or bowls of snacks around side tables and surfaces (protect surfaces to avoid damage from spills). Offer nibbles as you mingle, or move them near groups of guests and encourage everyone to dip in. Take platters of hot canapés around or enlist the help of a friend or co-host.

Below *Hire a range of different cocktail glasses for an authentic touch.*

Above *Avocado-filled eggs make excellent little canapés.*

Right *A selection of canapés and light bites suitable for a drinks party.*

Planning finger food

For stylish refreshments, present a modest range of excellent items. Select a number of complementary types of food, including variety in colour, texture and flavour. The following examples show how to match crisp and smooth textures and different ingredients and dishes. Broaden the variety by including a range of sandwich, tart or pastry fillings or toppings. In addition to the main snacks, distribute bowls of good quality bought (or home-made) nibbles, such as roasted nuts, breadsticks and Chinese rice crackers.

• Mini open sandwiches, crisp short pastry tartlets, fruit and cheese savouries on sticks, and crudités with dips.

• Filo-wrapped savouries, bread-based canapés, filled salad vegetables, and smoked salmon and/or ham rolls.

• Bitesize pizza pieces, Spanish tortilla squares, miniature fish cakes, cheese or meat croquettes, and crudités.

• Miniature kebabs, fish goujons, dried fruit wrapped in prosciutto, walnuts sandwiched with cream cheese.

• Smoked salmon sandwiches, marinated mini-mozzarella cheese skewered with cherry tomatoes.

• Excellent chocolate truffles.

Making canapés

The trick to making impressive canapés without an army of experts is by adopting a conveyor-belt method.

Buy large square sandwich loaves of white, wholemeal (whole-wheat) or rye bread and leave them unwrapped at room temperature for a day. Trim off the crusts, and then cut each loaf lengthways into large, fairly thin slices. Spread with the chosen topping, such as a savoury butter, flavoured soft cheese, pâté or spread. For speed, use a topping that can be piped, rather than spread, such as soft cheese or creamy mixtures. The bases can be prepared to this stage a day ahead; cover with clear film (plastic wrap) and pack in a plastic bag. Cut into squares or fingers.

Arrange the canapés on serving platters and then add the garnishes. For efficiency, prepare a tray that can be added to the topped canapés quickly and easily.

Fuss-free options include: lumpfish roe, peeled cooked tiger prawns (shrimp), stuffed green olives, pecan nut halves, halved cherry tomatoes, halved canned artichoke hearts or peeled and halved cucumber slices.

Portions

The amount guests will eat depends on the time of day and length of the party. The following is a rough guide to the number of bitesize canapés or snacks to prepare for comparatively formal occasions. It is as well to be aware that the more relaxed and lively the gathering, the more people are likely to eat.

• Allow 5 items per person as an appetizer with drinks before a meal.

• Allow 10–12 items per person for an early evening drinks party (assuming that guests will be going on to dinner elsewhere).

• Allow 12–14 items per person for evening refreshments following a late lunch party, wedding breakfast or reception. (Remember to increase this when inviting additional guests in the evening who have not shared the main meal.)

• Allow 14–16 small items per person for light lunchtime or supper refreshments.

at a time, keeping the rest of the pastry covered with clear film (plastic wrap) to prevent it from drying and cracking. Brush with a little melted butter or olive oil, or a mixture of both. Cut the sheet widthways into 7.5cm/3in wide strips.

For fingers, place a little full-flavoured filling across one end of a pastry strip. Fold the end and sides of the strip over, and then roll it up. To make triangles, place a little mound of filling in the middle of the strip about 4cm/1½in from the end. Fold the corner of the pastry and filling over into a triangle across one end, then continue folding the triangle of filling over along the length of the strip.

Perfect pastries

These can be prepared in advance; they are easy to eat, satisfying and versatile. Try the following tips for streamlined preparation:

Puff pastries: prepare three different full-flavoured, well-seasoned cooked fillings. For speedy preparation make squares, triangles and oblong shapes.

Brush the rolled-out pastry lightly with beaten egg before cutting it into 6cm/2½in squares. These can be paired to make square pastries or folded in half into triangles or oblongs. Use one filling for each shape and place a small mound in the appropriate place on

Above Little filled pastries are always popular party foods.

each square – centre slightly generous amounts for squares (leave an equal number blank for topping); in one corner for triangles; and to one side for oblongs. Top the squares and fold the others in half. Press the edges together and place on baking sheets. Brush with beaten egg and bake at 220°C/425°F/ Gas 7 for 7–10 minutes, until well puffed and golden. Cool on wire racks.

Flaky filo savouries: filo pastry triangles or fingers are extremely easy and quick to make. Work on one sheet

Kebabs and cocktail-stick snacks

For party finger food, make kebabs and snacks on sticks that are super tasty and neat:

• Thread no more than three miniature items on mini-kebabs.

• Cook trays of marinated ingredients, such as chicken or beef, then cool and thread them on to mini-wooden skewers. Reheat on ovenproof serving platters. Try cubes of chicken or gammon, mini-meatballs, mini-sausages, slices of spicy sausage, squares of (bell) pepper, small pickling onions, halved baby aubergines (eggplants) or cherry tomatoes.

Below Flaky filo fingers are easy to make for large numbers.

Below Individual tartlets make a substantial snack.

Below Soft cheese, herbs and nuts make a great pastry filling.

Filling ideas for pastries

- Mash a 50g/2oz can of sardines in olive oil with the oil from the can, 1 crushed garlic clove, 2 finely chopped spring onions (scallions), the grated rind of 1 lemon, a squeeze of lemon juice, salt and a pinch of chilli powder.
- Mix finely chopped or minced (ground) cooked ham with a little freshly grated Pecorino cheese, a generous dollop of wholegrain mustard and plenty of chopped fresh chives.
- Mix plenty of finely chopped sun-dried tomatoes, pine nuts, a few chopped raisins and a generous pinch of dried oregano into cream cheese.
- Mash feta cheese to fine bread-crumbs and mix with chopped spring onion, a little oregano and enough ricotta cheese to bind the mixture into a paste.
- Mix chopped, well-drained cooked spinach with chopped spring onion, 1 chopped garlic clove (optional), a little freshly grated Parmesan cheese and enough ricotta to make a firm paste. Season with salt, pepper and a little nutmeg.

- Make sure cocktail-stick (toothpick) bites are bitesize rather than too large to pop into the mouth in one go. (Biting savouries off sticks can mean that the piece left on the stick falls off.)
- Strips of tender foods that roll well are good spread with soft cheese or used as wrappers for firm ingredients. Roll smoked halibut or salmon, cured or cooked ham, salami, peeled roasted (bell) peppers or canned pimientos.
- Olives, melon balls, halved cooked baby new potatoes, cubes of

Above *Many supermarkets now sell good-quality prepared sushi.*

cucumber, pieces of dried fruit (prunes, apricots or dates) and radishes are tasty wrapped in cooked or cured meat.

Simply stylish sushi

Sushi is delicious and practical as it can be prepared ahead, arranged on platters, covered and chilled. Ideally, make the sushi a few hours in advance; however, it can be prepared the day before. Keep it well wrapped to prevent the rice from hardening. Remove from the refrigerator about 30 minutes before serving.

- Rolled sushi: buy mini-sheets of toasted and seasoned nori seaweed to make cocktail-sized rolled sushi rice. Top with dressed cooked sushi rice and add two or three strips of ingredients such as cucumber, spring onion (scallion), cooked carrot or cooked dried shiitake mushrooms marinated in soy sauce and a little sherry. Roll up firmly and neatly. Wrap each roll in clear fim (plastic wrap), twisting the ends firmly. Cut into small pieces before serving.

- Mini-moulded sushi: shape mini-sushi squares by pressing the dressed, cooked rice into ice cube trays. Place a small square of smoked salmon, smoked halibut, thin omelette or thinly sliced smoked or marinated tofu in the bottom of each ice cube compartment before pressing in the rice and topping each one with another square of the same or a piece of nori. Unmould on to a board and top with a suitable garnish, such as lumpfish roe, quartered cucumber slices and/or pieces of pickled ginger. Serve with small bowls of wasabi or light soy dipping sauce.

Below *A big mixed salad is almost a meal in itself.*

Fabulous Fork Food

Formal or casual, this type of food is fun to prepare, simple to serve and effortless to eat. Make light of the planning by adopting a completely practical approach to this style of buffet instead of stretching it beyond its limits.

Menu options

The fork buffet menu may be for a two- or three-course meal, laid out in stages, or a series of complementary refreshments presented together. Display a menu to let guests know what to expect and to encourage self-service. Although food must be complementary and marry well to form a meal if that is the intention, a party buffet is an occasional treat, so well-balanced nutritional value is not necessarily a priority.

Below *Cut large tarts into slices so that they are easy to eat with just a fork.*

When offering a first course, serve it from a separate side table before placing main dishes on the buffet to avoid any confusion over what should be eaten first. When serving a comparatively small number (10–20 guests) it may be easier to present the first course served on small plates, with accompanying cutlery. These can be arranged on a side table or handed around from trays.

For a stylish main course, focus on one or two main dishes and add easy-to-eat main accompaniments, such as creamy mashed potatoes, rice, pasta or couscous. To avoid overflowing plates, limit the number of vegetable or salad accompaniments to one or two that really make the most of the main dish.

When serving a range of savoury refreshments rather than a traditionally well-balanced main course, select dishes that are contrasting rather than complementary. However, avoid

Above *Individual vegetable terrines are light, elegant fork food.*

clashing flavours as guests often sample a little of each dish instead of eating just one or two.

Desserts are not likely to be confused with the main course, so they can be arranged towards the back of the buffet table to be moved forward when the main dishes have been cleared away.

Cheese can be seen as an alternative to main dishes, so if you want it strictly as a separate course, set the cheese board and accompaniments on a side table away from the main buffet.

Practical fork food

There is nothing worse than doing battle with food that is difficult to eat while balancing a glass and trying to make conversation.

• Serve ingredients in small pieces or that can be broken easily with the side of a fork.

• Select foods and dishes that cling together well and are easily scooped up on a fork.

• While moist dishes are successful, excess thin sauce can be difficult to eat and will drip easily.

• Match dishes or ingredients with complementary sauces or dressings

Above *Stuffed vine leaves can be home-made or bought from the deli.*

rather than serving a main dish and accompaniments in different sauces that clash or are too runny.

Favourite foods

The following dishes are always popular and are easy to serve:
• Baked pasta dishes, such as lasagne and cannelloni. Try fillings with seafood, poultry, vegetable or ricotta cheese as alternatives to meat.
• Dishes full of bitesize chunks in lightly thickened sauces – lamb or chicken curries, boeuf à la bourguignonne, beef casseroles, coq au vin made with boneless chunks of chicken, ratatouille.
• Comforting mince (ground beef) dishes – chilli con carne, moussaka and bitesize meatballs in tomato sauce.
• Moreish rice dishes, such as creamy risotto, slightly spicy kedgeree and rice

salad with a fine yet light, slightly creamy dressing.
• Creamy potato salad, fine-cut coleslaw, tomato and mozzarella salad made with halved cherry tomatoes.

Below *Savoury rice dishes are easily eaten with just a fork.*

Stylish options

Add one or two stylish variations to a fork supper. Try one of the following:
• Savoury moulds and creamy mousses, such as seafood or vegetable terrines, fish or seafood mousses, tender foods or eggs in aspic.
• Dressed salmon, Coquille St. Jacques or other seafood gratins.
• International specialities such as a saffron risotto with shredded Parma ham and basil, seafood paella or spicy Moroccan-style tagine.

Desserts

These are often overlooked for informal fork buffets: this is unfortunate because their are plenty of options. Individual pots or dishes are easy to eat but they do take up space. Large items and big bowls that cut easily or can be spooned out are most practical.
• Fruit salads, mousses and fools.
• Filo pastries with soft cheese, nut, fruit or chocolate fillings.
• Superlative trifle, light-as-air meringues, luscious chocolate desserts.
• Miniature portions of desserts, such as cheesecake, individual gâteaux, bitesize shortcake or tiny fruit tarts.

Below *Fresh feta cheese, good quality olives and bread are excellent party fare.*

Dinner from the **Buffet**

Balance dinner-party formality with self-service simplicity by offering a traditional menu buffet style. This is an excellent way of sharing a special meal with a larger number of guests than you would normally want to invite to dinner. The ambience can be stylish, with attractively garnished food, elegant table settings and all the trimmings that make memorable celebrations, but without the need for close attention from host or hostess during the meal. A buffet is a good way to entertain whether in a hired room or in a marquee erected at home.

Table tips

Lay out a buffet table to one side of the dining room or in a separate area – this may be another adjacent room, hallway or dining area within the kitchen. Prepare a separate side table for dessert, if necessary, and have the cheese course set out ready for self-service or to be taken to the table when appropriate. Allow room for guests to walk past the buffet without disrupting others seated at the table. Plan the "flow" of guests, arranging food to encourage logical movement in one direction. Prepare a discreet table, trolley or area on which to deposit used plates from the first and main courses, remembering to include a suitable container to take cutlery.

Set the dining table or several different dining tables – a conservatory, hallway or patio can be used instead of, or as well as, the usual dining area. When preparing several tables, take care to arrange them so that they are linked without any one being isolated.

Select a cold first course that can be plated and placed on the tables before guests sit down. Have table heaters, if necessary, for hot main-course dishes, so that they can be arranged on the buffet before guests sit down to the appetizer.

Simple dishes ensure success

The food does not have to be fork friendly – everyone will be sitting down to eat – but it should be approachable for self-service.

• A main course made up of individual portions looks neat and attractive, and

Below *Make sure there are plenty of napkins on or near the buffet table.*

Above *Choose a selection of dishes that are suitable for self-service.*

guests will not be intimidated by having to cut or carve. Individual pastries, fish steaks or rolled fillets, or chicken breast portions are typical.

• Casseroles made up of evenly cut ingredients are a good choice.

• Select dishes that can be kept hot successfully without spoiling. Sauced portions or wrapped ingredients that will not dry out easily are the best choices. Pan-fried or freshly grilled items that have to be served freshly cooked are best avoided.

• Instead of plain cooked vegetable accompaniments, select a gratin, purée, casserole or bake that will stay hot without spoiling.

• Bowls of refreshing complementary side salad can be placed on the dining table after the first course.

• Cold salsas, sauces or condiments for main dishes can be placed on the dining table.

• Platters of individual desserts look elegant and are easy to serve – try making individual versions of large recipes, such as little fruit tarts, mini-gâteaux, meringue pairs, little choux pastries and individual mousses or moulded sweets.

Menu reminders

Remember the usual rules for creating good menus: go for complementary flavours, contrasting textures and appealing colours. In addition, when serving the food buffet-style consider the following ideas:

• Easy appetizers: arrange stylish portions of salads that will not wilt on individual plates at the table. Try marinated roasted vegetables and mini or cubed cheese; cured meats with olives, Parmesan flakes and crusty bread; little cheese or vegetable mousses with crisp savoury biscuits (crackers); home-made fish or meat pâté with tiny dinner rolls; smoked salmon marinated with chopped fresh dill and mustard in olive oil; or pickled herring with shredded cooked beetroot (beet) and horseradish.

• Simple-to-serve main dishes: cubed boneless chicken or turkey breast; venison, beef, lamb or pork all make delicious casseroles enriched with wine and spirits; or cook breast fillets of chicken, turkey, pheasant or duck in wine sauces reduced to a thin glaze for coating. Cook boneless portions of fish, poultry or meat in filo or puff pastry, adding herb butter before wrapping. Game, poultry or vegetarian pies are suitable for formal and informal buffet meals, and whole cooked salmon is always popular.

• No-fuss accompaniments: simple leafy salads with dressings served on the side; creamy mashed potatoes flavoured with herbs, garlic, spring onions (scallions) and olives; roasted mixed vegetables dressed with citrus

Above *Whole meat joints can be carved and served at the buffet.*

rind and herbs after cooking; vegetable gratins; or casseroles of Mediterranean vegetables, such as ratatouille.

• So to dessert: for an elegant statement, make a simple salad of two or three fruits with an intriguing hint of additional flavour – try mango and raspberry dressed with orange juice and a little honey; strawberry and papaya with a hint of lime rind and

Above *Home-made truffles make a wonderful finishing touch to any party.*

juice; chilled pears poached in cider with melon and chopped preserved stem ginger; or pineapple marinated with cardamom and sprinkled with coconut. Classic individual dishes, such as crème caramel or crème brûlée and meringue nests, are all good for a buffet.

Below *Contrasting colours and textures provide an appetizing display.*

Dinner Party Planner

Many dinner parties may be sheer fun, others sedate and some involve a sense of duty but all should be sociable and stylish. Achieving the latter ultimate goal does mean putting in a little forethought and planning – but do not be daunted, entertaining is the most rewarding part of greeting and meeting. Ultimately, dinner parties should be enjoyable.

Style guide

Hitting the high point means making a few well-calculated plans:
• Scour the guest list for flaws to be sure of surrounding the table with people who will amuse each other (even if they don't entirely agree).
• Adopt a definite approach to ambience: relaxed businesslike, society smart, well-acquainted casual, lively and up-beat, socially sexy, friendly calm, or intimate.

Below *A rack of lamb is impressive for a formal dinner.*

Above *Home-made rolls add a special touch to a dinner party.*

• Plan the menu, table décor, room trimmings and lighting, background music, pre- and post-dinner nibbles and petits fours to fit in with the required ambience.
• Check out linen, crockery, cutlery and serving dishes in advance.
• Ensure cloakroom and other areas open to guests fit in with the ambience.

Above *Lobster claws make an unusual garnish for soup.*

• Be sure to allow time for spring cleaning – or organize cleaners to do so for you – a few days beforehand and last-minute tidying up.

Menu impressions

Effortless catering is always the most impressive. As a guest, there is nothing worse than acting as spectator to the host's or hostess's insecurities and kitchen inadequacies. Keep it simple and do not attempt anything out of your league.
• Check guests' diets beforehand if you do not know them well – just ring and ask if there is anything they do not eat.
• Plan a practical menu, with the majority of dishes ready in advance and requiring little last-minute attention.
• Buy the best ingredients you can afford and use simple methods.
• Use familiar recipes or try out new ones beforehand.

Planning and timing

From the menu, make a shopping list and then a list of "things to do" in the order in which they have to be done. Make sure you double check that you have included everything:
• Pre-dinner drinks and nibbles.
• Appetizer and bread.

- Fish or soup course.
- Sorbet (sherbet) to cleanse the palate.
- Main course.
- Vegetables and side salads.
- Dessert and biscuits (cookies).
- Cheese board and crackers.
- Coffee and chocolates or petits fours.
- Wine for each course, water and after-dinner drinks.

You may not want to include everything from this definitive list, but make a note of what has to be done and by when. If there is too much to do on the day or at the last minute, change some of the dishes to cook-ahead items or reduce the number of courses. Pre-plan shopping, cooking, serving and clearing up as you go along. Remember to allow time for relaxation and getting yourself in the mood well before guests arrive.

Quantity guide

The following is a rough guide when serving 4–8 people. The quantities vary according to the number of courses and type of dishes, but the amounts give some idea of the portions that "look" generous without being daunting. As numbers increase over about ten, the amounts per person

Below Asparagus in season can make any dish special.

tend to go down (except for individual items). You may well be preparing a multi-course menu with small portions for each course or you may know that guests have modest appetites.

When inviting people you do not know well, the solution is to opt for pre-portioned foods that you can count out per person and to prepare generous amounts of vegetables and salads rather than risk running out.

Appetizers, per portion:
- 250ml/8fl oz/1 cup soup.
- 75g/3oz shellfish or 115g/4oz prepared fish.
- 25g/1oz salad leaves (such as watercress or lettuce).

Main course:
- 175g/6oz prepared fish, 1 fish steak or 1 small whole fish per portion.
- 175–225g/6–8oz portion of poultry or meat or 1 modest poultry or game breast fillet per portion.
- 225g/8oz poultry, game or meat for casseroles per portion.
- 1 roast duck serves two to three.
- 1 roast pheasant serves two.
- 1 small game bird per portion.

Above Simple meat and vegetables can be beautifully presented.

Accompaniments, per portion:
- 75g/3oz vegetables such as beans, peas, broccoli and carrots, or salad.
- 1 baked potato.
- 3–5 boiled new potatoes.
- 2–3 roast potatoes.
- 50g/2oz uncooked rice.
- 75–115g/3–4oz uncooked pasta.
- 2–3 thick slices of crusty white or wholemeal (whole-wheat) bread.

Below Frozen soufflés are perfect for preparing in advance.

Fondue Flair

Although the fondue drifts in and out of fashion, it is always enjoyable and definitely a hassle-free option for light-hearted social gatherings. Serving fondue involves the minimum of time-consuming cooking, provides entertaining dining and allows guests to participate in the cooking process and select and sample as much or as little as they wish.

Fondue style

The following styles of fondue are open to interpretation and variation to create a variety of different menus:

• Classic Swiss-style cheese fondue is fabulously creamy with crusty bread and crisp vegetables or fruit.

• Fondue Bourguignonne consists of cubes of lean tender steak cooked in a pot of hot oil, and then eaten with accompanying sauces. Poultry and other meats are also cooked this way.

Fondue etiquette

Long-handled forks with different coloured ends (for identification) are used to dip ingredients into the fondue pot. Forgetting the colour of your fork is greatly frowned upon, as is leaving ingredients to cook in the pot for too long. When someone drops a piece of food off the fork into the pot, they are traditionally expected to kiss the other diners of the opposite sex!

Above *Garlic croûtes make a change from the cubes of bread that are traditionally dipped into a Swiss cheese fondue.*

• Fondue Chinois is an interpretation of the Mongolian firepot method of cooking a mixture of raw ingredients in simmering broth. Seafood, marinated chicken, little Chinese-style dumplings (dim sum) and vegetables are lowered into the broth, and then scooped out in miniature baskets. The wonderful broth is the final treat of the meal, usually with added vegetables, noodles or other ingredients simmered briefly before it is served.

• Dessert fondues are sweet dips served with pieces of fruit, finger biscuits (cookies) or cake for dipping. Chocolate fondues can be dark (bitter-sweet) or luscious with white chocolate and cream. Warm, thick fruit fondues laced with liqueur are perfect with mini-sponge cakes or cubes of brioche.

Dip and dine

Cheese fondue is simple to make and effortless to eat. Depending on the ingredients and accompaniments, it fits well into the simplest or most sophisticated dinner party setting.

Buy good quality crusty baguette early on the day or a day ahead, so that it is slightly stale, and cut it into bitesize chunks for dipping. Chunks of celery, fennel and apple also go well with cheese fondue. Firm, ripe cherry tomatoes and large juicy seedless grapes are easy to dip and delicious with a robust fondue.

Below *Croûtons make bitesize dippers, but slices of fresh bread are good too.*

Above *Always use long-handled forks to cook your food.*

Any other accompaniments should be simple – a crisp, refreshing side salad of leaves and herb sprigs clears the palate perfectly. Little new potatoes drizzled with a hint of good olive or walnut oil and sprinkled with chives balance the rich cheese, as does a simple salad of tomato strewn with finely chopped red onion.

Fondue sets

Sets are available that incorporate a pot, stand, forks and a burner. Cheaper sets with just a rack and burner can also be bought, as can individual pots and pans, forks and skewers.

Cutlery

Dinner forks can be used for dipping food into a fondue. However, when cooking food in the fondue, forks with wooden handles are needed, as the metal of a fork or skewer will get hot when left in the fondue. Small wire baskets can be used to fish out food that has been deep-fried or cooked in stock. Chopsticks or wooden tongs are the authentic equipment for cooking sukiyaki and tempura. For dipping, food can also be speared onto skewers.

Simple cheese fondue

For the simplest cheese fondue, the basic proportions to serve four as a main course (with accompaniments) are 500g/1¼lb cheese to 250ml/8fl oz/1 cup wine. The finished fondue should have a creamy consistency.

For a fabulous fondue, gently heat 1 halved garlic clove, 1 thin slice of onion, 1 blade of mace and 1 large bay leaf in 150ml/¼ pint/⅔ cup dry or medium-dry white wine until just simmering. Cover and set aside for several hours or overnight. Finely grate 225g/8oz each of Gruyère and Emmenthal cheese and 25g/1oz fresh Parmesan. Place the cheeses in a large bowl and thoroughly but lightly mix in 30ml/2 tbsp plain (all-purpose) flour with a little freshly ground black pepper until the cheese is evenly coated. (Take care not to compact the grated cheese into clumps or it will not melt as easily.)

Strain the wine into a heavy fondue pan and heat until boiling. Reduce the heat to low, so that the wine is kept hot but off the boil, and immediately begin to stir in handfuls of floured cheese. After adding a couple of handfuls, allow the cheese to melt before adding more. Continue adding the cheese, melting it gently and stirring constantly. Finally, add 45ml/3 tbsp Kirsch and bring to the boil, stirring, until the fondue is smooth and slightly thickened. Add salt and ground black pepper, if required, and a little freshly grated nutmeg. Transfer the pan to a spirit burner at the table and regulate the flame to keep the fondue hot but not boiling.

Alternative cheeses

Dolcelatte makes a creamy blue cheese fondue when used half and half with Gruyère. For blue cheese fondue that bites back, use Gorgonzola, Bleu d'Auvergne or Roquefort. Pep up blue cheese fondues with brandy instead of Kirsch.

• Other suitable cheeses include Beaufort, mozzarella, Edam, Fontina and Cheddar; try them for their subtle differences of taste and texture.

• For an economical choice, opt for mature (sharp) Cheddar and dry cider. Add a generous dollop of wholegrain mustard and omit the Kirsch.

Below *Classic Swiss cheese fondue with baby vegetables.*

Fondue Bourguignonne

This dish demands the finest beef and perfect condiments. Complementary side salads and warm crusty bread are the traditional accompaniments. Bring the beef to life with an imaginative mixed green salad, such as lightly dressed fine green beans on a bed of peppery rocket (arugula) and sprinkled with shredded basil, or try finely shredded fennel, celery and (bell) peppers on a generous base of rocket, watercress or salad leaves. Baked potatoes topped with sour cream, or crisp new potatoes roasted in their skins also taste terrific with the beef.

The choice of condiments and sauces can set the style for fondue Bourguignonne: they can be simple to prepare, such as a sophisticated béarnaise sauce or mayonnaise flavoured with garlic, chopped herbs, mustard or tomato. Chutneys, relishes, gherkins, pickled dill cucumbers and finely chopped onion are often served, and barbecue sauce is sometimes

Below Spicy potato wedges go well with a creamy fondue.

offered. Slightly spicy fresh tomato salsa or herby green salsa contribute a lighter feel.

Allow 175–225g/6–8oz good quality fillet or rump steak per portion. Trim off all the fat and cut it into 2cm/¾in cubes. Arrange the steak on small individual plates. Individual bowls of condiments and sauces are a good idea or large bowls can be passed around the table. Whatever the choice, the accompaniments can be prepared and chilled in advance.

Heat oil in the fondue pan on the stove, and then place it on the spirit burner at the table to keep it hot for cooking the meat. Remind guests that their forks are hot and the cooked meat should be scraped off for eating.

Fondue Chinois

This is quite different and light. The quality of stock is vital, so make it with 450g/1lb lean pork, 1 chicken leg and thigh quarter, 1 quartered large onion, 4 spring onions (scallions), 2 slices of fresh root ginger, 2 garlic cloves, a few sprigs of fresh coriander (cilantro) leaves and 1 lemon grass stalk or a strip

Above Crunchy vegetables perfectly complement a savoury fondue.

of pared lemon rind. Place in a large pan, cover with cold water and bring to the boil. Skim the stock, then reduce the heat and cover the pan. Leave the stock to simmer very gently for 1½ hours. Strain and season lightly.

To serve the broth: when all the ingredients have been cooked, taste the broth, which will be concentrated by this stage. Dilute the broth to taste with boiling water or adjust the seasoning and add some shredded spring onions and greens. Simmer the soup for a few minutes before ladling it into bowls.

Safety notes
- If oil is overheated it could burst into flames. If it catches light, carefully place a lid or a large plate over the top of the pan to cut off the air supply. Never pour water on to burning oil.
- Make sure that the food for dipping is dry, as wet food will cause the oil to spit.
- Protect your hands when moving a hot pan.
- Check that the fondue pot is secure on its stand on the table and that it cannot be knocked over accidentally.
- Never leave a lighted burner or candle unattended.

Above *Biscotti, small fruits and cakes are wonderful with sweet fondues.*

Right *Crab cakes cooked in oil with a chunky, spicy cucumber relish.*

Ingredients to cook
Prepare a selection of ingredients to cook in oil or stock – remember that dumplings for simmering can be bought from specialist stores. Try peeled raw tiger prawns (shrimp), scallops, cubes of chicken breast fillet or pork, pork meatballs flavoured with sesame, ginger and garlic, dim sum, tofu and

Below *Crème Anglaise with raspberry meringue and summer fruits.*

vegetables such as mustard greens or Chinese leaves. The ingredients can be marinated separately with aromatics or seasonings, such as soy sauce, five-spice powder, shredded ginger, spring onions or chopped garlic.

Dipping sauces and accompaniments
Whether plain or marinated, the cooked ingredients are dipped in a little sauce before they are eaten. Provide

individual dishes of dipping sauce for each diner. A mixture of soy sauce and dry sherry, with a drop of sesame oil, a little finely shredded spring onion and finely chopped garlic is powerful and delicious. Plain soy sauce, hoisin sauce or plum sauce also make good dips.

Shredded vegetables, such as cucumber, spring onions and Chinese leaves, are refreshing accompaniments, and plain boiled or steamed rice completes the meal.

Sweet fondues
• Some fruits, such as grapes and apples, are suitable for dipping into savoury as well as sweet fondues. Take advantage of fruits in season for sweet fondues: strawberries, cherries, plums, peaches, apricots and nectarines are all suitable, as well as exotic fruits such as figs, pineapple, papaya, mangoes, star fruit and lychees. Fruits available all year, such as bananas and the citrus fruits, also dip well. Underripe fruit can be lightly poached in sugar syrup, fruit juice or a fruity wine.
• Cakes, biscuits and cookies: slices of dense-textured cake and sweet biscuits or cookies make excellent dippers for sweet fondues. Try Madeira cake, meringues, biscotti or Danish pastries.

Brunches and Lunches

Parties between mid-morning and mid-afternoon range from laid-back indulgence time to lively and invigorating gatherings, from sophisticated low-key relaxation to fun with friends.

Dining and sharing

Brunch or lunch is often closely linked to shared activities, such as family excursions, sport or shopping; they may be part of a weekend house party; or a follow-on with overnight dinner or party guests. Food should be inconspicuously successful rather than dominating on these occasions, which calls for well-planned and completely practical menus. Prepare ahead or serve the easiest cook-and-share dishes; creative deli shopping is the clever choice.

Cook-ahead options include large or individual quiches, such as classic quiche Lorraine; set omelettes, such as Italian-style frittata or Spanish tortilla that can be served hot or cold; and chunky soups. Sweet breads, muffins and fruit compotes or salads are all good cook-ahead items. Refresh baked goods briefly in the oven before serving. Cook-and-share dishes are ideal for kitchen gatherings, when

Below Keep family and informal entertaining relaxed by using simple napery, crockery and cutlery.

guests congregate to help cook and serve and then eat in an informal atmosphere. Pancakes or waffles are ideal for eating over a long, relaxed joint cooking session. Egg dishes, such as fluffy omelettes or scrambled eggs, are also good options for sociable cook-together brunches.

Self-assembly open sandwiches are ideal for kitchen lunches – just lay out all the prepared ingredients and breads for guests to help themselves. For relaxed success, have all breads, ingredients and accompaniments prepared and laid out in platters, bowls and baskets.

Creative deli shopping makes a superbly simple meal. For menu sense and stylish presentation, focus on one type of food or, for larger gatherings, keep different types of ingredients separate. Display a selection of different salami and cured raw meats, such as prosciutto and bresaola, on a large platter. Arrange cooked or smoked poultry and meat on another tray, and seafood and smoked fish together. Present cheeses on a board. Garnish each platter lightly with herbs and wedges of citrus fruit. Provide olive oil for drizzling over.

Include dried and fresh fruit, pickles and breads to complement the savoury platters. Croissants, bagels and mixed breads can be served with savoury as well as sweet foods; brioches, sweet breads and fruit buns go with fruit conserves, marmalade, honey or maple syrup. Sour cream, fromage frais or cream cheese go well with savoury or sweet ingredients, including smoked salmon or croissants with fruit conserve.

Summertime chill-out

Light foods are ideal for relaxed brunches or lunches in the sun. Offer warm crusty bread, light rye bread, mini-rolls, croissants or thinly sliced bread and butter as accompaniments.

Above *Fish chowders are excellent for winter lunches and brunches.*

Below *American pancakes with crisp bacon make a tasty brunch dish.*

Below *Chive scrambled eggs in brioches are the ultimate brunch treat.*

Above *Iced melon soup with mint sorbet is a refreshing summer dish.*

Include one, two or more courses, or just set out an array of foods in a cool kitchen for everyone to wander and sample as they please, such as:
• Chilled fruit soups, lively citrus sorbets (sherbets) or fresh fruit salads are stylish and refreshing. Alternatively, serve prepared exotic fruit, melons and berries on a bed of ice.
• Muesli ingredients are satisfying with fruit – oat, barley and rye flakes, nuts, seeds and dried fruit can be mixed or served in separate bowls. Offer honey, maple syrup, yogurt and milk for moistening the fruit and grains.
• Offer simple grilled (broiled) seafood – lobster, large prawns (shrimp), scallops or oysters – dressed with butter and served with lemon.
• Summer dishes, such as dressed salmon, chicken salads or baked ham, are good cook-ahead main dishes.
• Asparagus or globe artichokes are a treat with melted butter and lemon.

Winter indulgence
Cold weather is the time for lingering over several courses of favourite foods and dishes.
• Serve warm compotes of dried fruit lightly spiced with cinnamon and cloves.
• Simmer porridge slowly, then serve it

with brown sugar and extra cream.
• Opt for an indulgent cooked breakfast, with gloriously aromatic grilled bacon, sausages, kidneys, tomatoes and crisp fried bread. Fried potatoes or potato pancakes and poached or fried eggs are essential.
• Poached kippers or smoked haddock are delicious with poached eggs, and buttered, lightly cooked spinach.
• Serve pats of butter creamed with chopped parsley and grated lemon rind to dress plain cooked eggs – baked, poached or boiled. Creamy scrambled eggs are special when served with smoked salmon.
• Remember to round off winter breakfasts with warm fresh American muffins or toasted English muffins with butter and marmalade.

House-guest breakfasts and brunches
A take-it-or-leave-it kitchen buffet of fresh fruits, yogurt, cereals and warm breakfast breads provides an informal and successful start to the day. This can be extended to include sophisticated cold platters or cooked dishes.
• Wake-up trays of tea or coffee and biscuits or cookies in the bedroom provide welcome refreshment.
• Prepare cook-ahead dishes to avoid early morning work before guests rise.
• Set the breakfast table or prepare everything last thing the night before, after guests have retired, if possible, so that you can relax in the morning.

Lingering over a roast lunch
The great British tradition of Sunday roast lunch with all the trimmings is still comforting in cool weather. Start by serving a tray of little canapés or nibbles with pre-lunch drinks – offer small quantities of tiny smoked salmon sandwiches, salted nuts and pretzels. Serve a small portion of smooth, light

soup as a first course. Then cleanse the palate with a melon or citrus fruit cocktail or a small portion of sorbet. For the main course, try the following traditional combinations:
• Rib of beef with Yorkshire pudding, roast and boiled potatoes, roast parsnips, buttered carrots, crisp, lightly cooked cabbage, rich port-reduced cooking jus, horseradish sauce and wholegrain mustard.
• Leg of lamb with new potatoes, baby carrots in tarragon butter, fine green beans, red-wine cooking jus, mint sauce and redcurrant jelly.
• Shoulder of pork with crisp crackling, roast potatoes, sage and onion stuffing, stir-fried red cabbage with raisins, creamy mashed swede (rutabaga), apple sauce and gravy.
• Chicken with parsley and thyme stuffing, salad or new potatoes roasted in their skins, roasted carrot wedges, crunchy broccoli, lightly cooked spinach and bread sauce.
• Desserts can be traditional favourites, such as fruit pies or crumbles and custard, or baked rice pudding with a poached fruit compote, or lighter alternatives, including crème caramel, fruit salad or a light mousse, chilled soufflé or creamy cheesecake.

Below *Succulent roast rib of beef cooked to perfection, served with horseradish, is a Sunday lunch treat.*

Children's Parties

Setting the scene for children's parties is enormous fun. Selecting a favourite character and using bought stationery and decorations is comparatively quick but it can be expensive. Picking an individual theme is more flexible and it can be based on anything from a popular figure to a favourite subject.

Below *Young guests will feel special with individual place name cards.*

Fun themes

The following are a few ideas to use as the basis for designing – or buying – invitations, goodie bags, decorations and games. They can be used as a theme for fancy dress or making masks, as well as on stationery and decorations. Draw simple images in bold black pen (or use a computer) and copy or print to make cut-out decorations to hang on the wall or stick on the corners of the table. Paint splashes of colour on the copies and add glitter. The birthday cake and novelty foods, such as cut-out cookies and sandwiches, should also match.

• Clowns – you could also hire a juggler to teach the young clowns.

• Pirates – a good theme for a treasure hunt; make sure everyone has a loot bag to take home.

• Witches and wizards – enlist a magician to add a little magic.

Above *A children's party is an ideal opportunity to create a bright table.*

• Dragons and monsters – friendly or fierce, hire a musician for musical participation and entertainment on the theme or set up a monster karaoke session.

Below *Sugar mice in bright colours will go down a treat with youngsters.*

Above *Decorate home-made letter cookies with pretty ribbon.*

• Wild animals – a great theme for hiring a face-painting entertainer or enlisting the help of a few willing adults to paint young faces.

• Balloons – use the balloon theme for decoration and fancy dress, and hire a balloon modeller to keep the youngsters entertained.

• Puppet party – have a hand puppet-making party and hire a puppet show.

• Girls' makeover – for little girls or teenagers, put together fun make-up kits and demonstrate a few beauty tips or persuade a gifted friend to help.

For a simpler party, all of these themes would work equally well combined with traditional party games, such as musical statues,

Below *Make simple place cards from coloured card cut-outs.*

musical bumps, pass the parcel, pin the tail on the donkey, simple Simon, sardines and hunt the thimble.

Table magic

Use disposable or wipe-clean table covers and disposable or shatterproof plates and tumblers with colourful drinking straws. Make a centrepiece of candies and sweets or floating balloons. Decorate plain paper tablecloths with colourful cut-outs on the party theme, sticking them firmly in place. Keep decorations towards the middle of the table so that they do not get in the way and cause more spills than necessary. Secure the table cover in place with sticky tape or ties so that it cannot be pulled to one side as little people jump off chairs.

It is better to have lots of small plates of food within easy reach than a few large platters. Have tuck boxes with bitesize foods ready at every place. Follow with little dishes of ice cream. Try a neat pyramid of fun little cakes instead of a big cake.

Small sweets

Children love sweet desserts, so opt for small portions of simple sweet dishes. Buy small colourful dessert containers for visual appeal.

Above *Bright plastic cups and crockery are practical for children's parties.*

• Fruit set in jelly is still a winner, especially with ice cream. Canned mandarin oranges, peaches or pineapple are all easy to eat. Halved or quartered fresh strawberries or whole fresh raspberries work well.

• Start ice cream sundaes in advance. Pile scoops of chocolate, strawberry and vanilla ice cream in dishes and keep them in the freezer. Add spoonfuls of prepared fruit and drizzle with chocolate or strawberry flavour sauce just before serving. Top with a whirl of whipped cream and a little iced cookie or jellied sweet (candy).

Below *Individual cup cakes can replace a large birthday or celebration cake.*

Barbecue Entertaining

Above *Serve small snacks that guests can nibble while the food is cooking.*

Below *Chargrilled pineapple with pineapple and chilli granita.*

Below *Sweet romano peppers stuffed with mozzarella cheese and olives.*

Achieving a relaxed atmosphere is the most important key to success for outdoor entertaining. The ultimate compliment guests can pay is being so at ease that they spontaneously become involved in cooking and serving at a barbecue. This *al fresco* impression of super-easy, impromptu entertaining is, in fact, usually the result of careful planning.

Barbecue food basics

The whole barbecue ambience is geared towards savouring the cooking process as well as the eating, so the menu should provide a relaxed first course that allows everyone to nibble while the main-course food items sizzle to perfection. For some occasions the idea of a main course of grilled food plus side dishes can be abandoned to a glorified sampling session. However, for the majority of occasions the following is a safe approach.
• An appetizer of dips, Italian-style antipasti or Greek-style meze works well. This may be finger food to nibble while standing around with drinks or trays of salads or marinated savouries to eat with bread at the table.

Above *Long, hot days herald the start of the barbecue season.*

• The main course can be grilled selected ingredients with planned accompaniments or a wider choice of "main" items and a range of side dishes. The latter can turn the whole barbecue into a relaxed and lengthy multi-course tasting session.
• It is a good idea to include fruit that can be grilled on the remains of the barbecue for dessert – bananas are terrific grilled in their skins and served with maple syrup and ice cream or cream; halved and stoned (pitted) peaches sprinkled with brown sugar and wrapped in foil can be cooked on the rack above dying embers; sliced fresh pineapple can be grilled on the barbecue or cooked in foil with rum and brown sugar; or marshmallows can be toasted on long forks.

Moreish morsels

Serve little dishes of the following to keep everyone happy while the barbecue heats and cooks the main course. Offer crusty bread and breadsticks with the savouries.

Above *Grilled bananas and ice cream are a classic barbecue dessert.*

• Mix thinly sliced garlic and chopped black olives with chopped fresh oregano and olive oil as a marinade for cubes of feta or mozzarella cheese.

• Halve baby plum tomatoes and toss with a little sugar, chopped red onion and plenty of chopped fresh mint. Drizzle with walnut oil.

• Buy plain canned rice-stuffed vine leaves and cut each one in half. Heat a crushed garlic clove with some dry white wine, plenty of olive oil, 2–4 bay leaves, a handful of pine nuts and a few fresh sage leaves. Bring to the boil, then remove from the heat and leave to cool before pouring over the halved stuffed vine leaves. Cover and chill for several hours or overnight. Sprinkle with lots of chopped fresh parsley and grated lemon rind before serving.

• Roast a mixture of baby carrots, pickling onions, turnips, radishes and chunks of red (bell) pepper together in olive oil in the oven until tender. Transfer to a serving dish, sprinkle with a dressing made from lemon juice, sugar, seasoning, a little mustard, capers and olive oil. Leave to cool and serve sprinkled with shredded fresh basil.

• Heat a few bay leaves and a handful of fennel seeds in olive oil in a large pan. Add cleaned button (white) or closed-cap mushrooms and season lightly. Cover and cook, stirring often, until the mushrooms have given up their liquid and are greatly reduced in size. Uncover and continue cooking until the liquor has evaporated, stirring occasionally. The mushrooms should be virtually dry and just beginning to sizzle in the remains of the olive oil. Transfer to a serving dish and drizzle with more olive oil. Leave to cool, then sprinkle with chopped parsley, a little chopped garlic and grated lemon rind. Serve with lemon wedges.

Bastes and glazes

Marinating is not essential but food should be brushed with oil, butter or another basting mixture to prevent it from drying out during grilling. The following can be brushed on foods during and after cooking.

• Olive oil flavoured with herbs, garlic, citrus rind or chillies.

• Dijon or wholegrain mustard diluted to a thin paste with sunflower or olive oil and sweetened with a little sugar.

• Equal quantities of tomato ketchup and wholegrain mustard mixed and thinned with a little sunflower oil.

• Sunflower oil flavoured and sweetened with clear honey and lemon or orange juice for a sharp contrast.

• A little tahini (sesame seed paste) stirred into natural (plain) yogurt, and

Above *Simple grilled vegetables make a delicious accompaniment.*

with a crushed garlic clove and finely chopped spring onion (scallion).

• Tomato purée (paste), a good pinch of sugar and a crushed garlic clove stirred into olive oil.

• The grated rind and juice of 1 lime mixed with natural yogurt with a pinch of dried red chillies, chopped fresh root ginger and chopped spring onion.

Below *Tongs are invaluable for turning and moving food over the hot coals.*

Marinating food

The point of marinating is to infuse flavour and moisten the food before grilling. Marinating also helps to tenderize meat. As a guide, a good marinade includes ingredients to keep the food moist during cooking – typically oil mixed with other liquid – aromatics and seasoning. Salt encourages moisture to seep from the food during marinating, so it is best to salt the food after marinating and just before grilling or partway through the cooking time.

• Always cool a hot marinade before pouring it over the food.

Grilling times

Cooking times are influenced by many factors, including the type of barbecue, heat of the coals, closeness of the cooking rack to the coals and thickness of food. All poultry, pork, sausages and burgers should be thoroughly cooked through. The following is a guide:

Total cooking time (turn items halfway through):
Fish steaks: 6–10 minutes
Small whole fish (sardines or small mackerel): 5–7 minutes
Large prawns (shrimp) in shells: 6–8 minutes
Chicken quarters: 30–35 minutes
Chicken drumsticks: 25–30 minutes
Boneless chicken breast fillet or turkey breast fillet: 10–15 minutes
Beef steaks (about 2.5cm/1in thick): 5–12 minutes (depending on required extent of cooking)
Burgers: 6–8 minutes
Lamb chops: 10–15 minutes
Pork chops: 15–18 minutes
Sausages: 8–10 minutes
Halved and seeded (bell) peppers: 5–8 minutes

• Keep food covered and cool during marinating – in the refrigerator if it is left for any more than an hour.
• Drain the food well before cooking and heat the marinade to boiling point in a small pan. Use this for basting food during cooking, then bring any leftover marinade to the boil and use it to glaze the food before serving. (Do not serve any remaining marinade from fish, meat or poultry without first boiling it as it will contain bacteria from the uncooked ingredients.)

Simple marinades

Lemon, thyme and caper marinade: for fish, seafood, poultry, gammon or game. Gently heat several sprigs of thyme in a little olive oil until they are just beginning to sizzle, then remove from the heat and add the grated rind and juice of 1 lemon. Whisk in freshly ground black pepper and some more oil, so that there is about twice the quantity of oil to lemon juice. Add 15ml/1 tbsp chopped capers and whisk well.

Orange, garlic and red wine marinade: this is good for all meats, game and red or green (bell) peppers. Peel a whole head of garlic and place the cloves in a small pan. Add 2 bay

Above *Fish brochettes with lime, lemon, garlic and olive oil marinade.*

leaves and 60ml/4 tbsp olive oil and cook gently for 5 minutes, stirring occasionally. Add the grated rind and juice of 1 orange, 5ml/1 tsp sugar, freshly ground black pepper and 300ml/½ pint/1¼ cups robust red wine. Bring to the boil and cook for about a minute, then remove from the heat and leave to cool before pouring over the ingredients to be marinated.

Mustard and rosemary marinade: a versatile marinade for oily fish, especially mackerel, and for poultry,

Below *Brush fish or meat frequently with a marinade during cooking to keep it moist.*

Above *Home-made beef or lamb burgers are popular dishes.*

meat, peppers, onions or mushrooms. Whisk 30ml/2 tbsp wholegrain mustard with 60ml/4 tbsp olive oil, 5ml/1 tsp sugar and pepper. Gently heat 250ml/ 8fl oz/1 cup dry white wine or dry (hard) cider with 3–4 fresh rosemary sprigs until boiling. Whisk into the mustard mixture and leave to cool before using.

Shortcuts for success

• Chicken joints, such as quarters and drumsticks, require lengthy cooking. For safety and speed when entertaining a crowd, pre-cook the portions in a covered roasting pan in the oven until just cooked but not well browned. Pour over a marinade or add seasoning. Cool and chill. Brown and thoroughly reheat the chicken on the barbecue.
• Potatoes take up lots of space, so pre-bake them in the oven until tender, then brush with oil and finish on the barbecue for crisp, well-flavoured skins.
• Boil small new potatoes in their skins until just tender, then toss with olive oil, a pinch of sugar, seasoning and a little mustard. Thread on metal skewers and grill until crisp and well browned.
• Grated potato pancakes are terrific on the barbecue. Make them in advance, cooking them until they are set but only very lightly browned. Cool, cover and chill. Grill on the barbecue until crisp and well browned.

Vegetarian barbecues

When cooking a mixed barbecue, organize a separate cooking area for vegetarian foods.
• Vegetables for marinating and grilling include halved and seeded peppers; slices or wedges of aubergine (eggplant); whole mushrooms; halved small beetroot (beet); par-boiled carrots; slices of butternut squash; halved courgettes (zucchini); blanched asparagus; and blanched fennel.
• For easy vegetable burgers, mix cooked and mashed carrots and potatoes, finely shredded white cabbage, chopped spring onions (scallions), finely chopped celery and chopped red pepper. Season, flavour with crushed garlic and shredded basil, then add enough fresh wholemeal (whole-wheat) breadcrumbs to bind the mixture firmly. Shape into burgers and brush with oil before grilling.
• Grill halved peppers cut sides down, remove them and fill with chopped fresh tomato, garlic and finely chopped fresh oregano, then grill skin sides down until well browned and tender. Serve topped with shavings of Parmesan cheese.

Food safety

• Keep food chilled until just before cooking.
• When serving food outside or keeping it ready for cooking, shade the table from the sun and cover food to keep insects off.
• Keep separate utensils for removing cooked fish, meat or poultry from the grill so as not to contaminate them with juices from raw or part-cooked items.
• Grill poultry and meat, and their products, high above the coals, or over medium heat, so that they cook through before becoming too brown outside.

• Marinate firm tofu with garlic and herbs in oil, then wrap in vine leaves and brush with oil for grilling.
• Marinate slices of firm halloumi cheese in olive oil with garlic and herbs, then grill until crisp and golden on both sides. Serve immediately.

Below *Langoustines are excellent barbecue food. Serve with mayonnaise.*

Packing up a **Picnic**

Individual adult hampers can be just as exciting and inventive as children's versions, especially when stylishly packed in extra-large linen napkins and tied into neat bundles. Try out a sample bundle, checking the amount and type of food it will hold and the number that can be stored in an insulated bag. Bundle contents can include portions of tasty cheese and charcuterie; small seeded rolls or baguettes, a small bowl of salad or marinated baby vegetables; and a little pot of condiment, salsa or dip. Individual bottles of champagne or wine can be included for a special touch.

Plan all the practical aspects of packing, transporting and consuming a picnic on separate lists compiled from menu requirements alongside the choice of food.

Picnic baskets are attractive and, while they are not the most practical choice for transporting food and equipment on large or informal family picnics, they are stylish for carrying china, cutlery and glassware for grand picnic meals. Lightweight crates that fit neatly into the storage area of a car are ideal for holding equipment. Wrap dishtowels and table linen around and between fragile items. Rigid plastic or disposable dishes, plastic cutlery and drinking containers can be stacked without fear of damage. Open baskets are light to carry and useful for bread.

Insulated bags keep food cool and in good condition. Soft bags are easy to carry and insulated backpacks are particularly practical when packing modest picnics. Although more awkward to carry, rigid chiller boxes protect delicate foods and bottles from damage as well as keeping food cool. Sort out or buy storage containers that stack neatly in chiller boxes to avoid tedious searching and shuffling when assembling the prepared picnic. Hi-tech

Above *A day beside the sea is an ideal opportunity for a summer picnic.*

storage boxes (designed for camping expeditions) can be plugged into the electrical supply of a car to act as a mini-refrigerator or as a modest oven for reheating food.

Relaxing in comfort
Folding chairs and tables may be *de rigueur* for flamboyant evening picnics but they are also comfortable for relaxed and informal meals. Decent chairs are far better than tiny, uncomfortable stools.

Rugs and cushions are a good choice. Damp-proof groundsheets or rugs with plastic backing are ideal. Pack umbrellas, sunshades and spare sun hats. Remember insect-repellent and storm candles.

Individual hampers
Children and adults alike love personal food packs and they are easy to prepare, distribute and eat. Colourful boxes that stack in a chiller bag can be filled with a selection of fun food packs. Drink packs can be packed separately and snack bags can contain fruit for a sweet course.

Above *Filled baguettes and fresh fruit form the basics of a tasty picnic.*

Below *Individual picnic packs are especially popular with children.*

Above *A wicker basket is practical when transporting bottles of wine.*

Safe carrying

Wicker baskets are good for carrying cutlery, crockery, loaves of bread, crackers, biscuits and cakes. Perishable foods that deteriorate in quality should be carried on chiller packs in insulated bags. Lightweight insulated bags and insulated lunch boxes are practical for out-and-about snacks. Stacking rings that are used to separate plates of food for microwave heating are useful for stacking plated items in a chiller box. Sturdy foods in plastic containers are easier to transport and more successful than delicate items with the potential for ending up as disasters.

Supermarket dash

Simple or special, it is easy to buy a complete picnic menu from a good supermarket or deli without having to compromise on quality. There is more to discover than the usual baguettes, cheese and fruit, so try adding some of the following to the shopping list:
• Breads: select interesting breads, wraps or flour tortillas for scooping up or holding salads, cooked meats or cheese. Try bagels, Italian-style crusty breads or ciabatta, rye breads, naan, mini pitta breads, chapatis, pancakes or crêpes.

Buy a full-flavoured extra virgin olive oil, walnut, macadamia or pumpkin seed oil to go with breads or rolls. Pour a little oil on to saucers and serve chunks of bread to mop it up.
• Salads and vegetables: select washed, ready-to-eat produce that does not have to be cut up but can simply be emptied into bowls and eaten by the sprig without cutlery or as crudités with sour cream, fromage frais, garlic and herb soft cheese, soft goat's cheese or garlic mayonnaise. Among the leaves try watercress, rocket and lamb's lettuce; and select from cherry tomatoes or baby plum tomatoes, trimmed sugar snap peas or mangetouts (snow peas), cauliflower and broccoli florets, baby carrots, baby corn or radishes. Washed parsley, coriander (cilantro) leaves, fennel and basil are also brilliant.

Plain cooked beetroot (beet), vacuum packed without vinegar, is excellent drizzled with walnut oil and sprinkled with ground black pepper; it is also irresistible with soft goat's cheese or mascarpone and a trickle of raspberry vinegar. Canned artichoke hearts are good drained.
• From the deli: smoked salmon or mackerel, pickled herring (packed in oil if possible) and peeled, cooked prawns (shrimp) are versatile with sour cream and lemon wedges. Cured and cooked meats, fish or meat pâtés and terrines are all ideal for picnics. Choose good quality olives and marinated (bell) peppers instead of the mixed salads.

Below *A stylish hamper for carrying china, cutlery and glassware for grand picnic meals.*

Simply different

These are just a few ideas for dishes that are easy to carry and simple to eat.

• Cut a large loaf into horizontal slices and sandwich them back together with complementary fillings. Wrap tightly in clear film (plastic wrap). Cut into vertical slices to make attractive-looking ribbon sandwiches.

• Slit a large baguette lengthways, scoop out the crumb and fill with layers of mozzarella cheese and roasted spring onions (scallions) and (bell) peppers. Drizzle the layers lightly with good olive oil and sprinkle with shredded basil. Replace the top of the

Below *Select alcoholic and non-alcoholic drinks to suit your guests.*

baguette, press firmly together and wrap tightly in clear film. Leave overnight in the refrigerator. Cut into wide chunks to serve.

• Sandwich soft wheat tortillas together into a neat stack with a filling of ricotta cheese, salami, cooked chicken and spring onions. Shred the salami and cooked chicken, and chop the spring onions. Spread each tortilla with ricotta and sprinkle with salami, chicken and spring onions before adding the next. Press the stack firmly together and wrap in clear film. Make a spicy tomato salsa to serve with wedges of the tortilla stack.

• Cut short fine strips of spring onion, carrot, cucumber and cooked ham. Thin smooth peanut butter with a little

Above *Filled baguettes in colourful napkins are practical and fun.*

tahini (sesame paste) and olive oil, then add a crushed garlic clove and a few drops of sesame oil. Add a dash of chilli sauce, if you like. Spread this paste thinly over Chinese pancakes and place a little of the shredded vegetables and ham on each. Roll each pancake up tightly and wrap in clear film.

Stepping out

The grand picnic party, so popular with gentility of previous generations, is still a fabulous way of celebrating at a special event. Summer season events such as a day at the races, sailing regattas or country-house operas typify picnic grandeur. The picnic may be served with ceremony and silver at a table (with chauffeur-cum-butler) or for stylish lounging on rugs and large cushions but always with linen napkins, proper cutlery, china and glassware.

• First courses: arrange smoked salmon sandwiches on a serving platter or plates and offer a separate bowl of lemon wedges.

Prepare individual pots of pâté, spread or mousse, sealed with clarified butter and garnished with herb sprigs.

Serve curly Melba toast, rye crisp breads or small shaped dinner rolls as an accompaniment.

Pack chilled soup, such as classic vichyssoise, gazpacho or a fruit soup, in a vacuum flask and take separate containers of cream or chilled garnishing ingredients to add to individual portions.

• The main dish: poached salmon steaks can be dressed at the last minute with a slightly thinned herb or lemon mayonnaise.

An impressive pie or pastry dish, such as game pie or pork pie in large or mini versions, travels well.

Cold roast whole or stuffed boned chicken, turkey, duck or pheasant can be served with a mayonnaise-based sauce or lighter salsa; alternatively, individual boned breast fillets can be coated with mayonnaise and aspic.

Baked glazed ham can be accompanied by pickled peaches poached in spiced syrup made with cider vinegar instead of water.

• Desserts: for exciting fruit salads combine a limited number of complementary fruits, such as

Above *Coleslaw, gherkins and creamy potato salad are all picnic favourites.*

strawberries with papaya and lime, pineapple with mango and toasted shreds of fresh coconut, or physalis with cherries. Whole tropical fruits such as passion fruits, rambutans and mangoes are delicious just on their own.

Fruit tarts and flans filled with confectioner's custard, vanilla custard or a sweetened cream and topped with summer berries are practical when the pastry case is baked in a serving dish.

Set custards baked in individual pots are easy to carry ready for turning out on to serving plates at the last minute.

• And finally, serve two or three perfect cheeses with finger oatcakes, classic Bath Oliver biscuits or plain crackers.

Pack home-made chocolate truffles or high quality after dinner mints in a cool box to serve with coffee. (Take a vacuum flask full of boiling water and instant coffee granules separately rather than keeping the coffee hot for several hours.)

Simple picnic feasts

Try these food combinations for escaping into simple indulgence or to excite the palate as part of an impressive menu:

• Creamy ripe goat's cheese with sweet fresh figs, and take a small pepper mill full of black peppercorns for freshly ground pepper.

• Fine slices of prosciutto, Parma or Serrano ham with little bunches of sweet seedless grapes and lime or lemon wedges.

• Ruffles of finely sliced smoked venison with halved strawberries and cucumber slices.

• Smoked loin of pork and succulent ready-to-eat dried apricots trickled with walnut oil, and lemon wedges.

• Mozzarella cheese slices layered with finely shredded fresh basil and chopped fresh coriander (cilantro) leaves, trickled with good olive oil and served with lemon wedges.

Above *A quick trip to the local deli can provide you with all the picnic basics.*

Outdoor escapes

Summer excursions and picnics may be the main focus for outdoor feasts but there are other occasions when food goes down well in the fresh air:

• On Hallowe'en or bonfire nights cook turkey burgers on the barbecue; wrap potatoes in foil to cook them on the barbecue or pre-bake them in the oven and then finish them on the barbecue. Finish with your favourite muffins, served warm with lots of whipped cream and chocolate sauce.

• The seaside can be exhilarating for winter walks, especially when seafood – large tiger prawns (shrimp) in their shells, prepared squid and skewered swordfish or tuna – is served straight from a portable barbecue and accompanied by pats of garlic and parsley butter with lots of crusty bread. A vacuum flask of light, clear vegetable or seafood broth with chopped herbs and finely diced vegetables goes well with grilled seafood.

• When the snow provides the opportunity for outdoor sport, assemble an impromptu afternoon party with toasted chestnuts, crumpets and English muffins on a barbecue. Mulled wine is a warming drinks option.

party basics

You do not have to be a five-star chef to throw

a good party bash but having a few snazzy

food and drink ideas to hand is a real help.

From exciting deli-selections to confidence

with basic recipes, inspiration and essential

information are the ingredients for

planning the perfect menu.

Just Nibbles

Tune in the party by serving the right type and quantity of snacks with drinks when guests first arrive. Too few or poor quality nibbles look mean and awkward; too many or filling snacks overfill guests before the meal. Flavours should preview the courses to follow; for example, it is not good form to serve powerful, spicy snacks before a delicate meal.

Off-the-shelf selection
The array makes it difficult to resist trying some of the amazing commercial creations, but it is best to do this in your non-entertaining time. Select plain snacks and classic products rather than bizarre concoctions. Many bought savouries are wildly over-seasoned and they completely dull the palate for a delicate meal. Plain salted nuts, Chinese-style rice crackers, simple breadsticks, lightly flavoured croûtons, and good quality crisps (US potato chips) and cocktail crackers complement home-made snacks.

Roasted nuts
Place blanched almonds and plain, shelled pistachio and macadamia nuts in a large, shallow ovenproof dish. Sprinkle with a little salt and cook at 200°C/400°F/Gas 6 for about 6–10 minutes, or until pale golden. Shake the dish well to coat the nuts with the salt and leave to cool. For a deliciously elusive hint of spice, sprinkle the nuts with two or three pinches each of grated nutmeg and ground mace.

Below *Feta cheese with roast pepper dip with chillies on toast.*

Below *Pistachio nuts, almonds and macadamia nuts are good party snacks.*

Above *Good-quality bread, cheese, olives and wine are essential party basics.*

Marinated olives
Lightly crumple 4 bay leaves and place in a small pan with 15ml/1 tbsp fennel seeds, the grated rind of 1 lemon and 2 peeled and sliced garlic cloves. Pour in a little olive oil and cook gently for 15 minutes so that the ingredients barely sizzle. Remove from the heat and whisk in the juice of 1 lemon, 5ml/1 tsp caster (superfine) sugar and a little salt and pepper. Stir in 250ml/8fl oz/1 cup olive oil. Drain a 250g/9oz can pitted black olives in brine, then add them to the oil and mix well. Transfer to a covered container and leave to marinate in the refrigerator for 2–7 days. Drain the olives before serving. (The oil is fabulous for dressing cured meats, vegetables and salads.)

Marinated cheese

Prepare the marinade used for olives to flavour bitesize cubes of feta cheese or mini-mozzarella cheeses. The fennel seeds are good with the cheese but they can be omitted and replaced by several sprigs of fresh oregano instead. Alternatively, instead of fennel and oregano, sprinkle the drained cheese with finely shredded basil when serving. Gouda or Jarlsberg cheese is excellent soaked in the same marinade with fennel, cumin or caraway seeds.

Vegetable crisps

Home-made potato crisps are special when combined with other vegetables, such as beetroot (beet), sweet potatoes, celeriac and carrots.

Peel and thinly slice the potatoes and/or vegetables using a hand peeler, food processor or mandolin. Rinse well in cold water, drain and dry thoroughly on clean dishtowels. Make sure all the slices are separate before deep-frying a handful at a time in hot oil until they

Below Lemon and herb marinated olives are tasty party nibbles.

are crisp and golden. Drain thoroughly on paper towels and season lightly with salt.

Roasted cardamom cauliflower florets

Split 8 green cardamom pods and heat gently in a large pan with 60ml/4 tbsp sunflower oil until the pods are just sizzling, then cook for 2 minutes. Break a trimmed cauliflower into bitesize florets. Add the florets to the pan and toss to coat thoroughly in the oil, then turn them out into a shallow ovenproof dish, scraping all the oil over them. Roast at 220°C/425°F/Gas 7 for 10

Above *Spiced plantain chips with hot chilli sauce.*

minutes, turning once, until lightly browned. Season lightly and cool. Discard the cardamoms when transferring the cauliflower florets to serving bowls.

Baguette croûtons

Cut a good baguette with good, soft centre crumb into quarters lengthways. Cut the quarters across into large bitesize chunks. Spread these out in a large roasting pan and bake at 160°C/325°F/Gas 3 for about 40 minutes, turning occasionally, until crisp, dry and lightly browned. Finely chop 1 garlic clove and cook lightly in 30ml/2 tbsp olive oil for 1 minute. Add 5ml/1 tsp each of dried oregano and thyme, then pour in a further 60ml/4 tbsp olive oil. Heat gently for a few minutes, then trickle evenly and thinly over the croûtons. Season lightly with salt and toss well, then return to the oven for a further 5 minutes. Toss with plenty of finely chopped fresh parsley and finely grated lemon rind, if you like, just before serving.

For lightly flavoured croûtons, heat 2 bay leaves, a blade of mace and the pared rind of 1 lemon with the oil instead of the garlic, oregano and thyme. Leave to stand for several hours before pouring over the croûtons.

Salsas, Dips and Dippers

A few good salsas and dips go a long way, and a repertoire of basic recipes can be varied to create exciting snacks. Try them as fillings for hollowed vegetables or halved hard-boiled eggs; spread them on soft tortillas, wraps or pancakes and roll up into tasty picnic snacks or slice them into stylish canapés.

Matching dippers to dips

Vegetable crudités, breadsticks, croûtes and crackers taste good with most dips. For a juicy dip, select dippers to scoop up and hold juice or absorb a little – thick, curly crisps (US potato chips) and tortilla chips work well.

Below *Crunchy tacos are perfect with tomato salsa and guacamole.*

Do's and don'ts for dips and dippers

Do …

• Make smooth, fairly soft, but not sloppy, dips for easy eating.
• Select sturdy and fairly short nibbles to dunk – chunky lengths of celery, carrot, (bell) pepper and fennel; mini breadsticks; pitta bread fingers and crackers.
• Use cocktail sticks (toothpicks) for small, firm bits to dunk.
• Match dippers to dips.
• Serve dips in small bowls on platters, surrounded by enough dippers for the entire bowlful of dip.

Don't …

• Make the dip too thick to scoop easily.
• Prepare dips that separate or become watery on standing.
• Serve fragile dippers that break or bend; avoid fine crisps (US potato chips), fine puff pastries and flopping wedges of pitta.
• Offer nibbles that are too small to dunk without putting your fingers into the dip.
• Serve a huge bowl of dip that does the rounds for 30 minutes only to become messy.
• Offer dressed or sauced dunks that discolour and flavour the dip.

• For crisp potato wedges cut medium to large potatoes into quarters lengthways and place in a plastic bag. Add a little sunflower oil and salt, and then mix well. (Add a generous pinch of dried oregano or rosemary if appropriate for the dip.) Turn out into a roasting pan and cook at 240°C/475°F/Gas 9 for about 40 minutes, turning two or three times, until crisp and browned. Serve freshly cooked.

These can be three-quarters cooked in advance, then finished in the oven at the last minute. Sweet potatoes and new potatoes also work well.

• For crisp skins, halve baked potatoes and scoop out the middle, leaving a fairly thick shell. Brush all over with oil, place in a greased roasting pan and season lightly with salt. Roast at 200°C/400°F/Gas 6 for about 30 minutes, or until crisp and browned.

Red salsa

Play with this basic mixture to impress your personality on it and excite your palate – add a little extra sugar or chilli, perhaps, and increase the paprika for a deeper, warmer flavour. To lighten the

salsa and add a lively zing, omit the tomato purée (paste) and stir in a little lemon juice. The salsa complements fish, poultry, meat or cheese; it makes a terrific dip with fingers of pitta bread or cheese cubes on sticks; and it is delicious on bitesize croûtes, topped with halved, hard-boiled quails' eggs.

Mix 60ml/4 tbsp tomato purée, 1 finely chopped red onion, 1 seeded and finely chopped red (bell) pepper, 1 seeded and finely chopped mild red chilli, 1 crushed garlic clove, 10ml/2 tsp caster (superfine) sugar, 2.5ml/½ tsp paprika and 30ml/2 tbsp balsamic vinegar until thoroughly combined. Peel and chop 450g/1lb ripe tomatoes, then stir them into the mixture. Add salt and pepper to taste. Cover and chill for 1–3 days in the refrigerator.

Cucumber and avocado salsa

This fresh, lively salsa complements fish and seafood, salami and cured meats, and grilled (broiled) and barbecued meats and burgers. It enlivens creamy cheeses. As a dip, it is wicked with potato wedges or skins, and chunky cheese straws.

Peel and finely chop 1 cucumber, then place it in a sieve. Sprinkle with

Below *Tomato-based salsas are very versatile: add chillies, coriander or garlic.*

salt and leave over a bowl to drain for 30 minutes. Meanwhile, finely chop 1 large seeded green (bell) pepper, 1 seeded mild green chilli, 1 bunch of spring onions (scallions) and mix with 15ml/1 tbsp caster sugar, 45ml/3 tbsp good olive oil and the grated rind and juice of 1 lime. Squeeze the cucumber and then dry it on kitchen paper before adding it to the salsa. Halve, stone (pit) and finely chop 2 avocados, then mix them into the salsa. Chop a big bunch of coriander (cilantro) leaves and stir them into the salsa.

Cover and chill for several hours or up to 1 day. Before serving, finely shred a handful of tender basil sprigs and stir them in.

Below *Pitta bread makes excellent dippers for creamy dips.*

Above *Spicy pumpkin dip served with cucumber crudités.*

Onion and chive dip

This is delicious as a filling for baked potatoes or with crispy barbecue-cooked new potatoes; it is a good accompaniment for baked gammon or a filling for cherry tomatoes.

Peel and quarter 6 onions. Mix 15ml/1 tbsp sugar, 15ml/1 tbsp wholegrain mustard, 30ml/2 tbsp sunflower oil and 30ml/2 tbsp cider vinegar in a shallow ovenproof dish just large enough to hold the onions. Turn the onions in this mixture, then roast at 200°C/400°F/Gas 6 for about 45 minutes, turning once or twice, until tender. Cover and cool.

Purée the onions with their juices. Gradually stir the onion purée into 450g/1lb curd cheese. Finely snip a handful of chives into the dip, add a little freshly grated nutmeg and mix well. Taste for seasoning, then chill.

Gorgonzola and parsley dip

Mash 225g/8oz Gorgonzola cheese and mix in 225g/8oz/1 cup ricotta cheese. Finely chop 50g/2oz flat leaf parsley and mix it into the dip with freshly ground black pepper. Stir in 250ml/8fl oz/1 cup crème fraîche and seasoning to taste. Chill before serving.

Salad Talk

In a flurry of curly leaves or a frisée of fine shreds, every salad should make a stunning statement. Move on from making irrelevant "side salads" to presenting classy creations by marrying vegetables with taste bud-tingling dressings and well-textured toppings.

Salad reminders

Harmonize all aspects of a salad; the base, main ingredients, dressing and topping or garnish should contrast and blend to perfection.

• Include a limited selection of complementary flavours and textures rather than a mishmash of ingredients – this is especially relevant with rice or pasta salads.

• Dress leafy salads at the last minute, otherwise they become limp. For buffets, serve the dressing separately.

• Sprinkle crisp or crunchy toppings over when serving, or offer them separately for buffets.

• Have a generous taste of the dressing to check the seasoning and balance of

Below *Classic Caesar salad is a popular party dish.*

sweet to sour. The dressing must complement not mask the salad.

• There should be enough dressing to coat but not drown the ingredients.

• Light-textured and thin dressings complement soft and crisp ingredients; crunchy and firm ingredients support creamy coatings.

• Unless they should be served chilled, remove salads from the refrigerator about 30 minutes before serving.

Full-of-flavour leaves

The palate-cleansing properties of fresh leaves are welcome with firm, substantial main dishes, such as grilled poultry or meat and hearty raised pies or pastries. They are also an excellent base for sautéed or grilled fish and seafood, finely sliced cured meats or crumbly or creamy cheeses.

For exciting leafy ensembles mix green flavours with subtly different textures. Crisp iceberg, cos or romaine lettuces contrast with lamb's lettuce, lollo rosso or Little Gem (Bibb) leaves.

Baby spinach brings a firm, rather than crisp, texture and a subtle, slightly musty flavour. Peppery watercress and savoury rocket (arugula) bring positive textures as well as lively flavour.

Above *Olive oil and ripe black olives add plenty of flavour.*

Herb sprigs are excellent in leafy salads, either singly or in a burst of mixed flavours. Chopping the herbs changes the result completely, distributing their flavour rather than providing the occasional interesting mouthful; so include small sprig ends with their tender edible stems.

Salad portions

Estimating salad portions for large gatherings is not easy; simply multiplying portion sizes for a meal for four or six by a larger number for a buffet does not work. Portion sizes are smaller for buffet salads. As a rough guide for gatherings of over 20, 1 large lettuce (lollo rosso, iceberg, cos or romaine) will provide eight portions, 500g/1¼ lb tomatoes will be enough for six, 1 small white cabbage will serve 12 when finely shredded, 500g/ 1¼ lb new potatoes will serve four and 500g/1¼ lb shredded carrots will serve six to eight.

The crunch factor

The greater resistance of crunch is different from crisp and it is a texture that supports substantial ingredients and flavours or creamy dressings very well. Fennel, celery, radishes, cucumber, carrots, celeriac, red or white cabbage, courgettes (zucchini), (bell) peppers, beansprouts and onions are packed with crunch. For super-crunchy salads, add drained and thinly sliced canned water chestnuts.

Tender not soft

Cooked root vegetables, tomatoes, mushrooms, canned bamboo shoots and olives are examples of tender ingredients that can be marinated in dressings to impart or absorb flavours. A suitable marinade should not spoil their textures but it will enrich the salad and give it depth.

Tip-top finishes

The decorative garnishes or toppings for salad add vital flavour and introduce interesting textures.
• Chopped, slivered or whole nuts can complement main ingredients or be a focal point. Walnuts, pecans, pistachios, macadamia nuts and hazelnuts are all excellent on salads.
• Lightly roasted seeds bring strength of flavour and texture. Linseeds, pumpkin, sesame, sunflower, mustard and poppy seeds are all delicious individually or together. Pine nuts are delicious, tender and nutty and go especially well with spinach.
• Lightly roasted grains bring texture and flavour, and they go well with seeds and/or bacon. Barley, rye and/or oat flakes can all be roasted in a dry, heavy pan until lightly browned and crisp.
• Croûtons bring crunch and they can be tasty with herbs and/or garlic.
• Crisp sautéed diced bacon or gammon, salami or chorizo are full of flavour and texture.

Above *White beans with green peppers in a spicy dressing.*

Asides to centrepieces

Salads make appealing first courses or light main courses and many are just a twist away from becoming impressive centrepieces for picnics or buffets. The trick is to marry punchy main ingredients with a salad base full of character, then link them with a sympathetic dressing. Experiment with the following examples:
• A substantial full-flavoured leaf and herb base is brilliant for pan-fried fish, poultry, cheese or tofu. Sliced scallops, peeled raw tiger prawns (shrimp), chunks of salmon, strips of chicken or turkey breast fillet, cubes of halloumi cheese or firm tofu can all be marinated with a little olive oil, garlic and lemon rind, then pan-fried and tossed into the salad while hot. Deglaze the pan with lemon juice or balsamic vinegar, a sprinkling of sugar, seasoning and a final drizzle of olive oil to make a delicious dressing. To serve the salad cold, transfer the pan-fried ingredients to a container, pour over the deglazed dressing and cool, then mix with the leaves before serving.
• Use shredded crunchy salad in a light oil-based dressing as a base for ruffles of thinly sliced cured meats; julienne of cooked meats; quartered hard-boiled eggs and diced smoked salmon or ham; or diced firm cheese. Add a creamy dressing and crunchy topping.
• A mixture of soft and crisp, lightly flavoured leaves (for example lollo biondo, lamb's lettuce and shredded iceberg) is a good base for fresh fruit, rich dried fruit and creamy cheese. Crisp and juicy green grapes, sliced dried apricots and sliced ripe Brie combine well. Add a topping of coarsely chopped walnuts and dress with a drizzle of walnut oil. Add lemon wedges as a little zest to taste.

Below *Refreshing tabbouleh with masses of chopped fresh herbs.*

Sauces, Dressings and Relishes

A good home-made sauce elevates plain cooked foods to a stylish dish. Here are a few classic recipes:

Tomato sauce

This good basic sauce freezes well. Thaw it for several hours at room temperature or in the microwave. Apart from the myriad of uses in compound dishes, the sauce goes well with plain cooked fish, poultry or meat.

For the simplest informal supper party, serve fresh pasta with tomato sauce, topped with lots of finely shredded fresh basil and coriander (cilantro), and shavings of Parmesan cheese. Add a punchy, crunchy salad of shredded fennel and white cabbage with chopped spring onion (scallion) and toasted pine nuts.

Chop 1 onion, 1 celery stick, 1 carrot and 1 garlic clove, then cook in 30ml/2 tbsp olive oil with 2 bay leaves and 1 large sprig each of fresh thyme and oregano for 15 minutes. Cover the pan to keep the moisture in and prevent the vegetables from browning. Add 1kg/2lb chopped ripe tomatoes, 30ml/2 tbsp tomato purée

Below Pickles add full flavour to accompaniments and condiments.

(paste), 15ml/1 tbsp sugar, 2.5ml/½ tsp paprika and a little seasoning. Heat, stirring, until the tomatoes give up some of their juice, and simmer then cover the pan and cook gently for 40–45 minutes, until the vegetables are tender and the tomatoes reduced. Discard the bay leaves and herb sprigs, then purée the sauce. Use the sauce as it is (slightly coarse) or press it through a fine sieve for a smooth texture.

Mayonnaise

Home-made mayonnaise is superb, and the flavour can be fine-tuned to your personal taste by adjusting the balance of sunflower and olive oils (or using different types of oil) and the quantity of lemon juice.

Home-made mayonnaise contains raw egg; pregnant women, the very young and the elderly are generally advised not to eat raw eggs.

Commercial mayonnaise, however, is pasteurized to destroy any micro-organisms in the egg and it can be a safer option for buffet dishes that are likely to be left sitting for several hours in a warm room.

Below Home-made garlic mayonnaise with crudités.

Above *Home-made mayonnaise is quick to make and so delicious.*

Use an electric beater to whisk 1 large (US extra large) egg with a little salt and pepper, 2.5ml/½ tsp Dijon mustard and the juice of ½ small lemon, until thoroughly combined. Mix 150ml/¼ pint/⅔ cup each of sunflower and olive oil. Whisking constantly, gradually add the oils to the egg in a very thin trickle, broken at first, then more constantly as the mixture thickens and becomes creamy. The finished mayonnaise should be thick, pale and glossy. Add salt, pepper and lemon juice to taste if required.
• The mayonnaise can be made in a food processor by processing the egg mixture first, then gradually dropping and trickling in the oil with the motor running. Scrape the mixture down frequently. A large food processor bowl may be too large for a single quantity.
• For a rich mayonnaise, use egg yolks rather than whole egg and allow 2 egg yolks to 250 ml/8 fl oz/1 cup oil.

Flavouring mayonnaise

A well-flavoured mayonnaise can be served as a filling for baked potatoes or a dip with potato wedges.
• Add 1 crushed garlic clove to the egg. For a mellow flavour, first cook 1 garlic clove in a little olive oil until lightly browned.
• Stir in 60ml/4 tbsp chopped fresh chives, parsley, tarragon, dill or fennel, or a handful of shredded basil leaves.

• Stir in the grated rind of 1 lemon, lime or orange. Use the juice of 1 lime instead of the lemon juice. (Orange juice is not sharp enough to balance the oil and egg mixture.)

• To make a spicy rouille, add 1 crushed garlic clove, 5ml/1 tsp paprika and a good pinch of cayenne pepper to the egg. Taste the prepared mayonnaise for seasoning and add a little extra cayenne if you like. Rouille is a traditional accompaniment for fish soups, served with slices of warm baguette, but it also goes with a wide variety of other foods or it makes a delicious dip for plain breadsticks.

Excellent salad dressing

This is a good basic oil and vinegar salad dressing, which can be varied to suit all sorts of salads. Different types of oil (sunflower, grapeseed, walnut, hazelnut or pumpkin seed) or vinegar (remember all the flavoured vinegars) can be used, and there are many types of mustard that will vary the flavour. Strong nut oils should be used in modest amounts with light grapeseed or sunflower oil.

Below Good quality olive oil adds a unique flavour.

Above Quail's eggs served with mayonnaise dip and olive oil.

Whisk 5ml/1 tsp sugar, salt and freshly ground black pepper, and 7.5ml/1½ tsp mustard (wholegrain or Dijon, mild or strong to taste) with 30ml/2 tbsp balsamic or cider vinegar until the sugar and salt have dissolved. Whisking hard and constantly, slowly pour in 150ml/¼ pint/⅔ cup olive oil. The dressing will emulsify and thicken slightly. Store in an airtight jar in the refrigerator and shake before serving.

Flavouring dressings

Try some of the following additions.
• Add 1 chopped garlic clove.
• Add 30ml/2 tbsp chopped parsley, mint, tarragon or chives.
• Add the grated rind of ½–1 lemon.
• To make a spicy peanut dressing, omit the mustard and use 30ml/2 tbsp crunchy peanut butter. Add the juice of 1 lime and a pinch of dried red chillies.

Beetroot relish

This sweet and sour preserve is terrific with hot or cold meats or with cheese. Serve it with a Christmas buffet or a summer barbecue.

Peel and coarsely grate 450g/1lb raw beetroot (beet). Peel, core and coarsely grate 450g/1lb cooking apples.

Finely chop 450g/1lb onions. Peel and chop 25g/1oz fresh root ginger. Mix all the ingredients in a pan and add 2 crushed garlic cloves, 5ml/1 tsp each of ground cinnamon and nutmeg, 225g/8oz/1 cup soft brown sugar and 450ml/¾ pint/scant 2 cups cider vinegar. Bring to the boil, stirring occasionally, then reduce the heat and cover the pan. Simmer the relish for about 1½ hours. Pot the relish in warmed sterilized jars immediately the pan is removed from the heat. Cover with airtight lids and store for at least 2 weeks before eating. It makes about 1.3kg/3lb.

Below Beetroot relish.

Making the Best of Bread

The advantage of baking your own bread is that you can create individual rolls or loaves to complement the menu or to become a real feature on their own, especially for breakfast, brunch, lunch or late suppers. Breads can be baked or bought well in advance and frozen. Seek out interesting breads and discover lots of ways of using them.

• Wholemeal bread: use wholemeal (whole-wheat) flour and add an extra 50ml/2fl oz/¼ cup water.

• Seeded breads: use all wholemeal or half and half wholemeal and white. Add 15ml/1 tbsp each of caraway and cumin seeds, and 30ml/2 tbsp each of poppy and sesame seeds.

• Rye bread: use half rye flour and half white flour. Add 30ml/2 tbsp caraway seeds and an extra 50ml/2fl oz/¼ cup water to the mixture.

Below *For a party, buy interesting bread flavoured with seeds and herbs.*

• Milk bread: use hand-hot milk instead of water for richer bread. Rub 50g/2oz/¼ cup butter into the flour before adding the yeast, salt and sugar then omit the olive oil. Do not glaze the bread before baking.

• Herb bread: add 10ml/2 tsp dried sage, 10ml/2 tsp dried thyme and 60ml/4 tbsp chopped fresh chives to the flour. Also try oregano, dill, fennel, coriander (cilantro) and parsley.

Shaping dough

Make interestingly shaped loaves for a special occasion.

• Braid: cut the dough into thirds and roll these into long, thin strips. Pinch the ends of the strips together, and then braid them. Leave to rise, brush with beaten egg and sprinkle with poppy seeds before baking. Use milk bread for a richer dough.

• Oval loaves: cut the dough in half and shape each piece into a roll about

Basic bread dough

Mix 450g/1lb strong plain white bread flour with 1 sachet fast action easy-blend (rapid-rise) dried yeast, 5ml/1 tsp salt and 5ml/1 tsp sugar. Make a well in the middle and add 250ml/8fl oz/1 cup hand-hot water and 30ml/2 tbsp olive oil. Gradually work the liquid into the flour to make a stiff dough. Turn the dough out on to a lightly floured surface and knead it for about 10 minutes, or until very smooth and elastic. Shape the dough as required and place on a greased baking tray. Cover with oiled clear film (plastic wrap) and leave in a warm place until doubled in size before baking. Bake large loaves at 220°C/425°F/ Gas 7 for about 40 minutes, or until well risen and browned. Bake rolls at the same temperature for 20–25 minutes. Turn the bread over and tap the base: the loaf should sound hollow. If it sounds damp and solid it is not properly cooked through so return it to the oven for a further 5 minutes and check again.

20cm/8in long. Leave to rise, then use a sharp knife to cut shallow diagonal slits across the top before brushing with a little warm water and baking.

• Rolls: cut the dough into 12 equal portions and shape these into round or oval rolls. To make a knot, roll a portion into a thin strip and twist it into a knot. For twists, divide each portion in half, roll into strips and twist these together. Transfer the rolls to a greased baking tray and leave to rise. Brush with beaten egg or milk, then sprinkle with sesame or poppy seeds before baking.

• Swirl: make up two batches of dough: one plain white and one

Above *Warm, fresh home-baked bread can be a real feature at parties.*

seeded half and half wholemeal and white. Cut each type in half. Roll out a portion of white into an oval, and then roll a portion of seeded into a equal-size oval. Lay the seeded dough on the white and roll up both into an oval loaf. Repeat with the remaining dough to make a second loaf. Leave to rise, brush with warm water and sprinkle with seeds before baking.

Buying guide
Buy bread on the day it is to be eaten or buy and freeze it in advance, then thaw it early on the day or overnight.
• Crusty breads, such as baguettes, French and Italian country breads, and the British bloomer, are good for mopping up dressings and sauces, and they go well with cheese. Cut them into chunks to make crusty croûtons.
• Rich breads, such as milk bread, brioche or challah/cholla, are a good choice for brunch or to accompany marinated vegetables and salads for lunch. They are excellent for picnics.
• Flat breads, such as pitta, naan or soft wheat tortillas, can be used more widely than in their traditional roles. They go well with dips or pâtés, and are good filled or topped with salads, roasted vegetables, grilled or cured meat.

• Individual breads are perfect for buffets, picnics, breakfast or brunch. Croissants, bagels, English muffins and crumpets, teacakes or currant buns are real treat breads, as good packed with fabulous fillings as they are served in traditional style.
• Close-textured or coarse breads bring out the best in smoked fish, seafood, cured meats, fine pâtés and cheese. While firm dark or light rye bread can be thinly sliced, the coarser grainy breads tend to be more crumbly and are good served in thick chunks.

Serving bread
Warm bread has a better flavour and texture than cold.
• Present a whole loaf on a cutting board, with knife. For a large party, when guests are less likely to slice their own bread, the loaf may be part or completely sliced and presented with the slices re-assembled to prevent them from drying out.
• Pile warm flat or individual breads in a linen-lined basket and fold the cloth over to keep the bread warm.
• Sliced baguette and thinly cut breads complement light first courses; chunks, wedges and hearty lengths of baguette are more filling with main dishes and substantial salads.

Hot savoury breads
Slice a baguette, bloomer or crusty French country bread ring, leaving the slices attached at the base. Spread one of the following fillings on the slices and press them back together. Spread a little extra filling over the top. Wrap the loaf in foil and heat in the oven at 200°C/400°F/Gas 6 for about 15 minutes. Serve hot.
• Garlic butter: cream 115g/4oz/½ cup butter with 1 crushed garlic clove.
• Herb butter: cream 60ml/4 tbsp chopped fresh herbs into 115g/4oz/ ½ cup butter.

Above *Serve garlic or herby buttered baguettes warm and with napkins.*

• Anchovy and olive butter: finely chop a 50g/2oz can anchovies in olive oil, and cream with 115g/4oz/½ cup butter, gradually working in the oil from the can. Add 115g/4oz chopped black olives, a squeeze of lemon juice and freshly ground black pepper.
• Spring onion, lime and coriander butter: finely chop 4 spring onions (scallions) and a good handful of fresh coriander leaves, then cream with 115g/4oz/½ cup butter, adding the grated rind of 1 lime and a squeeze of lime juice. Add a chopped garlic clove, if you like.

Croûtons and croûtes
These can be cut into small cubes or chunks to match any dishes. Sauté them in olive oil and butter or bake until crisp and lightly browned, then drizzle with a little oil. Alternatively, lightly brush slices of bread with oil and grill (broil) until golden, then cut into cubes.
• Croûtes are bread slices, brushed with melted butter or oil, and baked, grilled or fried until golden on both sides. They may be small and thin, or thick and crusty slices. Croûtes complement soft foods or make a good base to absorb juices.

Stunning Cheese Boards

Whether the cheese board is an international extravaganza or a celebration of one or two good cheeses depends on the occasion and the role of the cheese in the menu.

Dinner-party cheese course

When the cheese board is served as a dinner-party course among many there may be just one or two cheeses or a small selection of different types. Offering one fine example is quite acceptable, typically Brie or a similar universally popular type of cheese. It is fun to focus on something special you know your guests will appreciate, such as a good blue or tangy goat's cheese.

The more usual approach to the basic dinner-party cheese board is to include an example each of hard, blue and semi-soft cheese. One or two other cheeses are often added according to what is good at the deli. Availability and quality are important and it is better to limit the cheeses to a few good quality examples than to offer many second-rate selections.

Above *Keep to a few fresh, good-quality cheeses for the cheese board.*

• Vary the sizes, shapes and textures of pieces of cheese.
• Ensure that there is enough of each cheese for every guest to have a modest sample; buy more than one of a small cheese if necessary.
• Cheese may be served after the main course and before dessert, in the French style, or after the dessert and before coffee. If it is practical, the cheese can be brought to the table and offered at the same time as the dessert, allowing individuals to decide which they would prefer to eat first.

Cheese on the buffet

The selection of cheeses may be one of many courses of food or it may be the main focus for a buffet. The modern cheese and wine party is way beyond squares of hard cheese on sticks: it is a celebration of cheese.
• When serving a wide variety, keep the different types of cheese separate. Large pieces can be given their own

platters or stands. If there is more than one type of hard white, semi-soft or blue cheese, group them by type on separate boards or platters.
• Contrasting colours and shapes are important, so include cheeses with different rinds, and display logs, pyramids, squares, domes or rounds as well as wedges and wheels.
• One or more whole cheeses in perfect condition are a real delight. Order from a good supplier well in advance, requesting that the cheese be in peak condition for the party. A whole Brie and a half or whole Stilton are a good classic combination.

Presentation tips

Wooden or marble boards are traditional but china platters and glass or china cake stands work extremely well. Baskets lined with heavy linen napkins, topped with fresh vine leaves are an attractive backdrop for cheese.
• Remove cheese from the refrigerator several hours beforehand and leave it in a cool room. Unwrap any pre-packed cheeses and cover them loosely.
• Always have separate knives for hard, soft, blue and goat's cheeses.
• Allow enough space on the board or base for cutting.
• Do not clutter a board with grapes if it already contains several cheeses; it is better to serve the fruit separately.

Below *Remove cheese from the refrigerator shortly before serving.*

Accompaniments

Crackers should be plain. Oatcakes, water biscuits, Bath Oliver biscuits and Melba toast are excellent. Flavoured and salted biscuits ruin good cheese.

• Crusty bread with plenty of substantial, soft crumb should be offered as well as biscuits. When offering cheese as the main food for a meal or buffet, choose a good selection of breads that are light in flavour but substantial in texture.

• Serve bowls of watercress or rocket (arugula) sprigs with the cheese. A light green salad can clear the palate.

• Celery sticks and pieces of fennel.

• Fresh figs, apples, pears, grapes, physalis, fresh dates and apricots go well with all cheeses. Dried fruits to serve with cheese include apricots, dates, peaches, pears and figs.

• Nuts in the shell or shelled.

• When serving cheese as a main course, black or green olives, or sweet ripe tomatoes may be offered.

• Chutneys, pickles, relishes and salsas are delicious with a main-course cheese board. Sweet-sour flavours are particularly successful.

Below Chopped egg and onions with white cheese and olives.

Above Edible flowers, such as scented geraniums, add flavour and interest.

• Offer an excellent oil with the cheese – walnut, hazelnut, macadamia or olive oils may be trickled on a plate as a condiment for cheese.

Lower-fat options

Watching everyone else indulge in a lavish cheese course is dismal for guests who have to limit their intake of saturated fat. It is possible to offer lower-fat options without compromising on quality.

• Ricotta cheese is available in low-fat versions and is delicious with fresh or dried fruit. Slit and stone (pit) fresh dates, separate the halves leaving them joined underneath, fill with ricotta and top with a fine shaving of Parmesan.

• Creamy medium-fat soft goat's cheese is delicious with fresh figs. Slit each fig almost down into quarters, leaving them joined at the base. Fill with soft goat's cheese and serve with freshly ground black pepper.

• Sandwich walnut halves together with low-fat soft cheese.

• Slit ready-to-eat dried apricots and fill them with a little low-fat soft cheese, then add a young mint leaf to each.

• Ready-to-eat dried apricots are delicious with feta cheese. Place small cubes of feta in slit apricots.

• Make delicious potted cheese with nuts by mixing very finely chopped walnuts with low-fat soft cheese. Add a little walnut oil to intensify the flavour, if you like. Pistachio nuts and pistachio nut oil can also be used – do not chop the nuts as finely as the walnuts and use the pistachio nut oil sparingly as it is very strong. Serve with celery and fennel.

Cheese savouries

Hot savouries can be served instead of a cheese board. The important point is to keep everything small to add a final burst of flavour at the end of the meal or before the dessert rather than to introduce another filling course.

A small pot of cheese fondue, neat fingers of cheese on toast or Welsh rarebit are all suitable. Little croûtes topped with goat's cheese and grilled (broiled) can be served with peppery watercress or rocket. Miniature tartlets made with cheese pastry can be filled with warm Stilton topped with a grape.

Below A small pot of cheese fondue can be served as the final course.

Wine for All Occasions

The variety of drinks available, as well as attitudes to entertaining and drinking have changed significantly in the last couple of decades such that providing liquid refreshment involves more than buying a few anonymous bottles of red and white wine. There is better information in supermarkets, and wine merchants who provide reliable, practical advice are no longer limited to élite outlets. Parties offering an "open bar" are not common but it is usual to offer a mixed selection of pre-dinner drinks. Cocktail parties are fun occasions and can be combined with dressing up in 1920s style.

Whatever the occasion or refreshment, non-alcoholic drinks are important, as most people prefer to avoid alcohol completely when they are driving and many also prefer to drink small amounts. Generous quantities of table water are essential at every meal to complement wine, and a selection of sophisticated alcohol-free aperitifs should be offered on every occasion.

Below *Choose a selection of red and white wines to suit different tastes.*

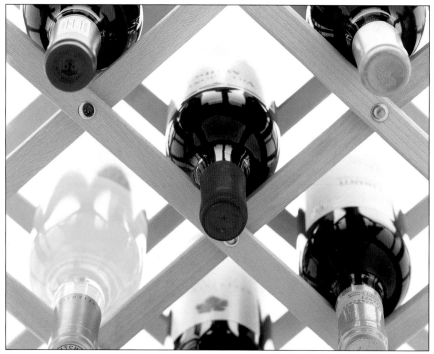

Above *There is a choice of several wine glasses from your wine merchant.*

Party wines

For the majority of parties it is still usual to provide white or red wine. Offering a choice of dry to medium-dry white is a good idea, especially when the menu is finger food rather than a main meal. Medium-bodied and soft reds are more flexible than their robust counterparts. Take advantage of wine-tasting opportunities at supermarkets, wine merchants or warehouses, particularly the latter where there is always a selection of wines for tasting.

Sparkling white wine is fun for parties, but always offer still wine as an alternative. Champagne is the choice for special celebrations. If you are planning a large gathering and want to serve expensive wines, it is worth taking expert and practical advice from a reputable wine merchant. You may well find expensive wines and sparkling wines offered there on a sale-or-return basis for whole cases.

Wine with food

The tradition of serving white wine with fish or poultry, and red with meat or cheese is still a good rule of thumb, but the vastly increased choice and changing cooking styles have widened the goalposts dramatically. Personal wine preference is just as important as bowing to expert opinion, so if you want to share your favourite wines with friends, do not feel inhibited even if they do not feature in wine guides or fashionable columns.

As a general rule, match light foods with light wines; crisp textures with crisp wines; and robust foods with characterful or full-bodied wines. Never

Below *Sparkling wine or champagne is popular for a special occasion.*

Above *Crisp, dry white wines complement seafood and poultry.*

make the mistake of using cheap and nasty wine in special cooking but use a good wine and complement it by serving the same or similar at the table. For example, when cooking fish, poultry or meat in wine or serving a wine sauce buy enough wine for cooking and serving with the meal.

First courses

When champagne or sparkling wine is offered as an aperitif it is often served for the first course. Light and crisp white wines complement salad-style appetizers and fine soups, while slightly more complex or fuller whites support fish or vegetables, pâté and egg dishes.

Fish, poultry and meat

• Fish and shellfish take crisp, dry white wines, including Sauvignon Blanc, Chablis, Muscadet sur lie or Chardonnay from Alto Adige. Firm-fleshed fish, shellfish and richer fish dishes or pâtés take the more robust whites, such as white Rioja, Australian Sémillon, oaked Chardonnays, and Californian Fumé Blanc.

• Chicken takes a soft red, such as mature burgundy, Crianza, Reserva Rioja or Californian Merlot. Light cooking methods, such as poaching in white wine, call for lighter wine but

Above *Choose full-bodied reds to accompany beef or pork.*

this could well be a rich white to match a creamy sauce.

• Turkey is slightly more powerful than chicken. An impressive red is essential for Thanksgiving or Christmas. St-Emilion, Pomerol claret, Châteauneuf-du-Pape, Australian Cabernet-Merlot or Cabernet Shiraz blends are all suitable.

• Duck benefits from a young red with some acidity, such as Crozes-Hermitage, Chianti Classico or Californian or New Zealand Pinot.

• Game birds take a fully aged Pinot Noir from the Côte d'Or, Carneros or Oregon while powerful venison is matched by concentrated red Bordeaux or northern Rhône wines, or Cabernet Shiraz and Zinfandel.

• Beef takes medium- to full-bodied reds. Serve reds from lighter Bordeaux wines or a medium Châteauneuf-du-Pape to the most powerful Zinfandels, Barolo, Barbaresco or Coonawarra Shiraz. Syrah or Grenache match mustard and horseradish condiments.

• Cabernet Sauvignon complements lamb, especially ripe examples from any of the producing countries.

• Pork takes full-bodied, slightly spicy reds, such as southern Rhône blends, Australian Shiraz, California Syrah or Tuscan Vino Nobile or Brunello.

Pasta

Match the wine to the sauce or type of pasta dish, for example the dominant flavours may be fish, poultry or meat. Light to medium reds go well with tomato-based sauces. Good Soave complements creamy pasta dishes, especially those containing seafood.

Desserts

Sauternes, Barsac and Monbazillac are classic wines for creamy desserts and custards. Rich Sauternes and high-alcohol dessert wines complement chocolate desserts. German or Austrian Rieslings or late-harvest Muscat from North America are great with baked fruit desserts and tarts. Slightly sweeter sparkling wines, such as Asti or Moscato d'Asti, are light and wash down Christmas pudding, gâteaux and meringues. Rich desserts, fruit cakes and nut-based specialities, such as pecan pie, will take a liqueur Muscat, sweet oloroso sherry or Madeira.

Cheese

Traditionally, cheese was always served with red wine, and although the combination of full rich and powerful

Below High-alcohol dessert wines go especially well with chocolate desserts.

Above Whatever type you select, always go for a good quality corkscrew.

cheese with a full red is an enjoyable one, the very heavy, tannic wines tend to mask the subtle nuttiness and lingering slight sweetness that comes with good ripe cheese.

Happily, the picture is now a little more varied. Any red wine or substantial white served with the main course can be finished off with cheese. Selecting wine to complement cheese is different and the idea of matching flavours and full-ness is a good one to consider. Fresh, crisp and slightly acidic and dry cheeses are best matched by crisp, fruity wines. Mellow, richer and creamy cheese takes a more rounded white, such as a full Chardonnay, or a light red. Blue cheeses are well matched by sweet wines.

• As a general rule, offer a choice of a substantial white and a soft red.
• Light whites, such as Sauvignon or Chenin Blanc, go well with light cheeses, such as the crumbly mild whites and fresh light goat's cheese.
• Chianti, Merlot or Rioja support the more substantial, ripe and well-flavoured semi-soft cheeses.
• New Zealand Cabernet Sauvignon or Côte du Rhône marry well with the medium-strong hard cheeses.
• Save Australian Shiraz and Californian Cabernet Sauvignon for well-matured hard cheese.
• Fruity wines, such as Vouvray, Chenin Blanc or rosé, match mild and creamy blue cheese while the stronger blues with a piquant flavour take the more robust reds.
• Sweet wines, such as Monbazillac, complement the stronger blue cheeses. Classic combinations include port with Stilton and Sauternes with Roquefort.

Serving wine

Much of the ceremony and paraphernalia of wine opening is conspicuous rather than practical.

Temperature

White wines should be chilled and reds served at room temperature. Over-chilling whites dulls their flavour – light whites should be served at 10°C/50°F, or just below, while the fuller Chardonnays, dry Sémillons and Alsace wines can be slightly less cool. The chilling time depends on the starting temperature of the bottle, but as a general rule allow a couple of hours in the refrigerator.

Leave red wines in a warm room for a couple of hours before serving. Heating them on a radiator is a bad idea as this clouds the flavours and aromas. Some light reds, such as young Beaujolais, can be served lightly chilled.

Allowing wine to breathe

Opening red wine in advance and allowing it to breathe before drinking is intended to take the tannic or acidic edge off the flavour of young reds. However, as the amount of air that

Below *Sniff lightly and long, with the nose slightly below the rim of the glass.*

Above *When opening sparkling wines, control the release of the cork.*

gets at the wine through the top of the bottle is minimal, unless the wine is decanted into a jug (pitcher) or carafe, merely opening the bottle normally has very little effect.

Decanting

This involves pouring wine off the sediment that has formed in the bottle. Leave the bottle to stand upright undisturbed overnight so that all the sediment sinks to the bottom. Open the bottle gently and pour the wine into the decanter in a slow steady

Below *A foil cutter removes a neat circle from the seal over the cork.*

Above *This type of corkscrew requires the minimum of effort.*

stream, keeping the bottle at a minimum angle the whole time to retain the sediment in the bottom. Keep your eye on the sediment and stop pouring as soon as it reaches the neck of the bottle. If there is more than half a glass of wine left, strain it through muslin.

Opening

Sparkling wine or chilled champagne will not go off like a cannon if properly opened, providing it has not been vigorously moved or shaken.

Have the glasses ready. Remove the foil and wire, holding the cork firmly in place. Hold the cork with one hand and the bottom part of the bottle with the other. Keep a firm hold on the cork. Concentrate on twisting the bottle, not the cork, until you feel the cork beginning to yield. Once it begins to go, the cork will push itself out, so the aim is to control its exit rather than leaving go and letting it pop out. The cork often needs a slight twist to help it on its way – just help it to move gently in the opposite direction to the bottle.

Pour a third to half a glass first to prevent the sparkling wine or champagne from overflowing, then go round again topping up the glasses when the first foam has subsided.

Organizing Drinks, Glasses and Quantities

If you intend making an open offer of drinks, make sure guests know what is available. Tell them or display the bottles on a table or set up a bar.

As a rule, include gin, vodka, whisky, sherry and dry white vermouth as a basic selection. Rum, Campari, red vermouth and sweet white vermouth are other options. Pimm's is a favourite summer drink. Tonic, American dry ginger ale, lemonade, cola and soda water are the usual mixers; Russian is a pomegranate-flavoured mixer that goes well with vodka. Have plenty of ice cubes and sliced lemons to hand.

After-dinner drinks may include a selection of liqueurs, Cognac, brandy and port.

Alcohol-free drinks

Have a plentiful supply of non-alcoholic drinks chilled. Still and sparkling mineral waters and jugs (pitchers) of tap water with ice and lemon are essential. Orange or tomato juice are

Below *Offer a selection of spirits for pre-dinner drinks.*

basic options, while apple, pineapple, exotic fruit and cranberry juices are popular. Alcohol-free beer is an acceptable alternative to beer.
• Add a generous dash of bitters to sparkling mineral water.
• Serve a squeeze of lime juice, lime slices and mint sprigs in tonic.

Beer

While beer is traditionally associated with informal barbecues and student parties, it is also an excellent drink to offer as an alternative to wine at drinks parties or as a pre-dinner drink on more formal occasions.

There is a vast choice of bottled beers available in most supermarkets. Coming from all over the world, they range from some light in colour and flavour to others that are dark, malty with a rich deep flavour. Fruit-flavoured beers are also popular. Colour and flavour are not necessarily related to strength – something to be especially aware of at parties – and some of the paler, light and fizzy beers are extremely strong.

Make the most of any specialist local breweries that offer particularly good or unusual beers not readily available outside the area. As well as selling live beer on its yeasty sediment, in casks or by the bottle, or bottled "bright" beer without the same level of active yeast (and therefore to be consumed within a couple of days), specialist breweries usually prepare seasonal beers. For example, for a limited period they may offer refreshing summer brews or warming winter ales. When buying a cask, always take advice from the brewery on the delivery and setting up of the barrel or storing the beer before the party, if appropriate.

When beer is offered as an alternative to wine, a light, lager-type brew that is thirst quenching and not too strong usually appeals to most tastes. This type of beer is good for barbecues, homely cooking (such as pasta dishes and meat sauces) and spicy meals (Mexican or Indian dishes, for example).

Fruit-flavoured beers are a good choice for drinks parties. The rich ales and very dark beers – such as British stout or the famous Irish Guinness – are a good alternative to red wine with robust, hard cheeses, such as mature (sharp) Cheddar. They are also excellent with meaty stews and casseroles and are popular instead of wine for informal lunches and suppers.

Light beers should be served well chilled. Darker beers are usually served cool – at cellar or cool room temperature – rather than chilled. However, this is a matter for personal preference and many prefer dark beers lightly chilled. Tall, slim lager glasses or large, stemmed balloon glasses are ideal for light beers. Larger tankards are traditional for the darker beers but they are not necessarily ideal for parties, when tall tumblers are much more practical.

Glasses

Disposable cups may be cheap and good for avoiding washing up but they do absolutely nothing for any drink, wine, spirits or otherwise. Even the most humble wine tastes better from a decent glass and a pleasing glass is one that is well balanced to hold, sturdy enough to feel safe but not chunky, and with a fine rim from which to sip. The bowl should be big and it should taper in towards the mouth to capture the aromas given off by the wine.

Conventionally, white wine glasses are smaller than red, which was thought to have more aroma and body to occupy a part-filled glass, but there is no good reason for this as whites are just as pleasing to swirl and sniff before sipping. The best solution for dinner parties is to have large white wine glasses and extra-large glasses for red.

Champagne and sparkling wines should be served in tall, slim, straight-sided flutes. These are designed to hold the bubbles, or mousse, of the wine for as long as possible, keeping it sparkling down to the last sip. The champagne saucers of the Sixties – wide and shallow glasses – allow all the bubbles to escape from the large surface area of the wine.

Fortified wines are served in smaller quantities, so smaller glasses are used, but they should still be large enough for the aroma and substance of the wine to be appreciated. Old-fashioned sherry glasses and even smaller liqueur glasses are sad receptacles.

Tumblers and tankards

In addition to wine glasses, medium to large plain tumblers (250ml/8fl oz/ 1 cup to 300ml/½ pint/1¼ cups) are basic, ideally the smaller ones for shorts and mixed drinks and the larger for water, soft drinks, juices, cider or beer. Large-bowled wine glasses with sturdy stems are excellent for light beers, cider

Above *Wine glasses are a preferable option to disposable cups.*

and substantial soft drinks. Tall, larger glasses are good for light beers, retaining the fizz and being well balanced to hold. Straight-sided glasses holding 600ml/1 pint/2½ cups are preferred for larger quantities of beer; jugs (pitchers) with handles or tankards are also satisfying for large amounts.

Quantities

A bottle of wine yields six average glasses. The amount consumed at a dinner party depends entirely on the company, ambience and attitude. It is always better to have more wine than needed and more than one bottle of each type than too little. When serving a selection of wines, remember that some guests may prefer to drink all white or all red rather than change with the courses. On average, allow one bottle for two non-drivers.

When catering for a large gathering, calculate the number of glasses based on six from a bottle. When serving sparkling wine as an introductory drink, allow extra unless the wine will not be served until everyone is gathered, as those who arrive first will probably consume slightly more. When selecting

Above *Serve beer in tall tumblers, pint glasses or tankards.*

special wines, such as good champagne for a large special-occasion party, it can be worth buying from a supplier offering sale or return. At informal parties, both large and small, it is common for guests to bring a bottle.

Below *One bottle of wine will provide around six average glasses.*

Classic Cocktails

The cocktail party can be a fun occasion for a Twenties or Thirties theme or a sophisticated contemporary gathering. If you are planning a fancy dress party, write fun invitations and ask guests to dress in style. Go to town on decorative, colourful cocktails, with novelty cocktail sticks, swizzle sticks and straws. Follow the theme through with music from the era and encourage guests to dance. Conversely, adopt a stylishly understated approach to a contemporary cocktail party, with smart drinks, canapés and nibbles. Keep the music low and lighting discreet, and concentrate on circulating and instigating stimulating conversation.

The cocktail bar

Invite guests to join in the mixing and shaking at a fun party, with the bar working from the kitchen. For more sophisticated gatherings, arrange a trolley or small table from which to shake, stir and pour, then use the kitchen as back-up. Hiring a good bartender will be worth every penny as long as the cocktail list, numbers and shopping list are discussed and agreed in advance.

Below *Cocktails will add colour and endless variety to a drinks party.*

Whether the party is fun or formal, focus on a few cocktails based on a limited number of drinks, and stick to that list. Have a recipe sheet and all decorations or accessories ready. Include a number of alcohol-free drinks.

Cocktail equipment

Bar measures and a small measuring jug (pitcher) are useful. The traditional single measure is 25ml/¾ fl oz/1½ tbsp and the double is 45ml/1½ fl oz/3 tbsp. If you do not have specialist measures, use a small sherry glass or similar. A set of measuring spoons is also essential.
Shaker: you will need several cocktail shakers for a party. Look out for those that have integral strainers. Make sure the shakers have tight-fitting tops and that they pour well.

Above *The choice of equipment is vast but you only need a few essentials.*

Mixing jug (pitcher): use for drinks that are stirred not shaken – look for one with a good pouring spout.
Blender: a goblet blender is useful for frothy cocktails. Do not crush ice in the blender, as this will blunt the blade.
Strainer: for straining mixed drinks into glasses.
Muddler: a long stirring stick with a bulbous end, which is used for crushing sugar or mint leaves.
Mini-whisk: a long-handled balloon whisk with a small balloon for whisking and frothing drinks.
Citrus squeezer: look for one with a deep container underneath and a good strainer to keep out the pips (seeds).

Zester and cannelle knife: these are usually combined in the one implement. Use for paring fine shreds of rind from citrus fruit. The cannelle knife cuts individual, slightly larger but thin strips and can be used to mark a pattern in the fruit rind. When sliced the rind forms a decorative edge.
Nutmeg grater: a small, fine grater for grating whole nutmeg.
Straws, swizzle sticks and decorative cocktail sticks: just some of the finishing touches for decorating drinks.

Glasses

Cocktail or martini glass: the classic V-shaped cocktail glass keeps warm hands away from cool drinks. This holds about 100ml/3½fl oz/½ cup.
Collins glass: the tallest of tumblers with narrow, straight sides, this holds about 250ml/8fl oz/1 cup.
Old-fashioned glass: the classic whisky tumbler, this is wide and short and it is referred to as a 175ml/6oz/ ¾ cup tumbler.
Highball glass: this is a 250ml/8fl oz/ 1 cup tumbler.
Liqueur glass: the smallest of glasses, this holds about 50ml/2fl oz/¼ cup.

Below A wide variety of different shaped glasses are suitable for cocktails.

Above Small whole fruit, such as cherries or strawberries, can be used as decorations.

Brandy balloon or snifter: the rounded shape is designed to be cupped in the hands to warm the contents while the narrow rim traps the aroma of the drink.
Large cocktail goblets: these vary in size and shape. Designed for serving longer or frothy drinks, these glasses have wide rims.
Champagne glasses: either saucers or tall narrow flutes. The flute is the best for sparkling wine and champagne cocktails; the saucer can be used for a variety of cocktails or drinks.
Red wine balloon: holding 250ml/ 8fl oz/1 cup, this should be filled about half-full to allow room for swirling the wine and releasing its aroma.
White wine glass: a long-stemmed glass held by the stem, so that warm hands keep away from chilled wine.
Pousse-café: a thin and narrow glass with a short stem, this is used for layered and floating cocktails.

Below Slices of lemon or lime add colour and flavour to many cocktails such as a Moscow Mule.

Drinks Checklist

Familiarize yourself with the flavours before writing your cocktail menu. The following is a basic guide:

Brandy: Cognac and Armagnac are the two French brandies. Fruit brandies or eaux-de-vie include peach, cherry and apricot brandy.

Champagne: dry (brut) champagne features in many cocktails. Champagne has the best mousse for making excellent fizzy cocktails, but less expensive sparkling wines, such as Spanish Cava, can be used instead.

Gin: familiar as an aperitif with tonic, gin is used in a variety of cocktails. It is flavoured with juniper berries.

Rum: dark rum is punchy but light rum is clear; this type is used for cocktails.

Tequila: a powerful Mexican spirit distilled from the juice of the agave cactus. Used in a variety of cocktails.

Vermouth: dry white, sweet white or red, or bittersweet rosé, there are many brands of these herb-flavoured aperitifs. The more expensive brands are generally better quality.

Vodka: as well as the basic, slightly peppery strong spirit, there are many varieties of flavoured vodkas, some subtle with herbs or spices, others distinct with fruit. A good quality plain vodka is useful for most cocktails.

Whisky: basic whisky is good enough for cocktails rather than masking the flavour of a long-matured single malt.

Liqueur flavours

Amaretto di Sarone: a sweet almond-flavoured liqueur.

Anisette: aniseed-flavoured liqueurs include French Pernod, Italian sambuca and Spanish anis.

Bénédictine: made by Benedictine monks of Fécamp in Normandy, this golden liqueur is flavoured with myrrh, honey and herbs.

Chartreuse: originally made by Carthusian monks at La Grande

Chartreuse monastery. This brandy-based liqueur is available as a green or yellow drink. Herbs, honey and spices flavour the liqueur. Yellow Chartreuse is flavoured with orange and myrtle.

Cointreau: orange liqueur.

Crème de cacao: cocoa-flavoured liqueur.

Crème de cassis: blackcurrant-flavoured liqueur – add a little to chilled dry white wine to make kir or use it to flavour champagne for kir royale.

Crème de menthe: mint liqueur.

Curaçao: orange-flavoured liqueur that is available coloured blue, clear or orange-brown.

Drambuie: malt whisky liqueur with herbs, honey and spices.

Galliano: golden liqueur flavoured with herbs, liquorice and aniseed.

Grand Marnier: French Curaçao, flavoured with bitter bergamot, orange and brandy.

Kahlúa: Mexican coffee-based liqueur with a rich flavour.

Southern Comfort: sweet fruity liqueur based on bourbon whisky.

Above Strawberry and banana daiquiris are popular cocktails.

Crushing ice

In the absence of an ice-crushing machine, lay out a clean dishtowel and cover half with ice cubes. Fold the other half of the cloth over, and then use a rolling pin or mallet to crush the ice fairly coarsely. Store in plastic bags in the freezer. If necessary, crush the ice finely just before using it.

Below Crushed ice can be prepared in advance and frozen until ready to use.

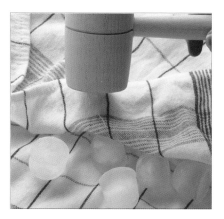

Making decorative ice cubes

These are particularly good for enlivening simple cocktails and mixed soft drinks.

1 Half-fill ice cube trays with water and freeze until firm.

2 Dip pieces of fruit, olives, citrus rind, edible flowers or mint leaves in cold water, then place in the ice cube trays.

3 Top up the trays with water and freeze until hard.

Below *Ice cubes with edible flowers.*

Frosting glasses

This simple technique adds a decorative and/or flavoured edge to the glass. Instead of sugar, the rim can be dipped into celery salt, grated coconut, grated chocolate, coloured sugar or cocoa powder. The flavouring depends on the type of drink you intend to serve. Place the frosted glass in the refrigerator until it is required.

1 Hold the glass upside down so that the juice does not run down the outside when you wet it. Rub the rim of the glass with the cut surface of a lemon, lime or orange.

2 Keep the glass upside down, then lightly dip it in a shallow dish of sugar, coconut, salt or celery salt. Re-dip the glass, if necessary, so that the rim is well coated.

3 Turn the glass the right way up and leave to stand for a while until the rim has dried. Chill in the refrigerator before pouring the drink into the middle of the glass.

Basic sugar syrup

Some cocktails include sugar syrup. This can be made in advance and stored in a sterilized airtight bottle in the refrigerator for up to 1 month.

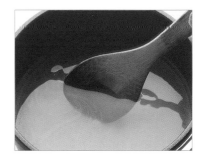

1 Mix 175g/6oz/scant 1 cup sugar and 600ml/1 pint/2½ cups water in a heavy pan. Heat gently, stirring, until the sugar has dissolved.

2 Brush the inside of the pan with cold water to clean any splashes of sugar that may crystallize.

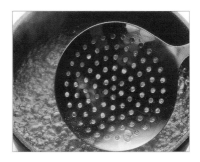

3 Stop stirring and boil for 3–5 minutes. Skim off any scum and, when it stops forming, remove from the heat. Pour the cooled syrup into sterilized bottles.

Traditional Cocktails

Knowledge of a good selection of classic cocktails is essential, and some favourites are given here, but you may also enjoy creating your own.

Black Velvet: combine equal parts Guinness and champagne.

Bloody Mary: mix 1 part vodka with 2 parts tomato juice. Stir in a dash of Worcestershire sauce or Tabasco and add a squeeze of lemon.

Brandy Alexander: shake together 1 part brandy, 1 part crème de cacao and 1 part double (heavy) cream. Serve dusted with freshly grated nutmeg.

Buck's Fizz: serve 1 part freshly squeezed orange juice topped up with 1 part champagne.

Daiquiri: shake 15ml/1 tbsp lime juice with 45ml/3 tbsp white rum and 5ml/

Below Bloody Mary served with celery, olives and cherry tomatoes.

1 tsp sugar on crushed ice. Pour into a sugar-frosted glass. Add fruit if desired, such as banana or strawberry.

Dry Martini: shake 2 parts gin with 1 part dry white vermouth. Pour into a glass and add a stuffed green olive. Some prefer to reverse the quantities, with 1 part gin to 2 parts vermouth.

Harvey Wallbanger: place some ice in a tall glass and add 2 parts vodka and 6 parts orange juice, then float 1 part Galliano on the surface.

Long Island Iced Tea: Mix equal parts vodka, gin, light rum, and tequila (optional) and lemon. Sweeten with a little sugar syrup and top up with cola. Serve on ice.

Manhattan: Mix 1 part each of dry and sweet vermouth with 4 parts bourbon or whisky.

Margarita: shake 1 part Curaçao, 4 parts tequila and 1 part lime juice. Serve in a salt-frosted glass.

Above *Brandy Alexander.*

Above *Martini with olives and chillies.*

Below *Strawberry Daiquiri.*

Above *Harvey Wallbanger with orange.*

Above *Long Island Iced Tea with mint.*

Below *Perfect Manhattan.*

Above *Margarita with lime.*

Below *Blushing Pina Colada.*

Pina Colada: shake 3 parts white rum with 4 parts pineapple juice, 2 parts coconut cream, 30ml/2 tbsp grenadine and 15ml/1 tbsp sugar syrup. Serve decorated with pineapple and a maraschino cherry.

Pink Gin: add a dash of Angostura bitters to a gin and tonic.

Rusty Nail: stir 2 parts whisky with 1 part Drambuie and serve on ice.

Tequila Sunrise: mix 1 part tequila with 2 parts orange juice. Pour 5ml/ 1 tsp grenadine into a glass and add ice, then carefully pour in the orange mix.

Whisky Sour: shake 1 measure whisky with the juice of ½ lemon and 5ml/ 1 tsp sugar on crushed ice. Pour into a tumbler.

Punches and Cups

Warming mulled wine, heady punches or delicate fruit cups are excellent welcome drinks for medium to large parties. Most well-seasoned party givers have their favourite recipes for a summer punch and a warming winter wine cup. The following are basic recipes to tempt you into experimenting further.

Mulled Wine: the classic Christmas drink for complementing melt-in-the-mouth mince pies. Stud 1 orange with 8 cloves and place it in a pan. Add 1 cinnamon stick and 60ml/4 tbsp sugar. Pour in a bottle of fruity red wine and add 150ml/¼ pint/⅔ cup brandy or rum. Cover and place over very gentle heat for 30 minutes. The wine should be just hot and aromatic. Taste and add more sugar if required. Serve hot.

Honey Glühwein: mix a handful each of raisins and blanched almonds with 1 lemon studded with 4 cloves, 1 cinnamon stick, 150ml/¼ pint/⅔ cup rum, 30ml/2 tbsp honey and 1 bottle red wine in a pan. Cover and heat very gently for about 30 minutes, or until the wine is just hot. Taste for sweetness and add more honey as required.

White Wine Cup: place 150ml/ ¼ pint/⅔ cup brandy in a bowl. Add ½ sliced orange, ¼ sliced cucumber and some mint sprigs. Cover and leave to macerate for several hours – this can

be left overnight. Add 1 well-chilled bottle dry white wine and top up with 900ml/1½ pints/3¾ cups chilled tonic water or lemonade.

Elderflower Strawberry Cup: rinse 4 elderflower heads and place in a bowl with 50g/2oz/½ cup halved strawberries. Add 750ml/1¼ pints/ 3 cups sparkling mineral water and 60ml/4 tbsp sugar. Stir well, crushing the elderflowers slightly and pressing

Above *Serve refreshing white wine cup with ice and garnish with borage.*

the strawberries without crushing them. Cover and leave to stand overnight, then chill well. Strain the mineral water into a bowl. Add 175g/6oz/1½ cups sliced strawberries and a bottle of chilled sparkling white wine. Taste for sweetness and decorate the bowl with washed elderflowers before serving.

Cider Punch: place 1 sliced lemon, 1 sliced orange, 1 quartered, cored and sliced apple and several mint sprigs in a bowl. Pour in 300ml/½ pint/1¼ cups medium-dry sherry. Cover and leave to macerate for several hours or overnight. Add 1 litre/1¾ pints/4 cups well-chilled dry (hard) cider and top up with 1 litre/ 1¾ pints/4 cups sparkling mineral water.

Sangria: slice 2 oranges and 2 lemons and place in a jug (pitcher) with 150ml/ ¼ pint/⅔ cup brandy or Grand Marnier. Add 1 bottle red wine, cover and leave to macerate for several hours. Add 2 cored and sliced apples and top up

Below *Warming mulled wine.*

Below *Cider punch with lemon rind.*

with 1 litre/1⅓ pints/4 cups lemonade and 600ml/1 pint/2½ cups orange juice, soda water, or sparkling mineral water (alternatively, use all lemonade).

Alcohol-free drinks

Although there is a wide choice of commercial soft drinks, there are many home-made cold drinks that are a real summer's treat for picnics or garden parties. Here is a selection:

Lemonade: grate the rind of 4 lemons and squeeze their juice. Place the rind and juice in a bowl and add 175g/6oz/scant 1 cup sugar. Add 600ml/1 pint/2½ cups boiling water, stir well and cover. Leave to stand overnight. Stir in a further 600ml/ 1 pint/2½ cups water, add 1 lemon cut into slices and some ice cubes. For picnics, carry the chilled lemonade in a bottle in a chiller bag.

Above *Sangria is a cool summer drink.*

Ice Cream Soda: place a scoop of good quality vanilla ice cream in a tall glass. Slowly add lemonade or soda water (lemonade is sweeter and tastes better

Above *Thirst-quenching St. Clements.*

even though soda water is correct), allowing the ice cream to froth up before filling the glass more than half-full. Decorate with berries, add a straw and long spoon and serve immediately.

Strawberry Banana Shake: purée 115g/4oz/1 cup hulled strawberries and 1 banana with 50g/2oz/¼ cup caster (superfine) sugar in a blender. Gradually add 600ml/1 pint/2½ cups chilled milk with the motor running. Pour into four glasses, add a large scoop of vanilla ice cream to each and decorate with fresh strawberries. For picnics, carry the chilled shake in a vacuum flask and omit the ice cream.

Mango and Lime Smoothie: peel, stone (pit) and dice 1 ripe mango, then purée it with the grated rind and juice of 1 lime. Add 600ml/1 pint/2½ cups chilled natural (plain) yogurt and whizz for a few seconds. Sweeten to taste with honey and serve immediately. For picnics, carry the chilled drink in a vacuum flask.

St. Clements: top up orange juice with an equal quantity of lemonade and serve with crushed ice.

Left *Old-fashioned lemonade is great at summer barbecues and picnics.*

Suppliers and Useful Addresses

Great Britain

Cake Art Ltd
Venture Way
Priors Wood
Taunton
somerset
TA2 8DE
01823 321 532
Wholesale suppliers of icings and equipment.

The Cooking Shop
The Old Estate Offices
Church Road
Sherbourne
Warwickshire
CV35 8AN
01926 624 444
www.thecookingshop.com
Kitchen supplies, accessories and equipment.

Epic Creative Limited
The Studio
38 Acacia Close
Stanmore
Middlesex
HA7 3JR
020 8954 3311
www.epic-creative.co.uk
Catering service.

The Garden Furniture Centre Ltd
Yew Tree Farm Craft Centre
Wootten Wawen
Henley-in-Arden
B95 6BY
01564 793 652
www.gardenfurniturecentre.co.uk
Suppliers of exclusive and innovative garden furniture and garden products.

Great Little Parties Limited
20 Burners Lane
Kiln Farm
Milton Keynes
MK11 3HB
01908 266 080
www.greatlittleparties.co.uk
Children's parties suppliers of invitations, party bags, tableware, balloons, gifts, candles and games.

Hobbycraft
0800 027 2387
www.hobbycraft.co.uk
Arts and crafts materials and equipment.

Invicta Bakeware Ltd
Westgate Business Park
Westgate Carr Road
Pickering
North Yorkshire
YO18 8LX
01751 473 483
Bakery equipment.

Non Stop Party Shop
214–216 Kensington High Street
London W8 7RG
020 7937 7200
www.nonstopparty.co.uk
Suppliers of party accessories, tableware, balloons and novelties and themed accessories.

Paperchase
213–215 Tottenham Court Road
London
W1T 7PS
020 7467 6200
www.paperchase.co.uk
Stationery, greeting cards, art materials and gift packaging.

Squires Kitchen
Squires House
3 Waverley Lane
Farnham
Surrey GU9 8BB
0845 2255 671
www.squires-shop.com
Specialist in sugarcraft and cake decorating products.

USA

A Cook's Wares
211 37th Street
Beaver Falls, PA 15010
800 915 9788
www.cookswares.com
*Bakeware, foods, appliances, pans,
cutlery and general utensils.*

Bowery Kitchen Supply
The Chelsea Market
460 West 16th Street
New York, NY10011
212 376 4982
www.bowerykitchens.com
Cooking supplies and equipment.

Broadway Panhandler
477 Broome Street
New York, NY 10013
212 966 3434
www.broadwaypanhandler.com
*Cooking utensils, knives, cookware,
bakeware, pots and pans and electrics.*

Chef's Catalogue
800 884 2433
www.chefscatalog.com
*Cookware, electrics, tools, bakeware
and cooking accessories.*

Party Suppliers & Rentals
4013 Oleander Drive
Wilmington
North Carolina 28403
910 791 0024
www.partysuppliers.net
*Supplies rental tents, tables, chairs,
party equipment, linens, china and
glassware and staging.*

Sur La Table
Catalog Division
1765 Sixth Avenue South
Seattle, WA 98134
800 243 0852
www.surlatable.com
*Bakeware, glassware, cook's tools,
housewares and specialty foods.*

Canada

Acme Tent Rentals
6999 Victoria Avenue
Montreal
514 342 5272
www.celebrationgroup.com
Quality rental equipment.

Gervais Rentals Inc
6570 Avenue l'Esplanade
Montreal. QC
H2V 4L5
514 273 3677
*Rental equipment for parties of any
occasion.*

New Zealand

Butler Gibpat
138 Ponsonby Road
Ponsonby, Auckland
PO Box 90998
AMSC Auckland
www.butlergibpat.co.nz
*Bakers supplies, catering equipment,
hotel and motel suppliers, kitchen
fittings and design, kitchenware and
restaurant supplies.*

Carlton Hire Group
0800 662 000
www.carltonhiregroup.com
*Cutlery, crockery, glasses, linen, tables
and chairs, marquees, sound and
lighting hire equipment.*

Australia

Barbehire
1236 Canterbury Road
Punchbowl
NSW 2196
02 9750 3390
www.barbehire.com.au
*Party hire for all occasions, catering
equipment, barbecues, marquee and
tables and chairs.*

Local Party Hire
38 Arden Street
Waverley NSW 2024
02 664 1399
Catering and party equipment rental.

Oxford Art Supplies
221-225 Oxford Street
Darlinghurst
NSW 2010
02 9360 4066
Arts and crafts suppliers.

South Africa

Jem Cutters
PO Box 115
Kloof
KwaZulu-Natal 3640
031 701 1431
Food supplies and manufacturer.

Index